# Here she comes!

The experienced man's guide to
deeply understanding his woman,
driving her crazy with desire,
and giving her ever stronger orgasms!

**Rod Govea**

**with Lu Abreu**

pum! Press

# Here she comes!

Cover design: Ryan Scheife, Mayfly Design
Interior illustrations: Rod Govea

ISBN: 978-85-64329-02-7

Published by pum! Press
www.pumpressworld.com

Note: The information in this book is true and complete to the best of our knowledge. This book is intended only as an informative guide on sexual practices, focusing on sensations, not on health issues. In no way is this book intended to replace, countermand, or conflict with the advice given to you by your own physician. We strongly recommend you follow his or her advice at all times. Information in this book is general and is offered with no guarantees on the part of the author or pum! Press. The author and publisher disclaim all liability in connection with the use of this book.

*To Bruno Salgueiro, 1973–2010.*
*The world became quite a boring place to be in,*
*after the funniest person left...*

*...and to all my wonderful friends*
*who are fortunately still around.*
*We have to seize that privilege!*

# Acknowledgements

First and foremost, I would like to express my deep gratitude to my wife, Lu Abreu. A clinical psychologist, she provided a big contribution to the concepts and theories contained in this book. Her contribution was so large that she became a co-author. Plus, she was fully supportive when I made the unorthodox choice of interrupting a well-paid career to write this book. But, most of all, I would like to thank her for being the perfect girlfriend first, and now the perfect wife. Only her could have turned this marriage-phobic guy into a loving husband.

I would also like to thank all my friends who reviewed the manuscript, for their relevant comments that deeply improved its quality (a special thanks to A.O. and R.P.), and to Sarah Cypher for her professional copyediting and helpful comments that also improved the manuscript.

A special acknowledgement is due to my friend David for showing me that one should always pursue one's interests in an educated manner, no matter how strange that might seem from the outside.

I would also like to thank all my previous lovers, who have been a very important part of my research.

My final acknowledgment goes to those special lovers who, sometime in the past, were an important part of my life. I loved every moment we shared and I will always keep you in my heart.

— *Rod Govea*

# What you are in for

On a single night, with your mouth and hands, you give your girl different kinds of orgasms, one after another. After a while, her orgasms fuse into a single one, lasting for minutes.

After a little rest, you start having sex—very smoothly, building a strong emotional connection and reaching new levels of intimacy. Then, you apply your new penetration technique. She feels ravaged as never before. She mumbles repeatedly how good you are in bed... and comes one time after another.

Afterwards, she lies so relaxed in bed. She stares at you with her sincerest smile. After some sweet and cuddly moments, you start telling her a story. You do so in a powerful and exciting manner. She is twitching in bed just by hearing your words. However, you don't allow her to get off. You just hold her tight. Soon after, she can't stand it anymore and she starts coming just by listening to your words.

Next day, the day after, every day—she wants sex again. Sex no longer requires a relaxed frame of mind, preparation, and romance. She just loves having sex with you. You become amazed by just how much pleasure she can feel.

Would you like to give this to a woman?
You only need to read this book and practice what you read.

# Praise for *"Here She Comes!"*

*"Here She Comes!* gives information not found in most sex books. Information that will help you to understand her and make love to her entire being. A must for the experienced man's book shelf. I melted just reading it." — *Sonia Borg, Ph.D., Author of "Oral Sex She'll Never Forget", "Spectacular Sex Moves She'll Never Forget" and "Marathon Sex".*

"Guys, when you read this book and practice the techniques you will have all the confidence you need to satisfy a woman. Rod makes it easy for you. Get on it!" — *Dr. Natasha Janina Valdez, author of "A Little Bit Kinky"*

*"Here She Comes!* by Rod Govea, is a must read for anyone, male or female who wants to experience all the glories of sexual nirvana.

My latest book *Don't Have Sex Until You Read This Book*, is a guide to a long, delicious, and lasting relationship. Once you have the relationship, and want to keep it strong and passionate, be sure to read *Here She Comes!* This book is full of practical, effective, inspiring experiences which will, absolutely, bring any woman to an awareness of her body and her passions. Her ties to you will strengthen with each incredible sexual release, leaving her purring, groaning, and laughing with spasms of ecstasy.

Govea, explores the depths of communication; spiritual and sexual. He teaches you to explore feelings, needs, and fantasies. His techniques create a foundation of trust, love, and need, which translate into a strong bond of pleasure and completeness.

Govea, brilliantly explores the female auditory pleasures. As the male love to look, the female excitation is in the words, the listening. Govea's ideas of storytelling, and speaking are very powerful keys to the female's door to orgasm.

Read *Here She Comes!* and join the very few who truly know the heights of passion and the physical intensity, which can be experienced by following these excellent ideas and techniques."

— *Carole Altman, author of "Don't Have Sex Until You Read This Book"*

"I have just finished reading *Here She Comes!* by Rod Govea. He understands that in order to make love to a woman, a man must understand her psychological motivations and desires. This is a fun and practical book that takes inspiration from a variety of sources from scientists to porn stars." — *Barbara Keesling, Ph.D., author of "The Good Girl's Guide to Bad Girl Sex"*

"*Here She Comes!* is quite an interesting read—it's a mix of personal hot experience, instructional tips, scholarly theories, and racy anecdotes—all in deference to a woman's pleasure and a man's adoration of goddess-love. It's definitely geared to a certain male reader who wants to become more adept at pleasing a woman, those who are willing, open, and savvy enough to enjoy and take it all in. That's the kind of man who'll make best use of new information. That's the kind of man I enjoy!" — *Adrienne Savine, author of "Crazy Hot Sex Secrets"*

# Contents

## Chapter 14: Creating Fantasies and Bringing Them to Life

Listening to fantasies is so exciting that some women orgasm just by listening to them. Learn how to use fantasies both to excite and to probe your partner. Then, if you both desire, make her live out her own deep hidden fantasies.

## Chapter 15: Giving Direct Orders to Her Unconscious Mind

Erotic dreams are wonderful experiences... if we could only remember them afterwards! Learn how to give your partner orgasms as in dreams. In fact, even better, as you can repeat these orgasms when she is awake. Sounds unbelievable, but it is true. Make her orgasm whenever you tell her to.

## Chapter 16: Toys, Beatings, Bondage, and Imagination

Toys, beatings and bondage can sometimes be really exciting for your partner. Read an intro on each of these topics. Who knows? You might want to follow up on some of them later! Finally, read some words on using your imagination to spice up your evenings together.

## Chapter 17: Being Sensual

The sensuality of the man multiplies his woman's sexual pleasure. Learn what sensuality is made of and how you can become a more sensual man.

# Introduction

*"If you don't do everything in your reach to be the first, you will not finish
second or third, but fatally as the very last." —Maréchal Hubert Lyautey*

*"I start where the last man left off."—Thomas A. Edison*

The first of the two quotes above, beautifully framed, stands on
top of my grandfather's desk. As a kid, I thought it showed clearly
how obsessed with work and unable to enjoy life the elder generation was. As I grew up, I came to realize that it reflects something
central about life: Life has amazing rewards and can be unbelievably
good, if you excel at doing something. If that "something" happens
to be sex, the rewards are extreme. However, to excel at anything
at all, you have to devote yourself to it wholeheartedly. Just being
"good" is not enough. Being satisfied on your current level does not
lead to the top—it leads to the bottom.

Fortunately, and contrary to the situation during my grandparents' time, self-improvement today does not derive from a lot of pain
and huge effort. We are blessed with a flood of information. Self-improvement derives from being smart and accessing the right information before putting in the effort. This is the single most efficient
way of improving in any area. You can learn from the experiences
of others without having to discover everything by trial and error,
saving yourself years of practice. If you learn from others, you can
then use your talent to discover a lot by yourself, but you do so from
a more advanced starting point. If you start from the plateau that
others have reached, you will be able to reach much higher peaks.

I wrote this book with that in mind: to put down, bit by bit, all
I learned about sex. As you will realize while reading it, this book
presents a very high level of sexual knowledge—and is a great base
for your own improvements.

This book is not to teach the general public about sex or to preach to men that they have to be more "generous" or "better." This book explains the techniques, details, and hidden female psychology that will allow grown-up, experienced men, who already strive to excel in sex, to swap their sexual brown belts for black-belts.

As you know, being great in something is not about excelling in a particular technique; it is about being great all around. What prevents us from excelling are the flaws, the missing bits, the stuff we never focused on. In sex, this becomes even more important, as there are so many different facets to it. This book mentions many of these, hoping that some of them will be relevant to you and that they contribute to continue your journey toward higher plateaus.

May it be a wonderful one!

## Who can read this book?

I wrote this book for curious, intelligent, interested adult men with experience in sex. This book describes advanced sexual techniques that I consider the most powerful in pleasuring a woman in a heterosexual relationship. More importantly, it provides a novel model for the female sensual mind and an original framework to fully satisfy it. To understand the female mind and the concepts of dominance, empathy, instinct, and unconscious mind require some maturity, intelligence, and openmindedness. Nothing else is required for you to start immediately applying what you read here.

## Who Should Not Read This Book?

People have differing views on sex. Some are repressed while others are bad-taste perverts (at least that is how they look at each other). Clearly, it would be impossible to write a consensus book that pleases everyone.

I belong to the group of people whom some consider improper, incorrect, and perhaps immoral, and I write this book accordingly. So, if you consider some people improper, incorrect, and immoral for performing legal sexual activities without harming or offending their partners, this book is not for you. You will probably feel offended by reading it and I definitely don't want to offend anyone.

If you are still not an adult and somehow got a hold of this book, or if you don't know the basics of sex, please put the book down. Despite its being a great book, it should not be anyone's first sex book. It does not focus on the basics of sex, such as kissing, petting, health considerations, and creating a relaxing and sensual environment in which to have sex. Not knowing the basics, you can't apply the advanced stuff—and this is definitely not a Sex 101 book.

Finally, a word to girls buying this book as an offer to their partners: This is not the perfect book to be read together by couples. It will be much better for both of you if your man reads the book alone.

For all non-repressed adults with some prior knowledge of sex, who are reading this book by themselves, welcome aboard!

## How to Read This Book

A lot of what is written here goes against the mainstream and will perhaps be enthusiastically criticized. Nothing new there: Good sex has always faced resistance from the forces of "proper social behavior." Actually, it was not only resisted, but clearly *defeated*.

So, in my life studying sex I decided to disregard all rules but one: If the woman likes it, and it is legal and harmless, it is good enough for us.

When you free your mind from some wrongheaded rules on how to behave, you become much more creative, able to communicate, and able to sympathize with other people. After all, that is exactly why we drink when we go out—and that is exactly why sex occurs more often when we drink!

This book is written in the same partying spirit. I ignore all the politically correct lies we usually tell each other and present things as I believe they really are. As you are probably reading this book in total sobriety, once in a while you will read something that will feel absurd, dead wrong, or impossible. But, if you were to read only consensual, straightforward stuff this book wouldn't be worth the time and money you will invest in it. Therefore, I ask you to approach this book with an open mind (or, okay, after a couple of beers if you like).

I don't ask you to believe anything without testing it—just that you don't dismiss it, either. Test everything in this book and see for yourself how well it works.

## Why should a man read this book?

Reading a book takes time. While some of the things in this book are techniques that can be applied immediately, others are mindsets that probably require a bit more effort. Plus, I present sex as something whose purpose is to pleasure the woman, never mentioning how the man should pursue his own pleasure or the fulfillment of his own fantasies. So, why would a busy man like you take the time to read this book and apply what I write here? What is in it *for you*?

There are plenty of good reasons for reading this book and applying its content. First, your partner will feel extremely happy. Second, most men find it exciting and rewarding to pleasure their partners more intensely. Third, giving immense pleasure to your partners is the best way to to fulfill your own sexual fantasies—your partner will become more sexual and feel indebted, eager to pay back the pleasure you give her. Fourth, you will see how your partner enjoys that you fulfill your own sexual fantasies with her—that should free you from any guilt feelings you might have regarding sex. Fifth, knowing that you can give immense pleasure to any woman will give you extra confidence—and women will spot it. Sixth, knowing how the female mind works will allow you to better understand women in general—and they will feel atttracted by that.

## About This Direct Style of Writing

This book is written in a very direct style, allowing lots of important information to fit in around three hundred pages, saving plenty of innocent trees and, much more importantly, a lot of your time. Plus, I will surely mention stuff you already know. Put together, this creates a writing style that will, once in a while, become irritating for you, as it will seem I am bossing you around on what you should do in bed. So please don't take it personally. It is just an objective and succinct way to express my method. It is a method that has served me very well in life and that I am eager to share. In the end, I will be very happy to hear your views on whatever we come to disagree on.

## Science and Logic

This book is different from others you might have read. I am not basing my opinions on hundreds of people suffering from sexual problems and I am not relying on sex surveys. In fact, I will mention just a few scientific studies on sex (sound ones), and I will often advise you against making simple deductions.

Does that mean that I am unscientific and illogical, perhaps even mystical? Not at all. Quite the opposite, actually. The reason I am careful about mentioning studies about sex is that they tend to suffer from one of three chronic problems:

1. They approach questions at the wrong level.
2. They fail to measure the relevance of their findings.
3. They look at individuals as isolated entities.

Let me detail what these mistakes are, one by one.

The mistake of approaching questions at the wrong level appears in studies that go very deep into physiology or anatomy to study something happening at higher levels, such as pleasure or attraction. For instance, there is a study that claims the nonexistence of the G-spot because the researchers did not find it after dissecting several female corpses. The fact that these scientists didn't find the G-spot only means that they didn't know what they were looking for. In the same way, when a neuroscientist dissects a brain, he can't tell whether its "owner" was intelligent or not. It is very tricky to understand high level properties (such as intelligence or sexual pleasure) based on inferences from lower levels properties (such as the number of neurons or nerve endings). Trying to do so is like defining the Sistine Chapel based upon the chemistry of the paint used to decorate it: a very bad idea. There are many levels between neurons and pleasure, and we still don't know them in detail. Surely, neurons are involved, but we don't know exactly how.

The second common mistake is to extrapolate some minor findings, giving them unmerited relevance. For instance, scientists asked some men to wear t-shirts for several days and then convinced women to sniff them and pick their favorites. They discovered that women preferred the scent of more genetically distant men. From there, people jumped to the conclusion that "chemistry between two people had been scientifically explained" and that "genetics drives partner choice."

However, the study only showed that "chemistry" is involved when dating is performed as a t-shirt-sniffing contest. I have a strong suspicion that if researchers made their tests on people hooking up in parties, or in long-term relationships, they would find the influence of scent to be less relevant.

The third common mistake is that of considering isolated individuals out of context. If a study shows that 70 percent of women prefer oral sex to penetration, what is the correct conclusion to be drawn? If someone asked you whether you prefer burgers or fries, what would you reply? Maybe you would imagine the best burger you ever had against the best fries you ever had. So, the correct conclusion might be something like: "Based on their limited sets of boyfriends, lovers, and one-night stands, 70 percent of women prefer oral sex to penetration, if they had to choose only one." Now, don't you prefer burgers and fries to each of them separately?

My main point is that scientific findings should be taken with a grain of salt, especially in regards to sex, given that we have better ways to form our opinions—through our own testing.

## Safety, Health and Legal Considerations

The broad topic of this book, sex, is one of the most positive topics in human life. However, sex books are usually filled with information about all kinds of diseases you can contract during sex. On the contrary, books on cars are not full of details about driving accidents. People know that car accidents happen and how they can avoid them. The same is true in regards to the dangers of sex. However, if you are not sure you know about the dangers of sex and how to avoid them by practicing safe sex, please don't buy this book. In case you buy it and you continue reading it from here, be aware that I will assume that you have the right background knowledge and that you are practicing safe sex in accordance to the official health recommendations of the country you live in. Again, this book is for brown-belts and above, not for beginners.

Chapter 1:

# Our Three Heads

*"Know thyself."* —*Ancient Greek aphorism at the Temple of Apollo*

*"People mistakenly assume that their thinking is done by their head; it is actually done by the heart which first dictates the conclusion, then commands the head to provide the reasoning that will defend it."*
—*Anthony de Mello*

### INTRODUCTION

This book uncovers the secrets on how to make women happier and sexually more pleased than they ever thought possible. The first step in that journey is to know what women want. The simplest and most logical way to take this step would be to ask women what they want. And, as you could expect, that has been done many times.

In public, most women answer this question by saying how much they appreciate a man who is kind, successful, tall, strong, and fun, and how they enjoy being treated with tenderness, care, and respect. They also add that sex is not the most important thing in a relationship—the connection is—but that sex should be an emotional and romantic experience. Finally, they say they want their relationship to be strictly monogamous.

Are women lying when they say this?

No.

So is the above correct and can we move on from there?

No. *Definitely not.*

Women are not lying, but the above is definitely not the whole truth—if you follow that advice, you are doomed to never please a woman. To explain this paradox, we have to understand how the human mind really works. Only then can we be able to deeply understand women and to become the man of their dreams.

WE AND OUR CONSCIOUS MINDS

### Are We Really We?

A very direct approach to understanding how the mind works is to literally open it and look at it. That was done in the following very interesting scientific experiment. The experiment was performed on individuals who had undergone a surgery to sever their *corpus callosum*, the central part of the brain that connects the left and right brain hemispheres. These individuals thus have two separate brains, the left brain and the right brain. One sees the world through the left eye, the other through the right eye. The left brain (which sees the world through the right eye) also happens to control speech and to harbor the conscious mind, which is what most of us, totally disregarding the rest of our brain, call "myself." In these individuals without a functional *corpus callosum*, the conscious mind is disconnected from the right brain. So, whatever these patients see or read with their left eye (and thus their right brain) remains totally unknown to their conscious mind.

Neuroscientists Roger Sperry and Michael Gazzaniga used this sad limitation to learn more about the conscious mind.[1] First, they placed a barrier on top of the patients' noses, so that they would see half of the world with each eye, but never with both eyes. Then, they presented to the left eye the order, "Walk." The patients rose to their feet and started walking, despite their conscious mind having no clue about receiving any orders—some other part of their brain read the order, understood it, and had the power to make the patient stand and walk. When the scientists then asked the patients (that is, addressing their conscious minds) why they stood up, the answer was surprising. Instead of an honest, "I have no clue," the patients

---

1 Roger Sperry was later awarded the Nobel Prize in Medicine for this work.

came up with an excuse: "To get a drink," "To use the restroom," etcetera.

This very surprising result is the key to understand human beings: What we call "myself," our conscious mind, isn't wholly trustworthy. Our conscious mind is a spin-doctor that tries to explain our actions in a favorable light. Our conscious mind is determined to make us sound rational and nice, both to ourselves and to others, but is not fully aware of the causes behind our every action. The conscious mind is not "all of us."

There is much more to each person than their conscious mind— and this book will tell you how to read and communicate directly with those other parts, because sex is not for the conscious mind. Sex is for the unconscious mind—or, as we usually call it, "the heart."

## CLUES FROM HUMAN SEXUAL BIOLOGY

### Our Very Sexy Bodies

In this book, sex and sensual relationships will be described as very important parts of human life, as sex in humans is definitely not just the means to ensure fertilization. Let's see how biology supports this view.

Humans are one of many dozens of species of primates. We have, of course, loads of differences from the remaining primates. Interestingly, some of these differences are related to sex. Compared to humans, the other primates have short and very narrow penises, sometimes full of spikes to hold on to the vagina, and they are stiff as bone—actually, it truly is as stiff as the bone within their penises. (Talk about a boner...).

Without having any inner bones (or spikes), humans have the thickest penises of all primates. For instance, the chimp penis, much thinner than the human one and supported by its inner bone, is more efficient than the human penis at ensuring fertilization—but would sell terribly at sex shops. It seems like Nature wanted humans to have a penis aimed at pleasuring the female, beyond simply ensuring fertilization.

Besides the marvelous penis, male humans excel in other aspects. Despite rarely getting any credit for it, the act of penetration between human males and females lasts much longer than those of the remaining primates, and women seem to feel much more pleasure than other primate females. Unlike most other primates, we have sex throughout the menstrual cycle, not only on the few days where conception can take place.[2]

We do not know why sex in humans is so distant from the minimum requirements for conception, but it clearly is. In fact, sex must have been very important in primitive human behavior for Evolution to "bother" favoring all these improvements.

Fig. 1.1. (Left) The penis of a Chimpanzee. You can't see it but there is a bone inside. (Right) The penis of the Loris Calabar Potto's. Even sexier... *(adapted from "Primate Sexuality," Alan F. Dixson, Oxford University Press, see Sources)*

As described in Leonard Shlain's book, *Sex, Time and Power,* if we were like most primates, men would still go around with practical penises, only think of sex when a female in heat was available, and spend the rest of their time happily not thinking about the sex they were not having. Women, on the other hand, would only think of sex when in heat, get lots of it (in ten-second bursts), and then forget about it until a couple of years later. Sounds weird? Yes it does—we surely are very different from most primates!

It seems clear that humans have somehow evolved to engage in sex for purposes other than ensuring efficient reproduction. In

---

2 The other primate exception is the bonobo (*Pan paniscus*), one of the two species of chimpanzees, our closest evolutionary relatives. The bonobos have sex many times a day with different partners of both genders, in different positions, and they also French kiss. Probably, the evolution for increased sexuality in the human lineage started before the evolutionary split between humans and chimpanzees, and was lost in the common chimpanzee (*Pan troglodytes*).

humans, sex became something more complex, more prevalent in many aspects of life, and much more pleasurable—especially for females.

## The Sex-test

What could these other purposes of sex be? Why did it become more pleasurable?

To answer these questions, Geoffrey Miller, in his book *The Mating Mind,* puts forward the following charming hypothesis: It is known that most mammalian species partially evolve by sexual selection. That is, individuals who are chosen to be sexual partners are the ones who pass their genes to the next generation. So, the set of criteria used to choose sexual partners by one gender directs the evolution of the other gender. That is, if females prefer stronger males, males become stronger at each generation. In general, males evolve to excel in the characteristics used as selective criteria by the females, such as strength, size, courage, beauty, etcetera. But Miller adds an important twist to this scenario. In humans, it is not only about strength, size, courage, or beauty. Humans use other complex criteria for sexual selection. And the fact we use these criteria can be the exact reason why humans are so different from other animals. Those additional criteria we use for choosing partners, such as intelligence, charm, political ability, and artistic ability are, in fact, very particular human qualities. According to Miller, maybe ancient humans started preferring talented artists as sexual partners, starting an evolutionary race to become the best paleoartist—and in the process, creating art. Even more important than the genesis of art, for the topic of this book, is another particularly human criteria for choosing sex partners, proposed by Miller: sex itself.

Humans would have evolved not only to be artistic, but also to be sensual, attractive sexual partners who would give their partners a good and pleasurable sexual experience. People would have sex more often with a partner they liked best, increasing their chances of having children with that partner. The most fascinating part of Miller's theory is that, contrary to other species, sexual selection would act on both genders. Besides, it would also act at two different stages: first, at the stage of being selected as a partner, and second, at the stage of being able to keep a partner.³

But why would sex itself be used as an activity to direct partner choice? Just for fun? Perhaps so. But perhaps sex served an even more interesting evolutionary function: Sex, in being so complex and demanding, could serve as a very good proxy for many human qualities such as intelligence, empathy, physical fitness, and beauty. A person could then evaluate all these qualities in a partner by having sex with them. That evaluation would be unconscious. People would just feel more attracted to the partners who gave us the best sex.

So, according to this view, not only have we humans evolved to become the sex machines of the animal kingdom, we have also evolved to fall in love and go totally crazy over that particular lover who really turns us on and gives us more pleasure than all the others before.⁴

## HOMO SAPIENS?

In this chapter, we have seen some evidence of how our unconscious mind can, in particular situations, even control our actions. We have seen how the conscious mind covers up for it. We have also seen the biological indications of a strong sexual drive. Finally, we have seen several interesting hypotheses to explain these facts.

We can, of course, choose to dismiss the evidence and the hypotheses. Maybe the results obtained in the Sperry and Gazzaniga experiment are a side-effect of the *corpus callosum* surgery. Maybe our highly sexual biological traits are irrelevant remnants of a previous evolutionary stage shared with the bonobos. Maybe we are, indeed, *Homo sapiens*, purely rational and wise, that can control not only his actions but also his thoughts, drives, and wishes, and pursue happiness in doing so.

Or we can do the opposite, and choose to look at ourselves as animals born to survive and reproduce through repeated sexual in-

---

3 Supporting Miller's thesis is the fact that it takes an average of several months of sex for a woman to become pregnant, unlike most other species.

4 To be that particular lover is what is taught in this book.

teractions, and that no matter how complex, civilized, wise, moderate, and altruistic our conscious mind becomes, it will never totally take over our unconscious mind. As Captain Kirk often explains to Mr. Spock, that is the core of humanity.

In this book, I take this second road. I believe that our pursuit of happiness will only succeed if we understand, listen to, and satisfy our instincts in a way that is not harmful to others or to us. So, I will analyze the interaction between humans during sex from an instinctive and experiential point of view, not worrying about our conscious explanations but trying instead to discover our real, unconscious motivations. I consider this approach more promising than to believe we are pure and rational while we choose to watch violence in every movie, watch porn regularly, or take Prozac daily. Let's be open. Let's embrace our humanity and our instincts. Our instincts are what make us humans and allow us to experience joy and bliss when we are intimate with another person. Our instincts are so important and so human that they deserve our non-judgmental attention.

Chapter 2:

# The Female Instinct as a Roadmap for Sex

*"If women did not exist, all the money in the world would have no meaning." —Aristotle Onassis*

*"Women dress alike all over the world: They dress to be annoying to other women."—Elsa Schiaparelli*

*"The desire of the man is for the woman, but the desire of the woman is for the desire of the man."—Madame de Stael*

## ORIGINS OF THE HUMAN SEXUAL INSTINCT

### The Prehistoric Instinct

From the dawn of mankind until a few thousand years ago, for a period of more than 100,000 years, humans lived as hunter–gatherers in tribes of up to 150 individuals. During that long period, human behavior had the opportunity to evolve toward perfection—for those conditions. That evolution generated a very special set of instincts and behavior. As any stranded person will tell you, a single human is a pretty lousy animal, and has a slim chance of survival. In a group, however, he is the most powerful animal to have ever existed.

Human evolution didn't pursue impressive strength, teeth, or claws. Instead it followed the path toward intelligence, language, and political abilities, enabling humans to generate extremely organized and flexible societies. This political ability of humans is innate. It is instinctive. Just by following our instincts, we organize into tribes and create complex social structures. This is visible in children. If humans had no innate political abilities, children would be a bunch of isolated individuals not interacting with each other unless a grown-up told them to, and how. Or, they could have a slight instinct for interacting, but not a real "political" instinct. In that case, they would interact randomly, not forming social structures—just playing with others when required. However, both these scenarios are very unlike the children we know, right?

Children form social structures even though their brains are not fully developed. They take roles inside groups, and they actively probe other children and adults to see how far can they push their boundaries. The instinct that leads humans to form social structures is very strong.

And, curiously, not totally separate from the sexual instinct...

## The Instinct Today

In the last several hundred years, humans changed their lifestyle. Instead of spending one's life in the same group of up to 150 people[1], many of us now live among millions. The human instinct that evolved during a time when everyone knew each other might not be so well adapted for today's conditions—perhaps an updated version of our 1.0 instinct would be more suitable for our survival and reproduction in the twenty-first century. After all, our instinctive behaviors lead to all sorts of problems, like fights, intrigue, murder, and war. Unfortunately, evolution hasn't had the time to adapt our instinct to modern life in large societies. Therefore, our behavior is still being influenced by this semi-obsolete version of our instinct, making our understanding of it a requirement for understanding behavior. Trying to do so, psychology looked into biology to learn how evolution could be used to clarify human behavior[2], giving rise to the

---

1 Anthropologists showed that hunter–gatherer human societies do not grow to over 150 individuals, the approximate size at which the family ties between individuals become too weak to overcome rivalry. Reaching that point, conflicts initiate and the tribe divides into two.

2 This only happened after decades of ignoring that the mind is inside a brain, that is

field of evolutionary psychology. Unlike other subfields of psychology, evolutionary psychologists study human behavior, acknowledging that it is influenced by an instinct that has evolved by natural and sexual selection; that is, it is optimized to increase the chances of surviving and reproducing. This perspective allowed evolutionary psychology to become a dynamic field, producing several interesting results—and a fair share of controversy. One of the topics under research is exactly the one we are interested here: the female sexual instinct.

From all the many fascinating things to be discovered on the topic, one has been the philosopher's stone, pursued by men over countless generations: "What the heck do women look for in men?" (With some alternative phrasings, of course...) As you could expect, there is still no definite answer, but there has been quite a lot of progress. Part of the discoveries in this field has been condensed in two models for the Ideal Man, as pictured by the female sexual instinct. I will next describe these two models and then introduce my own model.

THREE MODELS FOR THE IDEAL MAN

## The Warrior–Lover

One of the proposed models for the Ideal Man is the "Warrior–Lover," proposed by M.S. Salmon and D. Symons. The Warrior–Lover is strong, able of being aggressive towards other men, superior to them, and extremely dominant of both men and women. Men fear him, admire him, and follow him. Women desire him and he is therefore sexually experienced. The aggressive traits of the Warrior–Lover are softened with a special care for his woman.

This model resonates for most women, especially if they are somewhat ambitious, aggressive, or assertive[3]. Using male characters that follow this model[4], the romance literature sells millions of

---

inside a body, all of them a product of biological evolution....

3 For more details, see the article from Hawley and Hensley mentioned in Sources.

4 Or the other way around, as a lot of support for the model came from analyzing

books every year (around one out of four books sold in the U.S.). Millions of women around the world read these books perhaps lying in their beds, fantasizing they are being taken by a Warrior–Lover.

## The White Knight

Another model, slightly different, is that of the White Knight (proposed by L. A. Rudman and J. B. Heppen). Also popular in romance literature, this model seems to be favored by less aggressive and ambitious women. Perhaps because these women are not so interested in domination, are unable to dominate, or because they look negatively at aggression, they prefer a hero that, still being superior to other men and popular among women, does so by his chivalry, charm, and beauty instead of his assertiveness, aggression, and strength. The White Knight is romantic, devoted, and tender towards his partner.[5]

## The Queen & King

Despite the two previous models being helpful in describing the Ideal Man, I believe that women do not think of an Ideal Man. They think of an Ideal Relationship. In fact, women hardly ever think of an isolated man—they think about an eventual relationship with that man. Therefore, instead of a model for the Ideal Man, I propose a model for the Ideal Relationship.

To better describe this model, in the next few pages we will climb aboard a time machine, fly back some twenty thousand years, and sit down on a very comfortable rock while we observe the wishes of a regular girl from those days. Let's call this girl, symbolizing prehistoric women in general, Wilma (in honor of Mrs. Flintstone).

### Description of the Queen & King Instinct

Wilma is a girl living in a Paleolithic tribe. Her ambition is

---

these books.

5 We speculate that none of the traits of the White Knight are negative for the ambitious females. He just lacks the dominant aspect that is so important for ambitious, aggressive females. They don't mind romance or beauty—as long as it is paired with strength and dominance. A velvet glove over an iron fist.

straightforward: As any other girl, she wants to be the most beautiful woman and become the favorite lover of the most important man of her tribe—the King. Kings are strong and dominant. They hold power over the remaining tribe members. They are both admired and feared by men. Most women desire them and they do please some of these women. Wilma finds his dominance and popularity among women extremely attractive. She wants to use her beauty to seduce the King. She desires to become the King's lover. The King already has other lovers, but that is irrelevant for her. She wants to be his lover, but not just one more lover. She wants to become the first one, the favorite.[6] If she manages to do that, she will become the most important woman in the tribe—the Queen. In that standing, she will be very respected; she will be able to treat other women with superiority and dominance; she will get resources (material resources, labor, and protection) by everyone in the tribe, including the King. She will, in return, submit to the King, as everyone else in the tribe. However, in private, she will have her intimate powers over him...

It isn't yet clear to me whether this model is a broader view of the Warrior–Lover model or if it also includes the White Knight "fans." Maybe when women are ambitious and assertive, with potential to achieve a high social status, they go for the King. If they are more peaceful, less ambitious, or just feel that they can't hold strongly to a position of dominance, they search for a White Knight—to play it safe.

It is important to point out that the Queen & King instinct is just one of the several instincts humans possess, and not the strongest one (think of our very strong parental instinct, for instance). Our "general" instinct is a mix of all the different instincts we possess.

---

6 Scientific research shows that humans are not instinctively monogamous, but instead polygynous—some men having more than one female partner simultaneously. For example, of all the human populations studied by anthropologists, in 84 percent of them the most important men in the tribe are allowed to have several wives. Even in these populations, however, most men are monogamous (and all women).

*Differences Between the Queen & King and Previous Models*

Let us now look at what changed from the two previous models to the Queen & King model:

1.  In the Queen & King Model, one of the main goals of becoming Queen is to rule over other women. She wants power, acknowledged superiority, and dominance over other women.[7] In fact, the strongest criterion for the desirability of a man is how desirable he is to other women.

2.  The Queen & King model does not imply monogamy. She wants to be the favorite spouse of the King, not necessarily the only one. She might enjoy monogamy, but if given the choice, she prefers to share a King than having a regular guy just for her.[8]

3.  In the Queen & King Model, the social success of the woman depends on her union with the King and is attained through her beauty and charm. She wants to be the most beautiful and seductive woman, and therefore the most powerful—the Queen. She does not wish to dominate men by her authority, but by the attraction she stirs with her beauty and charm.

## The Queen & King Instinct in Real Life

Of course, I am only describing one of the several prehistoric *instincts*, not present behavior. Nowadays, women's actions are not so strongly guided by their instincts. But Wilma, in prehistory, probably followed her instinct. She was not rationally planning to seduce the most important man in the tribe. She just felt attracted to important men, as men feel attracted to beautiful women. She tried

---

7 In common chimpanzees, a patriarchal society, the female rank is important for survival of their offspring. In bonobos, a matriarchal society, the female rank is much more important. The patriarchal vs. matriarchal structure of human societies is a controversial issue, but all structures stand between these two extremes.

8 Women do not feel any attraction towards men other women don't want. This is quite unexpected, if you believe that exclusiveness is something women really desire. The reason women seem to value exclusiveness is that women who share a man have a terrible status in our current monogamous societies.

to evaluate the desirability of men[9] in the same way that men try to guess the shape of a breast through a woman's clothes—strong curiosity fueled by an irresistible excitation. It's not a rational act; it's attraction, and attraction is driven by instinct. Attraction is how our instinct guides us. That is why it is so hard to control: It's not conscious, but unconscious. So, without Wilma wasting too much time thinking about it, most of her actions had these underlying goals: to be beautiful, to compete with other women in beauty and status, to choose the most desired man of a given age group, to attract him, to be publicly chosen by him as his number one woman, and to have lots of sex with him.

Coming back from our time travel trip to prehistory and looking at the baby girls being born today, they carry with them the same instinct we saw in Wilma. Women of today still feel like doing the exact same things Wilma did in the past: to be beautiful, to compete against other women in beauty, to choose the most desired man, to attract him, to be publicly chosen by him as his number one woman, and to have lots of sex with him. That does not mean they actually do these things, but they definitely feel like doing them.

People do not blindly follow their instincts. When they believe that the best course of action is different from the one their instinct is suggesting, they (sometimes) consciously act otherwise—we call this free will. Plus, there are many social rules that prevent women from following their instincts.

Yet despite free will and social rules, it is undeniable that the female instinct still influences women's behavior. If women did not have the Queen & King instinct and were instead totally rational beings, wouldn't they be like a female Mr. Spock? That is, totally rational, conscious, and uninterested in any illogical act?

As we probe deeper into this question, let's call this totally rational woman "Mrs. Spock" and imagine her as a Leonard Nimoy look-alike, but with longer hair and thinner eyebrows (keeping the pointy ears).

---

9 The must-have book "The Mystery Method—how to get beautiful women into bed" explains the more complex criteria women use to evaluate the ranking of men (besides direct status), and how to use that in order to look like a King.

*Women Are Different from a Rational Mrs. Spock*

Mrs. Spock's goals would be the same as most women's stated goals: to become a good professional, a healthy person, a good mother, a faithful and supportive friend, and a loving wife of a good man who loves her for the person she is. Oh, and by the way, she would also hate when men stare at her cleavage. These would be Mrs. Spock's real goals and attitudes.

Mrs. Spock would surely use her time and money pursuing these goals. She would dress cheaply, modestly, and choose cheap purses. After all, she would dress to be seen as a good professional by her peers and as an attractive woman by her boyfriend or husband, who doesn't care about expensive purses.

Mrs. Spock would drive the cheapest safe car she could, have a cozy but not trendy home, avoid conflicts with her friends, avoid any intrigues in her workplace, refrain from competing in beauty or success with friends or sisters, and avoid wearing any provocative clothing that could elicit sexual thoughts in men.

She would not waste hours, money, and morning-afters going to discos, as she did not plan to meet the greatest man of her life drunk in a disco. When drinking socially, she would be as calm as always—there would be no unconscious desires or behavior popping out.

Mrs. Spock would save a lot of money. She would then set aside for her future children's education, and would never pressure her husband or boyfriend to make (or spend) more money. She would focus on making him feel happy with himself and in improving their relationship.

In the privacy of her home, with him alone, she would wear her more sexy clothes and put on some makeup. After all, she knows that men are totally driven by their insane instincts and she would use that knowledge to make their relationship more fulfilling and her boyfriend/husband a happier man.

Now look outside your window. Where is Mrs. Spock? Nowhere in sight? Fact is, women are just not like that. The few young women who do behave somehow like Mrs. Spock are either nursing small children or are very religious.

There are only two ways to justify this female detour from Mrs. Spock's ways. Either the stated goals of women are not their real ones, or their actions towards their goals are not rational. Be it one way or the other, or both, women's behavior is in fact strongly controlled by instinct. Their pursuit for happiness is driven by instinct. In fact, few women would be jealous of Mrs. Spock.[10] They would be miserable if they were in Mrs. Spock's shoes—their unsatisfied female instinct would make them so.

Therefore, to bring happiness to a woman, you have to give her something more than what she asks for. You have to totally satisfy her instinct—which is something really hard to do. It is much harder for a woman to become a Queen in a group of millions than it used to be in a group of 150. Women live constantly unsatisfied, comparing what they would like to be—the Queen—to what they are—average women. Nowadays, this is called "low self-esteem" and it's considered the result of high standards imposed on women by "society" (implying "men"). This "society" is, in fact, just all other women she competes against. Women have "low self-esteem" because they constantly, and unconsciously, worry about their place in the female pecking order.[11] Women compete with each other fiercely and this competition is central to their lives.

Given that this instinct exists and is responsible for so much unhappiness among women[12], the best thing their lover can do is to satisfy this instinct. But…

How the heck can you satisfy this female sexual instinct?

Don't worry, the answer comes in the next chapter. For now, let's make a small detour on a different topic.

## MARKETING, WOMEN AND MARRIAGE

Some women regularly buy facial lotions for hundreds of dollars, exclusive dresses for thousands of dollars, and spend a year pre-

---

10 Which supports the claim that their stated goals are not their real goals.

11 Their perception of their own place in the pecking order is likely distorted, because many select for environments full of good-looking women (including what they read, watch on TV, etc.).

12 Men also have their unsatisfied male instincts that make their lives miserable.

paring for their wedding day. If you asked Mrs. Spock why these women act as they do, she would have no clue. The reason, Mrs. Spock, is that "things" are not only "things." We buy things for how they make us feel when we buy them. Marketers know this very well, so they create products and advertise them so that women feel like Queens when they buy them—and women love it.

The best of these products—the Wedding—is the ultimate fulfillment of the Queen fantasy.[13] The bride is the Queen, dresses as a Queen (she even gets to wear some jewelry on her head), and is marrying a man who dresses like a King. She is exhibiting to all other women that she achieved what they all wish for: a marriage full of love and status. (The party is all about showing off the status.) In their eagerness to fulfill that fantasy, women forego all rationality and common sense. Their instinct totally takes over, making them spend huge amounts of time and money on an event that may even start eroding their relationship with the future husband.

That dream party is very good at luring a woman into marriage. I say luring, because marriage definitely won't make her feel like a Queen...

**The Problems with Marriage**

After the thrill of the wedding and the fantastic honeymoon, life is beautiful and the woman's love for her husband is at its peak—but her situation goes downhill from there. Fact is, a significant share of marriages doesn't last long. Many of the people divorcing feel frustrated with their failure to sustain their marriage or enraged with the partner who disappointed them. The problem is not with all these millions of people. The problem is with marriage itself.

First of all, we have to remember that marriage was not created to ensure the happiness of a bride and a groom. It was created to increase social stability and progress—even at the expense of the bride and groom's happiness. Actually, marriage included (and in many parts of the world, still does include) such sweet, romantic things as "parents choose who marries whom," "bride's dowry," "duty

---

13 Being "crowned" Miss Universe is even better than marrying—but only a selected few can achieve that glory. Weddings are for everyone.

of providing sex and obedience," etcetera—clearly not aimed at the couple's happiness.

If we look at how well a marriage satisfies the female sexual instinct (according to the Queen & King model), we will be disappointed. Women want to conquer their Kings and be Queens. They wish for their Kings to desire them intensely. They wish for fantastic sex. They wish to be attractive to all other men, as well. They wish to be admired by and superior to other women, measured by their beauty and their King's status.

But how can they fulfill all these wishes now?

When they are still single, it's pretty easy. They have the option of spending a large share of their income on clothes, hairdressers, and other means of exhibiting beauty and status. They can visit chic places where they feel important among the important people. They can go out to discos and feel attractive to the surrounding men. In reality, despite feeling sensually excited when dancing with guys they like, the highest point of the night is often when they and their friends compete and compare how many guys approached them. (Hence, the toilet visit is when discos really become fun!) Besides discos, they obviously enjoy going out on dates, where guys do as much as they can to amuse and impress them—after all, visiting nice places with someone who is doing his very best to entertain you feels great. And if it doesn't, she can just cut it short.

While single life can be fun and exciting, women usually don't feel fulfilled, as among other things (like feeling lonely) they can't feel like a Queen without a King. Having a King is required to satisfy the female sexual instinct. Of course, some people believe that women need a man as much as a fish needs a bicycle, but I do see a lot more women clinging to undesirable men than I see cycling anchovies.

The single woman's life improves the moment a highly desirable man to whom she feels deeply attracted declares his love for her. The previously single woman now goes to the same places as before, but this time she is next to a desirable man, making her look much better. Above all, she is in love, she feels relaxed, safe, fulfilled, successful, and extraordinarily happy (more even if sex with him is great).

Everything just feels so right, and she is so focused on her love that she wants an agreement to seal her happiness for the rest of her life.

But...

After some years of marriage, this happiness is gone. Sometimes, it is replaced by another kind of happiness, that of the true love that arises between people joined for life as family. Nevertheless, in many marriages, true love does not develop, and even in those where it does, life is not all roses. The woman doesn't feel as excited as she used to. Often, her husband doesn't look at her with the same desire as before. She is no longer the target of other men's attention as she used to be, she can no longer flirt as before. She doesn't wear the same sexy clothes anymore and she doesn't go on girls' nights out. She no longer feels attractive. She no longer feels like a woman.

When she started going steady with her husband, they went out often. Nowadays he doesn't feel like it. Deep inside, he used to go out in order to meet women. Now that he can't meet women, why go out?

In many cases, the relationship with her husband is not that great either. The wife blames all her sexual instinct disappointment on him—he doesn't take her out, he doesn't make her feel attractive, he is not successful enough, he is not great in bed, and he is pushing her to have sex when she doesn't want to (or he doesn't want to have sex when she wants to), and so on. He blames her for his own frustrations: If it wasn't for her, he could have sex with other women, she is not as sexual or free as she could be, she doesn't admire him for his manly qualities, and he can't do all those fun sports with the guys that often.

Add to this boiling pot all the problems faced by two people living and raising kids together.

Hardly a recipe for happiness, is it?

Marriage may bring many good things, specially the beauty of love. But for many women who have a strong female sexual instinct, their instinct is deeply dissatisfied, especially so because that same instinct was doing so well when they were single! Single life has improved dramatically since the time of our grandparents. Married life hasn't. We just postpone the inevitable evil for a bit longer and jump out of it when it gets too bad.

Can't we just think of something better? Can't we adapt married life to our sexual instincts the same way we did with single life?

Chapter 3:

# To Live Out the Queen & King Fantasy

*"Many men know how to flatter; few men know how to praise."*
—*Greek Proverb*

*"No woman wants to see herself too clearly."* —*Mignon McLaughlin*

### FULFILLING THE FEMALE SEXUAL INSTINCT

Fortunately, women are not doomed to keep their female instinct unsatisfied, because there is an interesting and efficient way of satisfying it: through sex.

It is during sex that our instinct dominates our mind the most—and this instinct can be best pleased then, too, as there is a strong mental component to sex. We all enjoy living out our fantasies. Adding a mental twist to the physical stimulation makes sex much better. Sex with an appropriate fantasy transcends sex. With an amazing fantasy, it transcends life, as it can provide us with what we want from life, a hundredfold.

That is what you can do for the female instinct. You can understand what it wants from life, sexualize it, and then satisfy that sexualized version in bed. You will then do something more powerful than just have amazing sex. You will bring her the satisfaction of her female instinctive desires—happiness.

As mentioned in the previous chapter, I believe that women have an unsatisfied instinctive desire: to be the Queen, lover of the King, ruler of other women. This desire can be easily sexualized, and then satisfied through a fantasy. When both sex and the couple's life together follow this fantasy, the Queen & King fantasy, both sex and life become much more exciting for the woman. Life can become a permanent fantasy.

To turn a sex session into the fulfillment of this fantasy, you need to follow six ground rules.

## Rules for the Queen & King fantasy

1. Stimulate the woman's sexual openness—let her reach out for her own instincts and live out the Queen & King fantasy.
2. Demonstrate being better than other men in bed—demonstrate that you are a King.
3. Perform sex in a dominant manner—give her what she wants from a King.
4. Demonstrate her superiority towards other women—demonstrate that she is the Queen.
5. Make her feel desired by you and other men and with power over you—as a Queen, the most beautiful woman of all.
6. Make her feel you are desired by other women—a King.

Let us now examine these six points in detail.

### 1. Stimulate the Woman's Sexual Openness.

Women are very sexual. They enjoy sex for sex, they need sex, and they have plenty of sexual fantasies besides making romantic love with their partner. They enjoy watching other people having sex, and they feel attracted in a sexual way to people they meet in their daily interactions.

Unlike men, they need to hide their sexuality to avoid being labeled with any of the many offensive words meaning "promiscuous woman." In most societies, women gain social respect by being beautiful and exclusive: The perfect women is so beautiful that all men desire her, but she only desires her husband/boyfriend, due to the love (not lust) that she feels for him.

A woman suffers in trying to live up to this image, even with her partner. She knows that most partners would lose respect for her if they knew how sexual she really was inside. And her partner's respect is fundamental for her. To ensure her partner's respect, she often represses her own sexuality.[1]

This repressed sexuality will become a barrier to the fulfillment of her female sexual instincts. That is why it is so important that you stimulate, from the beginning of your relationship, your partner's sexual openness. If you can show her that you will not look down on her by being extremely sexual and open, she will become much happier and relaxed, opening the way for the two of you to experience everything you ever felt you'd like to experience. If you don't blame her for being sexual and having "uncommon" desires, she will be much more likely to listen for her own unconscious desires, to be willing to embrace them, and to share them with you. This is really important if you want to enjoy a totally open and honest relationship—one that brings deep sexual satisfaction and total relaxation to your partner, and an equally satisfying sex life to you.

If you take the opposite road, supporting moralistic views, flattering her "semi-virginity," criticizing promiscuity or perversion in other women, being yourself sexually repressed, believing that sex is only a good thing when following a number of rules, she will be pushed to a role from which she can't escape, and she will live a whole life of repressing her instincts—like most women do.

She wants you to look at her with total respect. That can mean having a very simple, unadventurous sex life—if that is your idea of respect—or a no-barriers sexual life, if you can see how such a life could be respectful, too.

It is important that you don't believe or express that some sexual activities you fantasize about are "wrong" or "bad." If you do, she probably won't let you fulfill them with her. Remember, when talking about what is proper and what is not, she is walking on quicksand, so she won't be totally honest. She is not totally honest with herself, so she won't be with you either. So, don't even ask her about her feelings toward particular sexual activities before stating your opinions, and never ever change your mind if she considers something to be "bad." Don't ever apologize for having open-minded opinions. If you

---

1 A lot of men do this as well. Women, however, do it to a higher degree.

do, it will only confirm the "evilness" of your initial ideas.

### 2. Demonstrate Being Better than Other Men in Bed.

For her to live her Queen & King fantasy in bed, she has to look at you as a King during sex. Two things need to be in place: the way she looks at you in general, and the way she looks at you in bed. Probably, she already looks at you positively—that is why you ever got into bed with her in the first place. Even if she doesn't, don't worry. Deep in a woman's heart, being good in bed is one of the most important qualities a man can have.[2] No women will admit it in public, plenty of women won't admit it to their close friends, and some women won't even admit it to themselves. But for many women, it is like that whether they admit it or not. So try your best, so that she looks at you as a King in bed.

If that already happens with your current sexual partners, great! If not, after you finish reading this book and practice a bit, it will surely start happening. You will make your partner feel new, fantastic sensations and feel understood as never before—and she will look at you as a King. You should then act accordingly: always self-reliant, never bragging nor asking whether she liked it. Your Queen will deduce that your skills in bed and with the female soul, together with your confidence and your uninterest in impressing her, derive from superior genetics and your long track record with many other women—both characteristics of a true King. Let her think so.

### 3. Perform Sex in a Dominant Manner.

Women wish to abandon themselves in the embrace of their King, so that he devours them, giving them more pleasure than they would ever get if they were in control. To drive sex in a dominant and protective manner, you must permanently take the lead and ensure that everything is always to her liking, not letting sex get too mild nor too hasty. During intercourse, you should start on top of her, not under her.[3] You should avoid asking questions for guidance.

---

2 Besides being a man she already found good enough to take to bed in the first place, that is.

3 Key tip: In the first times you have sex with a woman, you should never orgasm with

That does not mean that you should not search for guidance—you must permanently search for guidance. However, don't ask her questions. When sex is over and she is flying high through the clouds, it is important that she feels that everything was so fantastic because:

1. You are really good in bed
2. You treat her with special attention and you care about her pleasure
3. She is irresistibly attractive to you
4. There is a mystical and spiritual connection between the two of you that takes sex to a higher level, proving that you were made for each other.

Even though it is not easy, it would be great if you could transmit at least the first three messages during sex. The fourth message depends on the girl, the kind of sex you had, your sexual chemistry and the kind of relationship both of you are after.

### 4. Demonstrate Her Superiority towards Other Women.

One of the key components of the Queen & King fantasy is that the Queen is the most attractive woman. You need to show her how much you admire her—as a person, as a woman, as a sex partner, or as any other role she takes. Exhibit your desire for her; she needs to see a lot of it.[4] Show her how she is the most beautiful woman in the world and that there is something special, perhaps mystical, in her personality and in the connection between the two of you. Show her—don't tell her.

Some men try to reach King's status by putting down their partner. That works well at the initial stage of meeting women and pickup, but at the point of having sex, that should change or else it becomes a shot in the foot. When you are having sex with a woman, you are already in the context of the Queen & King fantasy. You have to be the King, but she has to be the Queen.

Other men compliment their woman a lot without making them

---

her on top of you. If you do that, say bye-bye to your Kinghood....

4 Not an unspecific horniness, but a desire triggered by her.

feel like Queens. In fact, these men, by giving so many exaggerated compliments, lower their own status. They make themselves look like they are used to "much worse," and that finding her was a stroke of luck. And, in lowering their own status, they drag her status down as well. Bad idea.

Instead, show her that you admire her. Avoid romantic, inflated compliments like, "You are the most beautiful woman in the world." When you give her a big compliment, don't say it as though it is a big thing, in a romantic tone. Say it as a matter of fact, as if it were obvious. Something so obvious that you expect her to be aware of it already.

The best way to convince her that you find her awesome is to show her that she is exactly your type. In this way, she can believe that you really do find her awesome. In a general way, admire her and desire her in the ways she wants to be admired and desired. This is of critical importance: Do not contradict her own inner image. Two things are usually paramount for a woman's self-image: her beauty and something unique and spiritual that sets her apart from all other women. (Here's a tip—read Paulo Coelho's books for an insight into what "spiritual uniqueness" means.) In what relates to beauty, every woman self-evaluates deeply, determining how high she ranks in each feature of her body. She dreams of meeting a man that values the things she considers herself to be good at, while not caring about, or even appreciating, the things she is not so great at. Basically, a man whose type of woman is exactly her. Only in this way can she live her dream of being a Queen, the woman who conquered a King through open competition with all other women (as opposed to a woman who conquered a guy no other women wanted or a guy who doesn't care about appearance at all).

Besides beauty, she also has a unique spiritual side. Probably, someday, soon in the relationship, she will show you an intimate side of herself. In some women, who are rational and down-to-earth, this could mean showing her own works of art, her professional achievements, or just the sort of art she enjoys. She may even show you a part of her "dark side," but also some desires, qualities, and abilities that make her unique.

Less rational women will share with you their "sixth sense," their ability to forecast the future, etcetera. In either case, be grateful and careful when receiving these gifts from her, admiring them in an adequate manner.

Finally, it is not sufficient that you show her how fantastic you find her. You need to show her how she is superior to all other women. Don't miss out on chances of indirectly comparing her positively to other women. If your partner is on the chubby side, explain how unappealing catwalk models look like. Tell her that guys pretend to prefer models because that is socially well accepted. If your partner is more like a catwalk model, tell her how unattractive round asses are and how only primitive men find them appealing. Be careful, though, with stuff she might come to change, like hair... even, eventually boobs!

While you should do your best to let her know that she is your type, and that you chose her among all other women, don't make yourself look like a dork trying to please her. There is a fine balance that you will have to find, but the safe side is not looking dorky. Remember, the goal is not that she feels like a Queen. The goal is that she feels like *your* Queen. So wait until she looks at you as a King. Only then can you show her that you look at her as your Queen.

Finally, but also important: Don't miss out on any chances of making her look like a Queen in public. Any compliment is ten times more valuable if it is done in front of other women, especially if you compliment something that they can't evaluate by themselves, like her kiss.

## 5. Make Her Feel Desired by You and by Other Valuable Men.

Nothing is more fulfilling for a woman than to be desired by the most valuable men, on her scale of value. So make her feel desired by you.

Don't be shy about showing how attracted you are. In fact, exaggerate it. Grab her with desire, tell her how much you want her, compliment her body. Show your enthusiasm during sex.

But, if you do that, won't she feel that you wanted her because of her body? Yes she will—and she will love it! However, that does not mean that you wanted her *only for her body.*

Your desire alone, however, is not enough. Women in relationships deeply miss demonstrations of desire from valuable men. That is what they mainly search for when they go to holiday parties, girls' nights out, etc. You cannot overestimate how much women love to feel attractive. That is why it is so important for you to keep them feeling attractive to other men when they are with you. If you don't, they will either search for it when you are not around, or they will miss it. So, once in a while tell your partner how other men are staring at her. Don't blame her, and don't be jealous; tell her so as a compliment. She will feel happy that maybe men look at her more than she previously thought. She will feel so sexy, and so powerful. Finally, don't stick to men. Tell her how many women look at her with envy, admiration, and attraction in their eyes.

### 6. Make Her Feel You Are Desired by Women.

*"Women are the measure of all things."*

By the above sentence, I mean that women evaluate everything by how much other women desire them. And in nothing is this effect stronger than in evaluating men. Basically, a King is a man women want.

So, don't play the role of the faithful boyfriend/husband uninterested in women and social activities. Instead, dress your best when you go out with your partner and stir attraction in other women, without showing you are actively trying to do so. Don't worry if they, however, hit on you in front of your partner. She will find that exciting as well as a challenge. Act naturally, as if that happens all the time and seize the opportunity to demonstrate how great your partner is. Your goal is to make your partner feel that other women are attracted to you while you clearly show these women, in public, that your partner is better than them—a King and a Queen. If you want to learn about this topic in more detail, you can read my upcoming book *"Inside her Mind."* For now, generally speaking, act as if it is a natural and positive thing that women desire you, but that is not something you actively pursue or manipulate. It is just a consequence of your natural talents. Same goes for your previous experience with women.

## Conclusion

In this chapter we went over the six rules for the Queen & King fantasy: Stimulate the woman's sexual openness, show her that you are better than other men in bed, perform sex in a dominant and protective manner, demonstrate her superiority towards other women, make her feel desired and that other women desire you.

At this stage, the Queen & King Fantasy might sound too theoretical or too simple and obvious. However, the Queen & King fantasy is the foundation for the sexual interaction described in this book. It's just a small part of what we will see, but it pervades everything and it is required to bring sex to the fantasy level, satisfying your partner in a totally different manner and fulfilling all her desires—including the ones she is not even aware of.

Chapter 4:

# Dominance and the Deep Meaning of Power Relations

*A female view on this chapter:*

*You make her so happy. You are a real man and you know how to treat a woman. What she feels towards you is beyond attraction. She just wants to give herself to you—and she feels so proud when she does it!*

\*

*"In love there is always one who kisses, and one who offers the cheek."*
—*French proverb*

*"Pet me, touch me, love me, that's what I get when I perform. That's when I'm really getting what I want." —Connie Stevens*

DOMINANCE AND SUBMISSION

### In Humans, Dominance Is a Different Game

According to the Merriam–Webster dictionary, dominance is having a higher position in a social hierarchy. Being submissive is being under the rule of others.

When we look at the social structures of animals, we will very often encounter a few individuals who are dominant and a majority that is not. The dominants are privileged, as they have better access to material resources and mates. Because of that, individuals compete for dominance. The ones who are better in this competition—usually as determined by their superior physical strength—become dominant. The rest becomes submissive, accepting their lower status in exchange for not being attacked.

As you have read in the previous chapters, I say that a man has to be dominant towards his partner. Does that mean that he is superior to her? Does that mean that there is a threat of violence in a dominance relationship? Does that mean that a submissive individual is inferior, or that he enjoys being abused by dominants?

No, no, no, absolutely not, to all questions.

Although these questions seem logical, they are extremely wrong because they don't consider the two following key aspects of dominance.

First, the dominance competition happens inside each gender. Males compete with males; females compete with females, each gender in its own separate pecking order. This makes sense, as the main goal of the competition is to access the best mates of the opposite gender[1]. So, competition for dominance is gender-specific and it follows different rules in the two genders.

Second, dominance–submission in human societies is not the same as in animal societies.[2] Remember, we have unique and innate political abilities that make human groups far superior to animal groups. Among humans, dominance is granted to their leaders by the group. It is something the group gives to a particular individual; it is not attained by one-on-one fights. Therefore, to become dominant, two things are required: to demonstrate superior abilities, and to use them for the good of others. Dominance shows itself in two ways: by being obeyed, and by being admired. Primitive men achieved status not by beating up other men inside their own tribe but by being good warriors or good hunters, using their violence skills for the group's sake and not against the group.[3] To reach leadership among men, then, a man has to use his abilities for the good

---

1 The exception being, of course, homosexuals.

2 With the exception of our evolutionary cousins, the bonobos, who are somehow more similar to us.

3 We are talking about how dominance is achieved in representative human "tribes": small groups of both genders who need to work in order to survive. In other kinds of non-representative human groups, such as large totalitarian regimes or among jail inmates, the rules are different.

of the group, usually involving plenty of sacrifice, such as giving up resources, time, and sometimes even risking his own life. Those who have a stronger drive to achieve social status are willing to sacrifice more. Those that value social status less or have a lower drive to achieve it are willing to sacrifice less.

An extreme example of a powerful, dominant individual was the village's Catholic priest. Priests were more educated than the villagers (superior abilities) and had only one mission: to save their flock (the good of others). They were also prevented from having interest in any of the material rewards of dominance, such as mates or money. So, the priest was not seen as a competitor by other men and he could then become extremely powerful. It is not a coincidence that the word for priest in Latin, pater, means father. When we are children, our parents have superior abilities and they use them to our benefit. We then obey and admire them. We are submissive and we feel great about it. That is what the figure of a priest does. The dynamic triggers this natural human submissive feeling, which is the key for human domination: To achieve domination over adult humans, one has to make them feel like sons or daughters. To feel like a son or a daughter, the person submitting has to feel that the valuable dominant cares specially about him or her and provides him or her with goods, as mother and father did.

That is very different from what we see in many animal species, where there is a violent competition for dominance. In animals, what we call dominant and submissive individuals are the "best" and the "lesser" animals. In humans it is different. Dominant and submissive are words used to describe personalities. Dominants are secure; they make decisions quickly, take initiative, like to direct others, and worry deeply about their personal status. Submissives are the opposite: Less secure, they don't like to direct others or make decisions, and they are not so worried about personal status. Dominance and submission are personality traits, not measures of success. Dominants are not winners and submissives are not losers. Dominants are the ones who want to be social winners. Some do end up as social winners—others as jail inmates, the ultimate losers. Submissives, on the other hand, are not losers. They are the ones who value other things besides social status—and they get these other things, often from dominants. Therefore, they don't consider the dominants to be in a privileged position at all.[4] Only from the point of view of dominants, who value status above everything else, are submissives losers.

That is why many dominant authors have tried to explain the "puzzling" fact of submissives accepting their submissive condition. But, as the human dominance–submission relationship is totally different from master–slave relationships, the existence of willing submissives is very simple to explain. Submissives grant social status to dominants in exchange for goodies they receive—it is an exchange both parties perceive as beneficial. Dominants are after social status and submissives are after the goodies (resources, pleasure, knowledge, planning, protection, etc.). Despite social status bringing its rewards, dominants tend to overvalue it—and submissives to undervalue it.

Being dominant does not mean that one is better, just that one wants to be recognized as better, to be admired. That drives people to perform, to give, to sacrifice other areas of their lives, to look for less able companions, and to take chances—for them, the prize is worth it. Being submissive means that one is more focused on getting the best one can. The submissive wants to meet the best people he/she can and wants to receive resources, knowledge or pleasure from them—he/she does not mind paying for this with recognition and temporary obedience. Willing submission in humans results from an unconscious calculation of profit between a perceived benefit and the loss of status. If the individual perceives the gains from submission to pay off the loss of status, he/she will submit. Almost anyone can be submissive or dominant in a relationship; it depends on the calculation above.

---

4 Those jealous of Olympic athletes or CEOs "forget" that these achievers have devoted almost all their free time to training or work. If they really wanted to be in these people's shoes, they could do the same—but they don't, because for most of us, it just doesn't pay off.

## Dominance and Women

The reason people compete and sacrifice for status is that these struggles bring advantages. And because much of this struggle remains unconscious, we might predict that these advantages will be of an evolutionary nature—and they are.

As we know from the previous chapters, men have very good reasons to pursue high social status: Women feel attracted to Kings. Persons of high social status in leadership positions (such as Kings) have a particular way of acting: they make decisions and give orders, but they also assume responsibilities, organize stuff, and take care of others—they act as people who have superior abilities and who are willing to put them to work for others. That is how leaders lead. As women feel attracted to high social status and leaders, they likewise feel attracted to this way of behaving. It is the behavior of a dominant (even if he or she has no status whatsoever). So, women indirectly feel attracted to the dominant attitude, as it looks the same as a leadership attitude. Women feel so attracted to a dominant attitude that they try to make their man have one, thus making him look even more attractive. Contrary to most dominant–submissive relationships, she does this without loss of status. As she is not in the same pecking order as the man, she does not feel that she is competing with him, so she is not showing inferiority by submitting—as she would by submitting to women. So, dominance between a man and a woman is not a totalitarian "one bosses the other" relationship. It is more like a democracy: "You direct stuff as long as I vote to keep you in office." The woman grants the man dominance in order to receive pleasure. She can then just sit back, enjoy and relax as her dominant man plans, organizes, directs and performs.

In public, however, she does not want to be dominated. She wants to be treated as a Queen and be made clear that she has power over her King. In detail, here is the exact deal she wants: She grants him dominance in order for him to give her pleasure. He is allowed to be dominant towards her as long as that does not challenge her social status—while he should act as a dominant man in public (mostly towards others), he has to preserve her image, treat her like a Queen, and make her rise in the female pecking order.

Meanwhile, in private, he can be slightly dominant, and in bed he should be dominant—that makes her excited. Being dominated in bed is the exaggerated, sexualized satisfaction of the female sexual instinct—extremely exciting and powerful.

If she can cut this deal, she will be very happy.

## The Three Types

We have been looking at what the perfect dominance–submission relationship is for most women. Now let's look at what they get in real life.

I believe that there are three fundamental types of men, as regards their dominance–submission relationship with women: altruistic dominants, selfish dominants, and non-dominants.

### Altruistic Dominant

An altruistic dominant proactively looks for what is best for his partner. Every time she lets him lead, she has a fantastic experience, better than if she had taken the lead herself. Besides, she never has to worry about anything, as he takes care of everything. She becomes super happy in the relationship. She feels how everything is much better with him. She gains a lot without losing anything. In regards to sex, if the altruistic dominant brings her new sensations, she will be very open to any new experiences he leads her toward.

To go out at night with his partner, the altruistic dominant buys tickets to something the partner likes to attend or do. In bed, the altruistic dominant leads the sexual interaction with the clear goal of giving his partner pleasure while paying full attention to her reactions. He might slap her and call her all sorts of bad names, if (and only if) he realizes that is what she enjoys. If she doesn't, however, he can be very sweet and tender. Usually, he is sweet, tender, and rough at the same time.

The altruistic dominant is the one that satisfies the Queen & King fantasy. Women love him. Despite having named him the altruistic dominant, I don't want to mislead you regarding his intentions. The altruistic dominant is not moved by real altruism (whatever that is). He loves to be adored and admired as a King. He himself is living out his fantasy of becoming a King, by conquering his Queen's heart.

### Selfish Dominant or Domineer

A selfish dominant (usually called domineer), neglects his partner's needs, although he still expects appreciation and recognition. In the dominance–submission bargain, he does not hold up his end of the deal. Although he leads the interactions, he does so considering his interest, not hers. With him, she eventually becomes disappointed and feels "not valued enough." She accepted a dominant man so that she would be taken care of and treated as a Queen he admires. Not to be treated as an underling.

Despite her dissatisfaction, she will still feel attracted to this man, because, as David deAngelo brilliantly says: "Attraction isn't a choice." A man that acts dominantly is extremely attractive to women. Being unable to control him just makes her more excited.

In bed, the selfish dominant leads the sexual interaction, exhibiting his dominance over her. When he enjoys slapping or calling her bad names, it is because he likes it. His fantasy is being a King. Period—"Queen not included in the package." Many women find this type of behavior exciting (due to its dominance aspect). However, it is not always satisfying (due to its selfish aspect).

### Non-dominant

The non-dominant men are a large and heterogeneous group of men. Most have little desire to take initiative, and believe that success derives from obeying rules and norms. It includes the politically correct men, the men who believe that all differences between genders are socially constructed, the men who believe women are either fragile or morally superior, the men who feel guilty about having sex, the men who have an overly objective view of things—nerds—and submissive men (both altruistic and selfish).

When going out with their partner, the standard non-dominant usually asks the fatal question: "What shall we do tonight?"

In bed, the non-dominant does not lead the sexual interaction, which is done "together." He won't act or talk in a way that could be seen as disrespectful—he fails to see that sex does not follow social rules. Sex is primitive. It follows human instincts and it is much more important than social rules.

Yet sexually submissive women are ambitious. They want the best man they can get. So they feel attraction to men they consider above or on par with in the male social ranking, not below. Instead of a Queen & King fantasy, a man who respects her excessively is asking for a Queen & Serf fantasy. While children's books are full of Queen & King stories and Prince & Princess stories, look as much as you want, but you won't find Queen & Serf stories. Non-dominants do not see the world through the lens of dominance, however—as the world actually is—and they very often are caught in Queen & Serf relationships.

## How to Implement Dominance

Dominance is extremely exciting in the male–female relationship. It allows the woman to live out her Queen fantasy. She deeply desires a King to whom she can give herself so that he pleases her as she cannot imagine. A King whom she admires and who will take possession of her in bed. Two things need to be in place for a man to fulfill this fantasy of hers.

First, that she looks at the man as a King. Second, that he is dominant and exhibits signs of dominance.

If she doesn't look at you as a King yet, then you should be careful with exhibitions of dominance. A good strategy to implement dominance is to start by being good in bed, thus earning your status of dominant, and then proceed to exert your dominance. Women do not crave to be dominated by men in general. They crave to be dominated by the King, who is so superior that he dominates everyone (in her fantasy). That is why you should not start by dominating her, but by placing yourself as King before you do. If you act as if you are a dominant without backing it up, you will look like a too-obvious selfish dominant.

### Demonstrations of Dominance

There is, however, an exception to what I am saying here. Women are so turned on by dominance that acting dominant before she considers you a King can be helpful in making her consider you a King.

If you live in a misandrous culture or generation—and you probably do—she will probably consider that "most men are dorks and unworthy of her." If you act slightly dominant, you will stand out from the over-submissive crowd of men she is used to interacting with, and she will consider you attractive. As the dominance of a man is so important for her, she might test how submissive or dominant you are during your first interactions: She will perform a demonstration of dominance over you to see how you react.[5] If you allow her to do so, you are accepting your submissive status towards her. She will then continue performing these demonstrations, because you are giving her power and she wants to enjoy it to the fullest. Despite her enjoying that power, she won't feel attracted to you.

If you block her demonstration of dominance, showing that you understand what she is doing and will not submit, she will probably feel excited. The interesting thing is that she will then expect you to progress, making your own demonstration of dominance. If you do, she will probably feel very excited—and happily submit. She wanted to submit all along, but only to a man who understands submission, and who can lead her to a positive experience.

What are, in more detail, these demonstrations of dominance? They are actions whose major purpose is to exhibit a dominant position. For instance, she can give direct orders to you; she can push you to bed or control your movements (such as forcing you to sit); she can ask for abusive favors (such as asking for you to get up and fetch something for her); she can touch you but not allow you to touch her, etc., etc. In bed, she can also try to give orders, control your movements, or slap you (usually while showing her excitement and giving you compliments). All these are clear demonstrations of dominance. Usually, she will love if you slap back harder, in a more dominant way. In general, that is the correct thing to do when facing demonstrations of dominance: Act in a way that shows that you understand what she is doing, show that you are not offended, and with good humor, reject submitting to her. Then do your own dem-

---

5 These are called shit-tests in the pickup artists' community.

onstration of dominance, in a calm and polite manner.

When you do that, you are signaling, "I understand dominance. Not you or anyone else can dominate me. I will be the sexually dominant one. Are you interested? You can now relax and submit to me during sex. Just enjoy." How come are you signaling such a complex message by slapping her ass harder? Remember what I said before about dominance being like a democracy—that you dominate only after you win your election? That is what you just did—you did not jump to impose demonstrations of dominance on her; you waited for her to do her demonstration—or was it just a request? Then you showed her how dominant you are. She asked for it. You took a stand. You won your election.[6]

As a general rule, don't impose demonstrations of dominance on her until she shows interest. Let your dominance flow as a positive force to give her pleasure. Show off your dominance by exhibiting your physical strength (lift her in the air), your sexual experience (give her pleasure), both together (give her pleasure while having hard sex with her) and your general coolness about sexual issues. Don't be interested in demonstrating your dominance, per se—that is a selfish dominant desire. Be as dominant as a strong bull elephant that impassively looks at a lion, not like a nervous dog barking at other dogs.

Inside a longer-term relationship, women also make requests for dominance, although in a different manner: They misbehave. They misbehave very obviously as a request to feel your strong dominance. This misbehavior can take different forms but usually comes out as a totally illogical argument over something irrelevant. When she starts behaving illogically and aggressively, she is usually asking for you to have rough and dominant sex with her. It is like a child losing self-control, being aggressive without really wanting to be so. In a similar way as how parental behavior calms a child, having rough dominant sex calms her down and makes her relax. She

---

6 Submissive women crave to be dominated, so as soon as you show dominance, they just enjoy their submissive position. So she slaps once, you slap her once, she enjoys, end of story. However, if the woman slaps back, be careful. She is probably not interested in submitting and you should not impose it on her.

will feel dominated, protected, secure, and back in control of herself.

This is not to say that arguments between couples should be solved through dominant sex—I believe that both parties should listen to mutual criticism attentively and always try to improve their interaction. What we are talking about here is not about serious, constructive arguments but about silly, illogical arguments over irrelevant issues that might come out of the blue. Not illogical because the man finds it illogical (as he sometimes does with many female issues), but illogical to the point that will seem illogical even to the woman, as soon as she calms down. The reason they are illogical is because they are just made-up excuses. She can't tell you that she craves you to take an attitude, so she makes up excuses for being annoyed, and those excuses often end up sounding illogical.

Of course, I only recommend that you *try* having dominant sex with her in those moments. If she wants it, she will be very happy you understood her. If not, she will let you know and you should obviously cut your attempt short!

**How to be Dominant in Bed**

Being dominant is about taking care, making things happen, giving protection, being secure, giving orders, and demonstrating power over the other—allowing the submissive to enter a state of absolute no responsibility, no need to make decisions or even to think. The submissive enters a state that can be described as a child being spoiled on Christmas Eve: the child has to follow some pleasant orders and will, in return, get lots of gifts. It is very important that your partner feels like a child being spoiled.

Start applying your dominance in bed the moment you begin foreplay: Lead her around the room, almost like dancing. Slowly turn her around to kiss her back, turn her again to kiss her. Do this by slowly pushing her. Don't worry if it looks dramatic—that is a good thing, within some limits, of course. Kiss her lightly, but hold her tightly—exhibit your physical strength while being gentle. If you want her to move, get her off the ground and place her where you want her next, but only if you can do this easily. If you can't, don't worry; it is just a detail. When you lie down in bed, embrace her, holding the back of her head with your hand, like you would do to a baby. Then slowly lay her down in bed, with exaggerated care. Once in a while, don't be shy of doing the opposite: Lift her in the air and throw her on the bed.

Do foreplay with a dominant stance, deciding what to do and when to do it. Take off her clothes. Talk to her in a dominant way, as described in Chapter 12. Look for body contact. Grab her. Grab her lightly and grab her strongly, to discover what she prefers. Wrap your legs around hers. Get as much body contact as possible. Proceed slowly. Dominate her by preventing her from going too quickly.

All you do, all the "orders" you might give and all the positions you lead her into, however, are for her pleasure. To say, "Suck my cock!" and push her head against your dick is not altruistic dominant behavior, and will not make her feel like a spoiled child, because you are giving yourself pleasure. While it still might excite her, it isn't the approach I recommend.

Being dominant in bed is the very essence of sex between a man and a woman. To be treated to immense excitement and pleasure is what most women crave for in bed. To do so, start very softly, but control the situation. At a later stage, control her position (pinning her down, for instance.) Slowly and softly develop from there, giving her immense pleasure with foreplay and oral sex before starting sex in a very soft manner, focusing on the emotional connection. Only then increase your dominance and use the powerful penetration movement (explained in Chapter 8). The loud sound of your pelvis banging against her pelvis or ass will make her extremely excited.

You can progressively increase your dominance according to her wishes. Try grabbing her really strongly and see how she reacts. Slapping her ass and calling her some slightly bad names in a nice manner, as explained in Chapter 12, are the next steps. If she approves this and enjoys—many women usually do—you can progress, step by step, with her implicit approval, until you find the appropriate dominance level for her. Sometimes, her tolerance may be quite advanced: You might end up slapping her very hard, saying some very strong words, and even spitting on her, but always, always, to her pleasure. Most times, she will enjoy just an occasional slapping, sweet offenses, and some hard banging, but not more. As the spoken word is extremely important in dominance, be sure to read Chapter 12 before you start acting dominant.

Finally, keep being dominant when sex ends. Take good care of her, cleaning her if you happen to get her dirty, and making sure she is comfortable. Offer to fetch some water if she needs some, etc., and cuddle for a while—in a dominant position, obviously. Let her rest her head on your shoulder or something of the sort. Be a gentleman.

*Bonus of Being Dominant*

The acts of feeling responsible, leading, focusing on your part-ner's pleasure, applying the powerful penetration movement, and feeling her admiration for you actually allows you to have a much better control of your ejaculation. Your brain shuts down those dis-turbing pleasure signals from your penis as it is focused on doing the job. You enter the state of Flow, where pleasure and pain have no room.

## How to be Dominant in the Non-sexual Environment

As I said before, most of the time, being dominant is about mak-ing her feel like a child who is extremely well taken care of. So, when you are not having sex, take some actions that trigger those same positive feelings, such as the following:

- As she sits in the living room, bring her some of her favorite cookies and tea.
- When she leaves the shower, wrap her in a towel. Comb her hair.
- When she falls ill, be the best nurse/daddy in the world.
- Cook for her.
- Always know what to do. Be the strong daddy who is always there for her.
- Help her in anything that is giving her trouble.
- Take the responsibility of planning your dates
- Don't allow her to misbehave.
- Never ever misbehave, yourself.

The analogy with the child treatment should not be taken too far. It is meant to make your partner feel the positive sides of being a child, not the negative ones. So, for instance, you should never treat her like a child during conversations or decisions, nor look at her as a child, nor act as though you know better. Especially, you should not try to control your partner, inquire about her whereabouts, preach to her, etc., as parents do with their children.

My point is that you should adopt a caring and diligent attitude, dedicating yourself to her well being as a good father does with his children—but in a seductive way. Do this not because women are any more juvenile than men are, but because the topic of this book is how to make women extremely happy.

## Not Becoming Suffocating Dominant

To be dominant does not mean to "impose" anything on her. To be dominant means that you promise permanent action, but not against, or regardless of, what she does. You will not wait for her to take the lead in any aspect of life, but when she does, by all means listen carefully and adapt to her wishes.

Even if she is a very submissive woman, she will still want a chance to show off her qualities. She doesn't want to have to perform, but she will enjoy performing when she feels like it. You need to give her room to show off her qualities to you. This is not hard to do, of course—just let her lead whenever she starts doing anything dominant (but not involving demonstrations of dominance), and give her lots of compliments on whatever she does.

## Do Not Suffocate Yourself

You should also be careful in not becoming suffocating dominant to *yourself*. As in everything in this book, I don't mean to suggest that it is your moral duty to do anything. I am just describing a strategy to achieve a goal. Being dominant is tiring, especially outside the bed. If you feel that being the dominant is too much of a burden or something that does not make you happy, it is better to give it up. Despite the importance of dominance, it is much better to be a motivated non-dominant than to be a dominant that feels the relationship is a burden instead of a pleasure.

## Where Are All the Altruistic Dominants?

Unfortunately for the fulfillment of the female Queen & King fantasies, there are not many of those altruistic dominants out there. They are rare. Most men act non-dominantly towards women, and most of those who act dominantly do it selfishly.

Girls do not hide their strong attraction for dominant men, but after a few experiences with selfish dominants, they become disappointed, feel humiliated, generalize, and assume that all dominants are selfish. They then start fighting the craving for dominant men consciously, and eventually choose a non-dominant.

When women, sad and hurt, pout and complain to their non-dominant male friends about their selfish dominant boyfriends, these friends find it ironic that she is complaining, given that she is the one who chose them; but they are wrong. She searched for an altruistic dominant and what she criticizes is his selfishness, not his dominance. She doesn't deny wanting a King. She just wants to also be the Queen by her King.

Why is this? If it is so simple to be dominant, and so rewarding in sexual terms, why aren't most men altruistic dominant?

Recent research on feminine submission, by Patricia Hawley and William Hensley at the University of Kansas, gathered some very interesting data that might be able to explain this "paradox." These researchers found that not only the majority of women prefers a fantasy of sexual submission to one of dominance[7], but also that the majority of men prefers it, too! This is not so surprising if we look at submissives as we have been doing: people who are interested in getting the best for themselves without having to take risks or have the trouble. If we, however, had looked at female submission as a result of male oppression and as a trait of inferiority, the above results would be indeed very surprising. Dr. Hawley's research sup-

---

7 The submission fantasy was the following: a dominant stranger (attractive and sexually experienced) met the submissive at a hidden area of a party they both attended, and proceeded to kiss him or her, despite the submissive's unconvincing protests.

ports the idea that being a submissive is pleasant and that women are not weird or inferior by preferring the submissive role—they are just lazily looking out for pleasure. After all, the submissive is never rejected in an advance, nor accused of rape, nor of being easy (on the contrary, the dominant demonstrates to the submissive to find him or her attractive.) The submissive lets the dominant take chances. The submissive has neither performance anxiety nor guilt—only pleasure.

This research also sheds some light on why there are so few dominant men: because most men, like women, are interested in having the goodies without the trouble. They prefer to be sexually submissive. From here, understanding why there are so few altruistic dominants compared to selfish dominants is also pretty easy. Unless the man really enjoys feeling women attracted to him or has a deep wish to please a particular woman, he simply isn't motivated to put the woman's interest in front of his.

So, in broad terms, we all like to feel pleasure and to be admired. Most of us just wait around for others to come and please us, without having to bother much about it. A few of us proactively go and get from others what we want: pleasure and admiration. A small minority plays a different game. First it gives to others as much as it can without being submissive: then waits for them to pay back with pleasure and genuine admiration.

This last group, the altruistic dominants, is the group you should belong to be an extraordinary lover. Being an altruistic dominant will help you achieve a different kind of relationship where she is utterly happy. To do so, you have to focus on how to make sex better for her, and how to make her live out her Queen & King fantasy. Be her King and make her your Queen.

I don't claim that being altruistic dominant is the only way to have a satisfying relationship with a submissive woman. Other kinds of relationship can be extremely fulfilling and exciting—but they are just not the same. They won't unleash and then satisfy all unconscious desires of a woman. I am talking powerful stuff here.

## Becoming an Altruistic Dominant

We all have a submissive side and a dominant side. We all crave pleasure and for social recognition. Where pleasure is more important than status, we take a submissive role; where status or a genuine care for the submissive matters most, we take the dominant role. We all have been born submissive to our parents and become dominant towards our children; and even the nicest among us has probably taken a selfish dominant slip somewhere down the road.

So, dominance is something you achieve easily if you want to, especially when the other person actually wants you to take that role.

If your goal is to sexually satisfy your partner to the extreme, I warmly advise you to step into the altruistic dominant's shoes.

## What If You Meet a Real Dominant?

I believe that the large majority of women is submissive to the men they are attracted to, even if these women start by looking dominant on the outside. There are, however, a few that are dominant all the way. So, how shall you act if you meet one of these?

At first, it might seem logical that, if you meet a dominant woman, you should be submissive, so that the fit is perfect. Despite being a logical reasoning, it is plainly wrong. You should never be submissive to a woman, as she will never feel deeply attracted to you.

So, let's see how to behave with dominant women: first with the altruistic dominants, then with the selfish dominants.

### Being with an Altruistic Dominant

If you meet an altruistic dominant, you should start a duel, with one altruistic dominant facing another. It is really a duel—a duel of titans. The duel is not for blood but for excitement, with each opponent trying to excite the other.

Your altruistic dominant partner is probably extremely sensual to begin with, and she will use her talent on you. She will tease you. She will get you excited and then deny sex. If you move away, she will come after you, make you all horny again... and then stop. She will make you absolutely crazy with desire. She will stare you in the eyes to see the effect she has on you.

However, her goal is not to show power over you. Remember, men desire women and women desire the desire of men. So, while a male altruistic dominant wants to see women crazy with pleasure, an altruistic dominant female wants to see you crazy with excitement. She just wants you to feel as excited as possible before you translate that into amazing sex. Deep inside, altruistic dominant or not, she is a woman and, as such, she wants passionate dominant sex from the man.

So, with an altruistic dominant woman, don't be over-controlling, let her perform her act and give her lots of compliments. However, be equally exciting to her: this relationship is altruistic dominant versus altruistic dominant. Let her perform some of the time, but then take your turn to please and excite her, even if that goes against her will (and it usually will). You see, she doesn't feel comfortable with being pleased. Sex is her performance, and is not for her pleasure—though she will get pleasure at the very end; by submitting to the pleasure you offer her, she will feel that she is mundane, just one more of your conquests, and that you will fail to see how amazing she really is in bed. So give her compliments on how great she is, even at receiving pleasure. Either make her feel she is performing when she is receiving pleasure, or just force it a bit. But, eventually, receiving pleasure is not what she wants, so she will come back to tease you again. When she teases you enough, show her the man you are and how hot she makes you feel.

For example, let's say she has placed your penis at the entrance of her vagina more than twice, and when you pushed into her, she stepped back with a sly naughty look, obviously teasing you. Altruistic dominants do this all the time. Even though it might not seem so, she is as horny as you are, but she is making the game last. She will ask you how much you desire her. She will make you "beg" to let you have her. She will do this until you understand how the game is played.

The way to play that game, when enough is enough, is to be more cunning than she is, and through your irresistible desire, just get what she wants you to get. For instance, by saying:

"Wow, I am so hot for you. So let me just push the tip of my dick in. I promise it will only be the tip."

"Really?"

"Really."

"OK, just the tip then..."

You slowly push just the tip of your penis into her. Then, give her a couple of compliments, show how irresistible she is, and when she says:

"Just the tip...," answer:

"Just the tip..." and slowly and carefully, slide a bit more in. Then ask: "Like this, just the tip?" and keep on slowly pushing the rest in.[8] You can do it like this or in many other ways as long as you play her game. Then, start having passionate sex with her. She wants to drive you crazy and have sex with a man that is totally crazy for her. She wants no boring regular stuff done by people in control. She prefers not to have sex than to have sex with a man who doesn't seem to be crazy for her.

So, once it starts, enjoy it fully and show her how crazy she drives you. She wants to see you totally crazy with passion, fucking her like an animal or totally crazy with passion making slow and intimate sex, melted by love, desire, and horniness for her.

In this battle of titans, simultaneous orgasms are common. Nothing is more exciting for an altruistic dominant as the orgasm of their partners, so it just happens naturally. Besides, simultaneous orgasms are the best result for the battle of titans: no winners, no losers, and a definite need for a rematch...

That is not to say that altruistic dominant versus altruistic dominant is the best possible sex. While it is a very exciting experience, it is an unstable equilibrium where both partners want the same and, sooner or later, one or both will feel they are not getting enough appreciation.

### Being with a Selfish Dominant

Selfish dominants look at sex as the means to get off and at their

---

8 Remember, this is a game to be played with an altruistic dominant woman, who is clearly playing a game and obviously interested in having sex. Besides, because you are doing it very slowly without restraining her, she always has the option to stop.

sex partners as the instrument to achieve that. They have no interest in the sexual needs and desires of their partners, unless they clash with their own or if they can use them to manipulate their partners. A selfish dominant does not please her partner for free. Nevertheless, a selfish dominant feels it is her right to be pleased whenever she wants and in the exact way she wants it.

Sex with selfish dominants is sometimes non-sensual and mechanic, as they are often non-sensual women. For a selfish dominant, the goal of sex is for her to get off and the rest is either hot air or hidden ways to force women to submit to men. When a selfish dominant starts behaving sensually, don't be fooled: it is with the hidden agenda of performing demonstrations of dominance.

Selfish dominants are often proponents of the more extreme versions of feminism. It is an appealing ideology to them, as it provides a justification for their desire to act only on their own behalf, disregarding their male partners. These women are only a slightly watered-down version of the selfish dominant machos of the nineteenth century. So, it is not a surprise that I have no clue—nor interest—in finding out the best psychological frame of mind to please them in bed. Nevertheless, sex is sex and they will enjoy the physical techniques taught in this book.

The most important point to remember when dealing with a selfish dominant is that, when she says no, she really means no—and will feel very offended by any insistence. In fact, she is being fair, as she is objective and direct in her "no" and she does not even understand why other women can act in a different way.

**Never Be Submissive**

If you are submissive to a selfish dominant, she will abuse you more and more. In the end, she won't value you anyway.

If you are submissive to your altruistic dominant partner, she won't have as much fun and she won't feel so attracted to you. She wants to feel she is the best, and to be the best means that she can drive even the most experienced man crazy. So, by showing her how aware, valuable, and dominant you are—and still be driven crazy and conquered by her—you are making her happy. But to be sustainable, you have to permanently "put up a fight," let her win some battles, but never the war.

Finally, if you are with a submissive partner, being submissive is not the answer. Sex will be boring, she won't value you, and she might even have to jump into the dominant role, which is exactly what she does not want to do. She will feel like you do when you hire a professional to do a job and you end up doing the job yourself.

## Where Is the Power?

Power and dominance are two different things. Powerful people know the difference between the two. Most people ignore it—and that is why most people have no power whatsoever.

Many sex books and magazines advise women to once in a while play an extremely (selfish) dominant role towards their partners, emphasizing demonstrations of dominance. This brings out the powerful woman in them and gives them power. Besides this advice, we are currently surrounded by the concept of "girl power," which is basically the idea that women should capitalize on men's chivalrous ideals and on the sexual arousal women cause in men, all to the practical effect of behaving abusively towards men.

Does this really bring power to women?

Yes and no.

The ultimate female-specific sexual power is to have power over a King; to feel his uncontrollable desire and love for her, to see how he puts her above everything else, and to witness his willingness to sacrifice so much for her—and be in control of that. That is Power.

A woman that performs demonstrations of dominance on a willing partner or behaves abusively towards men in general does have some power. True, she feels great and she manages to extract resources from men. Best of all, she feels powerful in relation to other women: She feels powerful when she abuses guys and she feels powerful when she laughs about it with her girlfriends and shows how "powerful" she is with men.

However, the reason she can get away with those actions is because she is not dealing with Kings—and, probably, she never will.

Women become more powerful when they avoid doing demonstrations of dominance. And they become more excited when their partner prevents their demonstrations of dominance than when he accepts them. They realize they have power of securing a relationship with a more worthy man—and having this sort of power over a King is ten times more exciting and valuable than dominating an underling.

## Sexism?

Some people will not agree with the Queen & King model, saying that it is chauvinistic and wrong because it does not advocate for equal, identical roles between the genders.

Like it or not, Kings and Queens are different, because our unconscious mind looks at them differently. A country won't feel properly represented by a monarchy featuring a metrosexual King visiting fashion events and a sporty Queen who joins the army. Similarly, most citizens want to live in a country whose males do well internationally in sports and which has the most beautiful female models in the world, not a country whose women are famous athletes and men distinguished models.[9] Of course, if the country also has the best women in sports and the best male models, great! Nothing against beautiful men and athletic women... It's just that, for most people, those qualities have different value in the different genders. A woman is more attractive if she looks good. A man is more attractive if he is a champion; we want our Queen to be the most attractive woman and our King to be the most attractive man. There is nothing necessarily chauvinistic about this.

Some women, however, don't want to be socially or sensually appreciated for their looks, but only by their academic, professional, or athletic achievements. Great for them. What is absurd is that they assume that they are either representative of women or that other women are inferior to them. Unlike them, most women also want to be socially appreciated for their looks, and this does not make them inferior beings. In the same way, some men value their looks immensely. Great for them, too. However, most men will definitely

---

9 Male athletes make much more money than female athletes. Female models make much more money than male models.

not feel fairly represented if that small minority of men starts talking on their behalf...

Let us not forget that Kings and Queens are representative roles for the social and sensual lives, not for the professional life. I am therefore not arguing that one gender is more adequate for any kind of work or that women should be promoted based on their looks or men on their athletic achievement. I am also not saying that in professional or otherwise non-sensual relationships, men should behave dominantly towards women.

In bed, however, we are not interested in the professional abilities of our partner; we are interested in his or her quality of attraction, which is triggered by our unconscious desires, which differ between genders.

## Dominance Is Not the Whole Story

My strong focus on dominance does not mean that being an altruistic dominant by itself is enough to sexually satisfy your partner. Not at all! It is just one of the several qualities a lover should have. Other qualities, such as sweetness, sensuality, sensitivity, beauty, and technique are also important, and will be dealt with in other chapters.

Contrary to what some people might think, being dominant is not the opposite of being sweet. In fact, being dominant allows you to look even sweeter in her eyes, without seeming dorky. Do not confuse submissiveness with sweetness—and be very sweet.

Chapter 5:

# Relaxation, the First Step of Sex

*A female view on this chapter:*

*She doesn't know how to explain it. She just knows that you make her feel so relaxed. No fears, no worries, nothing. With you she can be herself. With you she can be at her best.*

\*

*"The main thing to do is relax and let your talent do the work."*
*—Charles Barkley*

*"Making love is like hitting a baseball. You just gotta relax and concentrate." —Susan Sarandon*

## RELAXATION

There are two emotional keys for sexual "success", be it a woman's or a man's. If you turn these two keys in the right way, your partner will be better able to engage in sex, to perform, and to experience pleasure. The two "magic" keys are these:

1. Relaxation, and
2. Excitement.

This is not surprising, but it is extremely important. Excitement is the level of sexual arousal, and translates into a desire for physical stimulation. Increase the women's excitement and she will be increasingly more willing to engage in more advanced sexual activities and increasingly more able to enjoy them. A big share of this book focuses on increasing your partner's excitement.

Relaxation is the other emotional key—and the focus of this chapter. It is critical during your first experience with a particular partner, but becomes less of an issue as time goes by.

Women are typically anxious. As their anxiety prevents them from enjoying and having sex, they crave chances to relax in a romantic environment. This environment is directed at relaxing the woman in the presence of the man she will have sex with later on. Candlelight, drinks, a full stomach, movies, two isolated persons, no one watching; all these are helpful in relaxing the woman[1], who is particularly anxious when she is about to have sex with a man for the first time. When moving to bed, a very nice room properly decorated to look both beautiful and safe keeps helping her relax. But why do women need to relax in order to have sex?

Because to have sex is, biologically, more dangerous for women than for men. A woman can eventually get pregnant—so she better know what she is doing. To ensure that she does, she has evolved to get unconsciously anxious when facing sex. The evolutionary point was not to screw her sex life, but to be sure that she really wants to have sex before she does it. This is, however, just one of the several reasons behind her anxiety. Another derives from the weird relationship with sex our societies have developed. On one hand, women see sex in the media all the time, and they talk about it all the time. It sets a performance bar, giving rise to performance anxiety before sex. On the other hand, we have a strong puritan legacy that makes her feel guilty and wondering whether she is doing the proper thing and with the proper timing.[2] There is also a power issue: Before she has sex, she has power over the man. She knows he wants her and the ball is on her side. Finally, the man she will have sex with will evaluate her sexual performance, her looks and, paradoxically, her purity—adding to her performance anxiety.

So, it's actually not surprising that women feel anxious. Both the romantic environment and a few drinks can lower her anxiety. They are actually very helpful, but can we do something more? If we take a

---

1 The first few drinks are for simple bodily relaxation….the next ones are for another type of "relaxation": to get the conscious mind out of the way.

2 On Chapter 12 there is a section on how to deal with repression.

step back, we can see that the root cause of all these kinds of anxiety is the chronic female insecurity. Their insecurity breeds anxiety, so they crave relaxation.

So, another way of making women relax is to aim at the root-cause, the insecurity. Women will relax once they know that there is no reason to be insecure.

## Some Common Causes of Female Insecurity

There are many different causes for the female insecurity regarding sex. They mostly derive from the different fears she has before sex occurs: that sex won't be good or that the man loses interest. Most women will stop feeling insecure once they believe that their worries are unfounded. They will relax if their partner, besides being romantic, demonstrates that he can be trusted for the following:

1.  To not harm her;
2.  To allow her to stop in case she wants to;
3.  To not lower her social status;
4.  To not judge her morals;
5.  To find her beautiful and sexy;
6.  To not require her to perform;
7.  To please her;
8.  To be pleased.

Some of these things she will get to know through intimacy. By being with you for a longer period, she will feel closer to you and more trusting. Other things, she can discover through sensual intimacy. By dating you for some time, she can find out whether you excel in all the above eight points, and then relax for sex more easily.

Great, but how about if you don't want to wait that long? How can you make her relax quicker?

The way to do that depends on the dominance stance of your partner: You have to do it in one way for submissive women and in a different way for dominant women.

## How to Ease the Submissive Woman's Insecurity

A good starting point to ease a submissive woman's anxiety is to behave as an altruistic dominant. The woman can then take a submissive stance and relax. A dominant man ensures that he will make things happen and by being altruistic, he transmits safety and relaxation. By switching to submissive mode, women lower their chronic anxiety and insecurity—they know they don't have to do anything but enjoy. Besides behaving altruistic dominantly, there are specific things you can do to address each of the eight causes for insecurity in women.

### Do Not Harm Her

To make a submissive woman know that you won't harm her requires that you show yourself to be a trustworthy and harmless person.

This is when being a dominant man brings some problems. Their fears increase when they see that they can't control you, so you must demonstrate safety. This is not easy to do, because women are terrible at detecting trustworthiness. Most of them trust bank account managers, advertising, astrologists, etc., so you can't expect them to find you trustworthy just because you are. Increase your trustworthiness score by being very normal, totally fitting into a tribe stereotype, and by using chivalrous speech.

Fortunately, once you are having sex, trust builds from real stuff. You can build trust by showing that your interest is totally aligned with hers: Show her (don't tell her) that you are interested in her feelings and her pleasure, and that you know what you are doing in bed.

As your foreplay and sexual interaction develop, and as she notices how you use your talents to please her, she will gain confidence. She will see that it is in her interest not to question or block you, and will put down her guard because there is nothing to fear.

### Allow Her to Stop

Despite your taking control of what happens, never insist or push her to do more "advanced" stuff. Focus on making her more and more excited, so that she will be eager to progress. If she says she wants to stop[3], obey—stop what you are doing, but keep on making her feel more and more excited, without progressing.

## Do Not Lower Her Social Status

Status is so important for a woman that she must feel that you will not lower her status, either in public or in private. Keep a secret of whatever happens between the two of you and be extremely discreet if you mention past relationships. Show concern regarding her public image, act like a gentleman, treat her like a Queen, and take her to nice places.

## Do Not Judge Her Morals

The woman's fear of being seen as a slut is strong, and a major obstacle for happiness in the world. Fortunately, you can easily make it disappear. It is just required that you are neither sexually repressed nor judgmental, and that you give the right incentives.

The first step is not to make moralist remarks or jokes regarding the sexual behavior of any woman or any homosexual.

The next step is to encourage her small steps towards sexual freedom. Whenever she does or says something in a way that you find desirable, say "I love when you do that! You look so sensual and free," then kiss her—works perfect.

## Find Her Beautiful and Sexy

Let her know by your words and expressions how attractive you find her. This is especially important as you undress her for the first time. To make her relax as you undress her, dim the lights, compliment her body, and touch and look at it with admiration and horniness. Then keep on complimenting her body regularly.

## Do Not Require Her to Perform—Please her, Be pleased

All these points can be tackled by having a dominant attitude

---

3 Yes, many women say no, meaning yes, to feel like irresistible sirens, but I advise you not to play that dangerous game. Just make her so horny she will beg you to have sex with her.

towards her (backed up by sexual competence[4]). You will ensure that everything will be great without requiring anything from her.

## How to Lower the Dominant Woman's Insecurity

The points above, together with being romantic, will help relax a submissive woman. How about a dominant woman?

A dominant woman will choose a different path, first of all. She will assume some amount of control, so there is less to fear. Being dominant, she will love to perform, so performance anxiety is not an issue for her. She will take it as her responsibility to please the man and please herself, so she is not anxious about that, either. Also, she won't be anxious about your judging her morals—being dominant, she doesn't really care.

Her serious concern is only whether the man finds her beautiful. To minimize her anxiety she will probably choose a man that has signaled strongly that he finds her beautiful. So, to help her relax, you should give her plenty of compliments and let her perform. She is a dominant, so she likes compliments above anything else. Give fantastic compliments and enjoy her, and she will totally relax. Nothing else is needed.

---

4 You will need no more sexual competence than that which you will acquire by reading the coming chapters of this book.

Chapter 6:

# Touching the Woman's Skin

*A female view on this chapter:*

*You tenderly caress her entire body. She feels relaxed and excited. Then more excited. Even more excited as you keep on touching her skin. You make her very excited and her pussy is eager to be touched. The moment your tongue touches her pussy is magic. You then progress to use your tongue to play with her clit until you find the exact way she loves to be licked. Your tongue seems wonderful to her and soon you feel your head clamped between her contracting thighs, as she yells in orgasm.*

\*

*"Touch seems to be as essential as sunlight." —Diane Ackerman*

*"To be able to feel the lightest touch really is a gift." —Christopher Reeve*

## INTRODUCTION

In the previous chapters, we have focused on the psychological stuff. I repeated again and again how important it is to be an extraordinary lover—without telling you how to do that. I will make up for that absence in the next chapters. I will describe in detail the physical techniques for giving your woman extremely powerful orgasms. Apply them correctly and you will make her discover the potential of her own body, feel fulfilled as never before, and crave sex with you again, and again, and again, and again, and again... Actually, you should start considering putting your TV and DVD player on eBay.

The description I provide in the following chapters is detailed enough for you to be able to successfully reproduce the techniques described. First, let's start with some general tips that apply to all techniques.

- Your movement should always be as rhythmic and predictable as you can make it. No breaks, no bursts. Smoothly transit from one technique to the other, as in a sensual dance, so that she can relax.
- While performing the physical stimulation, always provide a compatible psychological stimulation, both from the excitement point of view and from the relaxation point of view (Chapter 12 will explain how).

Despite being quite long, the following chapters are not a showcase of all existing techniques. They are a selection of my favorite techniques. I do not include the very basic or the very common: For instance, as an average lover already knows that kissing is important, I decided not to include it in this book. As there are hundreds of books on body massage, I didn't try to reproduce them here. My goal is to give you a real and advanced vision of what really works and what is a priority in giving women extreme sexual pleasure. I do not want this book to contain all the different ways of touching and kissing or fifty different sexual positions, as if they are a priority for sexual excitement or satisfaction—they are not. The most important factor is the *movement* used in those positions, which is deeply analyzed in Chapter 8.

So, what you are about to read in the next four chapters is what I consider the best physical stimuli to give extraordinary sexual pleasure to women.

Before I give you the goodies, however, there are two topics I would like to mention: how women differ from one another and how careful you must be not to injure her or yourself.

### Don't focus on the orgasm

Women vary. That is not news, of course. But let's reinforce the point. Some women have orgasms like mad, orgasm after orgasm. They orgasm without a particularly skillful stimulation. That is just the way they are. If they had been born boys, they would be struggling to control their quick ejaculation. As they were born girls, they are very happily coming all the time, and making their partners very proud.

Some women, however, don't orgasm when the wind blows harder on their nipples. They require a careful, skillful, appropriate stimulation while being in an excited and relaxed frame of mind. Maybe they would be proud of their non-stop hours of sex if they had been born boys, but as they were born girls they are not so happy about being that resistant to orgasm. Often, both they and their partners feel frustrated. They read in magazines how other women orgasm easily and they feel sad. Because of that comparison to other women, sex becomes a source of frustration and lies. (I may have mentioned once or twice by now that women are always comparing to other women.)

When you are with your partner, focus only on giving her as much pleasure as you can. Focus on creating an amazing experience. *Do not focus on the orgasm*—it does not depend only on you and is an over-simplification. If she comes ten times, there might still be some room for improvement. On the other hand, if she didn't orgasm at all, don't feel frustrated, because your frustration will add to hers in a vicious cycle. Focus on her pleasure, not on her orgasm or number of orgasms. Those will come by themselves, and while their number is a good measure of your progress, it is not what you should focus on.

Sex is so much more than orgasm, and the intensity of female orgasms varies immensely. Focusing on just orgasming will cause you to miss out on a big part of her experience. If her interest in sex were to orgasm quickly, she would stay home alone and buy a Magic Wand or use her fingers for a few minutes. Sex is much more than getting off.

That is not to say that you should not make her orgasm. Of course you should. But you should do much more than just make her orgasm. The wonderful thing about female sexuality is that it is highly plastic. A woman who has never reached an orgasm might, after proper "training," come very often. That training will require that you focus on her pleasure, and not put pressure on her to orgasm.

## Safety Precautions and Warnings

Here comes the warnings and safety precautions section. Pay attention, because these coming chapters include some hardcore stuff. Therefore, you need to be even more cautious than you are when practicing regular lovemaking.

- Always practice safe sex and follow the Surgeon General's recommendations—and the laws of the place where you live.
- When inserting your fingers inside your partner's vagina, be sure they are clean and present no cuts. You can carry with you a small package of disinfecting gel.
- Keep your nails short, smooth, and round.
- When putting on a condom, don't touch the inner side of it with your hands if they are drooling of female juices…
- Always remember where each of your fingers has been. Don't touch the vagina with fingers that have been inside the anus.
- Minimize friction on the skin, ensuring there is always plenty of lubrication. For anal sex I recommend using lubricants (water-based when with condoms); for almost everything else, I recommend using your partner's own lubrication or a bit of spit. If that is not enough, then maybe you are going too fast[1]—get her more excited before you proceed.
- Don't persist in movements that give you or your partner any discomfort. Something that feels slightly uncomfortable done once can become quite nasty if repeated a hundred times. On top of this, we are not good at noticing pain during sex—but sex hangovers happen!
- When applying a technique, start doing it in a way that feels comfortable. Don't wait until your muscles are tired to look for a better position—then you might be too tired and it might be the totally wrong time to stop!
- Only perform heavier techniques in a situation where you can constantly check you partner's reactions.
- Be very careful not to climb to acrobatic positions from

---

1Except if your partner has real lubrication issues.

which you can fall.
- Always be in total control of what you are doing.

## FOREPLAY

### The Five Goals of Foreplay

Foreplay is wonderful. By becoming systematic and crude for a moment, we can dissect its purpose into five different goals:
1. It relaxes your partner.
2. It excites your partner.
3. It excites you.
4. It shows your partner that you know about women.
5. It allows the two of you to establish an empathic and emotional connection.

Important stuff, isn't it?

So, no reason to look at it as "fore" play. Do it before but also during intercourse. Don't let intercourse become mechanical penetration, or oral sex something you do with your tongue. Keep foreplay going throughout the entire sexual experience. Continue interacting with her through your kisses, your words, your body against hers, your hands on her body, your legs wrapped around hers.

The five goals of foreplay are as important before intercourse as they are during intercourse.

### About Kissing

Kissing is a world in itself, but fortunately quite common. So I will be brief in this section. For me, without a doubt, the most important thing about kissing is the *interaction*.

In many areas of sex, one lover is active and the other is passive. In a kiss, however, there are no active and passive lovers—both mouths are exactly the same. When French kissing, focus on interacting with your partner. Interaction is the key to great kissing. Kissing is a key to great sex.

Interaction does not mean kissing in a particular way and then waiting for her "reply." Interacting means kissing while feeling what she is doing and immediately adapting to it. Kissing is like "mouth-telepathy." When kissing, you communicate with her at deeper levels. You communicate more than in touching, than in looking in her eyes, than talking with her. It is the most intimate form of communication. I wouldn't say it is magic, because I do not believe in magic, but when two people kiss well, it is like they have an emotional tunnel straight to each other's hearts. So, as it is something for the heart, when kissing, use your instinct. Let it flow. Be smooth. Listen to her kiss while telling her your feelings for her with yours.

As kissing is so important, kiss a lot. Do it before, during, after, and out of the sexual interaction. Do it in different ways, reflecting the emotional and excitation climate you and she are experiencing.

Having said that, I still think you should master a few kissing techniques before you let it flow. So…

1. Make your lips soft when kissing.
2. Use one hand to grab the back of her head and the other to embrace her body. In more tender moments, use both hands on her head, one on each side of her face, very lightly. Word of caution: many women invest a lot in their hair, so be careful not to ruin her hairdo with your hands. At least not at the initial stages…
3. Use many variations, like using your lips to kiss each of her lips separately, or playing with your lips on hers. Always be slow and interactive. When using your tongue, connect your tongue with hers. That is, find her tongue with yours, press lightly against it to maintain contact and then move it with hers. Then you can really let it flow.

While you should not behave dominantly in your kissing technique, you can still apply your manly dominance during your kiss: Once in a while, grab her tightly and strongly in your arms and rub your pelvis against hers; but always be gentle with your lips and tongue.

Teasing is usually a good thing in a kiss. So don't "over-kiss" her. Make her want more. Take a few breaks, kiss her face, kiss her neck, kiss the magic path from the collarbone to back of her ear lobe, etc.

(just avoid the forehead, that looks like a selfish dominant trait), and then return to the kiss. When she is craving your kiss in her mouth again, kiss its corner before finally kissing her mouth again.

## Touch

Like kissing, your touch is also extremely important. Touch is not just a source of physical stimulation for your partner; it is also a way of communicating with her, as touch transmits feelings. When we touch, we express ourselves more openly than when we speak. It is easier to fake a smile than to fake a tender touch. Touching creates and develops the empathic connection between two persons.

Touching is a key factor to be successful in bed. To touch properly depends on experiencing adequate feelings for the person being touched and on having the skill to convey them. A certain kind of touch can make her feel admired, desired, and excited while another kind, slightly different, can make her feel only one of the above or... nothing at all. Therefore, let's focus on how to improve the basic touch.

### Exercise for Improving Touch

First, sit down in a chair, wearing only your underwear, exposing your skin. Close your eyes and rest your right hand on your left arm, slightly above your elbow. Slide your hand up to your shoulder. Remove it.

Next, repeat the above in a more delicate manner: when you are resting your hand on your arm, first touch your arm with the tip of your fingers, then slide them around your arm, until your entire palm rests in your arm.

Then, slide your hand to your shoulder, as before, but lift your hand from your arm in the opposite way as it landed, that is, start with the palm and end with the tips of your fingers.

Can you feel the difference between these two ways of touching? The latter transmits a feeling of tenderness and sensuality. The former does not.

I suggest that you experiment and practice on your own body several variants of touch until you are satisfied with it. Touch your

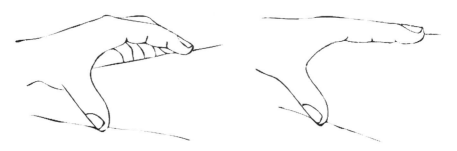

Fig. 6.1. The hand landing on the skin. (Left image) Touch first with your fingers, and then... (Right image) slowly slide the rest of the hand toward to the skin. Then grab, with a tighter grip, if you want to use a hornier touch. Even tighter, for a dominant touch.

arm, legs, thighs, and chest. Notice how each part of your body prefers a different pressure.

While you are practicing, try rotating your hands, from palm-touching to back-of-the-hand-touching; touch only with your fingers or only with your nails. Use your imagination. Feel how different kinds of touch convey different feelings.

While kissing gets all the credit for being the gate to a woman's heart, touching is extremely important and neglected. By touching your woman well, you will get easy credits.

## Massage

Massaging is a nice way of exciting your partner. I don't mean a real and long massage[2], but just a few minutes sliding your hands on your partner's body, with the five goals of foreplay in mind.

Not forgetting that the most important thing is your touch, slide your hands along the sides of her spine, up to the shoulders, then grab the areas between her shoulders and neck between your thumb and the remaining fingers (by the way, this is a typical demonstration of dominance, and she will enjoy it...). Slide your hands along her legs and thighs, then along the rest of the body (not forgetting

---

2 There are hundreds of books about massage that you can read in order to improve. I nevertheless believe that a big share of the sensual value of your massage resides in your touch. Focus on improving the sensuality of your touch. It is more important than learning complex massage movements.

the buttocks and breasts). Use dominant movements that make her feel taken, not petted. These are movements in which your hands seem big and "holding" her. For instance, slide your right hand and lower arm along the outside of her right thigh as you simultaneously slide your left hand along the inner side of the same thigh. She will feel you climbing up her legs. Your left hand can then slide really close to her vulva and then under her body, almost meeting your right hand, that is sliding all the way to her waist. Then come back, and repeat.

As you might have noticed, you should be kneeling by her feet not standing by her side, to be able to do this movement. That is the best position to be in when you are starting an erotic massage, if your back can endure it. You can then proceed to kneel over her butt. Notice that most massage movements have two components: one that makes your hand slide across her skin, along her body, and one that applies pressure to the body. The former is associated with tenderness, the latter with dominance. When you massage, focus on sliding your hands in a sensual way, and adapt your pressure to the area being massaged. On more muscular areas you can touch with more pressure by, for instance, compressing her muscle between your four fingers joined together and the palm of your hand. On more sensitive areas, like the belly, you can just slide/scratch it with your nails. When massaging the face, be extremely sweet, light and caressing, using only the tips of your fingers.

It is a good idea to end the massage with massaging her hands. Go down the arms, from shoulder to hand, and finish off massaging her hands in a very sensitive manner. As touching is a way of communicating, during the massage she will be receiving your messages, unable to respond. She will be eager to touch you. Only when your hand touches hers will she be able to communicate in return. That will be a special moment. Respect that moment and use it as the end point to the "innocent" massage and the starting point for the erotic massage. For instance, start smoothly kissing her body or start sliding your body on hers.

To evolve as a masseur, a very good strategy is to go to professional masseurs and imitate the most pleasant techniques. The ladies giving you the massage will feel very proud if you tell them that you want to learn from them to impress your girlfriend/wife, so they will probably explain to you in detail what they did.

After the massage, a good progression is to start kissing her entire body... Your partner's body, that is—not the professional masseur who taught you the techniques!

## Kisses along the Spine

When you feel you have done enough sweet-not-clearly-sexual-foreplay, using the kisses and touches that you find more appropriate, there is one technique that makes most women become very aroused. It is a great technique to make her want to say, "Please, please, please, lick my pussy right now!"

As your partner lies on her stomach, smoothly and slowly lick along her spine, from her buttocks all the way to her neck. (By the way, this starting point, the lower spine, is extremely erotic in some women. Take your time testing that on your partner.) Flick your tongue up and down as you progress. Flick at a rate of 3 lps (licks per second). This should make her really hot.

When you arrive at her neck, do one of the following:
- Kiss the side of her neck and eventually go down to the collarbone or climb to the earlobe. Gentle bites in the area between the earlobe (inclusive) and collarbone are very interesting, as well as touching with your lips or tongue behind the ears or in the more external part of the ears. Use a very gentle and non-intrusive touch.[3]
- Tongue-kiss the back of her neck, but only if she is already very excited.

### ORAL SEX TECHNIQUES

Before we move on to these fantastic techniques, let's do a brief review of the female outside genitalia, the vulva, to be sure we are

---

3 While for some women getting your tongue all over her ears can be very exciting, for many it feels terribly intrusive. Unless you know that she likes it, don't take that chance. Even if you decide to try it, maybe it is better to do it at a later stage and proceed step by step: gentle bites, light tongue touches, etcetera.

using the same names.

Let's look at Figure 6.2 from top to bottom. Starting from the top, the clitoris has a hood, protecting the top of the clitoris in the same way the foreskin protects the glans penis—to maintain its extreme sensitivity. Smoothly pulling the hood back (by pushing the

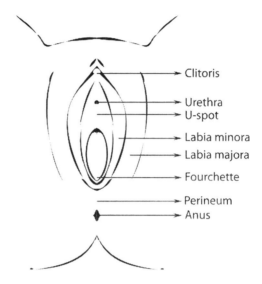

Fig. 6.2. The vulva.

skin that lies above the clitoris towards the girl's head) exposes the clitoris head.

Going down from the clitoris, we find the urethral opening; slightly below it, the U-spot, a sensitive area some women enjoy having stimulated. In a few women (a very few), this area is even more exciting than the clitoris.

Below it comes the vaginal opening, an organ with extreme inner beauty (we will look at the vagina and its opening in the coming chapter). On its sides, we find the labia minora (small lips, in Latin), and on the outside, the labia majora (big lips). The labia minora are very sensitive and should be given some attention. The labia majora are the female equivalent of the male scrotum, the outside skin covering the testicles. So, presumably, the sensitivity on the labia majora might be similar to that of the scrotum, which is a lot less than the labia minora.

Continuing downwards, we will find the perineum—the area between the vaginal opening and the anus. By the way, the area inside the vaginal opening closest to the perineum is called the fourchette. Finally, after the perineum, we will find the anus, another organ with some inner qualities of its own (again, more details will follow in subsequent chapters).

As you see, there are many exciting areas in the vulva. Still, the most pleasurable area in probably more than 95 percent of women is the clitoris. Therefore, the techniques I show here are mostly devoted to it—but I suggest that you explore also the neighboring areas, such as the small and big labia. It can be exciting and stimulating for your partner in the same way that getting your balls licked spices up a blowjob. Stimulating these areas alone can be very exciting when you are initiating oral sex, so I recommend that you do not move straight to the clitoris. Spend a little time before teasing her with your fingers or your tongue.

Even when you are already directly stimulating the clitoris, stimulating these areas together with it will increase her pleasure.

## Simplest Technique

The simplest oral sex technique is just to pass your tongue over the clitoris, back and forth. Despite being the most basic technique, you can already perform a lot of variations. You can vary:

- The contraction of your tongue
- The target (where in the clitoris you touch)
- The amplitude of your movement
- The inclination of your head
- The pressure
- The speed
- Whether you just touch her clitoris on the upward movement or if you do it on both ways
- Whether you touch her with your lips or not
- Whether you press your face against her vulva

Try plenty of these variations until you tune into what your partner enjoys best. (See the tips on how to tune your techniques in Chapter 10.) When you tune in to exactly how your partner likes it, this simplest technique is as good as any other and sometimes the best. In fact, taking the time to tune in to your partner's preferences and anatomy is so important that all the techniques described in this chapter should be seen as general frameworks to be fine-tuned to each of your partners; not techniques that should be performed exactly as described.

Coming back to the simplest technique, after you have done your oral foreplay (kissing and licking around the clitoris, but not on it), place your upper jaw against the region above her clitoris, so that your tongue can comfortably reach her clitoris. Then, as you start performing oral sex on her, it is usually good to begin smoothly before picking up speed or pressure.

While your mouth is busy, use your hands to provide other pleasant sensations. Softly caress her thighs for tenderness, or hold her hands for connection; grab her ass for horniness, or grab her breasts for pleasure... And then start doing your variations. As a good initial guess, I recommend using some contraction on your tongue and touching all the lower side of the clitoris and a bit of the top as well. The lower side is the most sensitive part (as it is in the penis). Start very softly, so that you transmit a feeling of care, admiration, and tenderness. Later, I will tell you to convey the feelings of horniness and dominance—but that is for during intercourse, not oral sex. Apply mild pressure and use a slow speed, touching the clitoris both on the upward and downward movements. For now, don't use your lips, and especially not your teeth.

As you progress, start trying out the variations described in the previous page—not for the sake of variation, but to discover how exactly she prefers it.

**Twister**

To perform the Twister technique, you should rotate your tongue around her clitoris. You use the upper side of your tongue to touch under the clitoris, and the underside of your tongue to touch the topside of her clitoris. It is only your tongue that rotates, not your head.

This technique is quite sensual. Performed slowly it shows some tenderness and engagement on your part. It is a good starting technique, sometimes even better for that purpose than the simplest technique.

## Hummingbird

The tip of your tongue touches the clitoris in an extremely light, featherlike manner. Why is it called the "hummingbird?" Because you do it really quick. Really quick. You must flick the tip of your tongue as quickly as you can, touching her clit on both movements (upwards and downwards). Practice in front of the mirror. If you can see the tip of your tongue, try to do it faster.

The other key to success is that you first locate the most pleasurable point on her clit. Pull the clitoral hood back (by placing your hand on her pubis and gently pulling the skin towards her head; the hood will follow). This technique is so light that you really should do it on her naked clit.[4]

While performing the technique, search for the hotspot with the tip of your flicking tongue. It does vary from woman to woman. Start on the top center and then move around. Search in both directions—very often the most sensitive spot is not in the center of the clitoris.[5] Not every woman finds this technique exciting, but some love it.

## Licking Her Hard

Open your mouth wide, exposing your tongue. That is sometimes visually exciting for her. To lick her really hard, focus more on applying pressure against her clitoris than making a licking move-

---

4 Most techniques work better when you pull the hood back. Pulling her hood back is, however, something that should do with some care, after you have performed oral sex on her for some minutes and shown her that you know what you are doing.

5 Chapter 10 tells you exactly how to look around in search for the most pleasurable spots.

ment. In fact, the up and down movement along the clitoris is very small, and it is done by moving your head, not using your tongue muscles. How much pressure you should use really depends on the girl. Doing it smoothly is exciting. Doing it very hard can bring her to orgasm.

Doing a long movement, like a dog, is very often a turn-off. Think of this movement as the complement of what she does when she sits on top of you and rubs herself hard against your tongue.

## Lower Lip Push

Instead of your tongue, use your lower lip to press hard against her clitoris, with upward movements. You can add a tongue touch, touching first with your tongue, then with your lip. With this technique you can apply heavy pressure on her clitoris without getting tired—you use your neck muscles, not your tiny tongue muscles. By the way, shave properly before you do this technique. Her clit will slide across your lip and into your chin—an unshaved chin will hurt her.

## Sucking Her Clitoris

Take her clitoris in your lips, and suck it into your mouth like a nursing baby—actually, not that hard. This technique has different variants for different goals. When you do it with *extreme care*, it is so smooth that you can do it—in a few women—just after their clitoral orgasm, during the most sensitive period.

When you do it with a lot more intensity, it is one of the best techniques for giving women who have problems orgasming through oral sex their first oral orgasm. In this more intensive manner, suck the clitoris inside your mouth and slide your tongue along the body and the tip of the clitoris. Suck it in and partially out, at approximately 1 sps (sucks per second). You can also try to keep it in your mouth and just perform the tongue movement.

Gradually increase the intensity on this technique. As always, be careful not to overdo it.

**Sucking the Entire Pussy**

As said, sucking the clitoris can be very pleasurable for her...
and, interestingly, so can sucking the entire pussy into your mouth,
labia majora included. Open your mouth wide, suck it all in. Keep on
using the clitoris as the "epicenter" of your sucking.

This is a great technique to catch her by surprise. If she is unaware, reading or watching TV, her vagina will be unexcited and
closed. This technique is great for that short moment...

**Heavier Stuff**

Some girls have a fantastic resistance to pressure on their clitoris. One way of finding how strong she likes it is for her to sit on
top of you, and make her move her clitoris against your tongue until
she comes. I do not recommend doing this during your first dates,
as it is quite submissive from you and that can turn her off at initial
stages of the relationship. (It does not turn her off sexually at that
exact moment, but it turns her off from you). When you decide to
do this, tell her what she should do, so that despite your being in a
submissive position, the command comes from you. Then, let her
enjoy her dominant position.

If she feels very happy about it, there is no problem in letting
her play dominant for a while. Show that you enjoy her doing it. She
might be afraid of pushing too hard. Make her feel comfortable to
push as hard as she wants, by pulling her butt against you. She is
usually submissive to you, so you had better transmit the idea that
you don't find submissiveness offensive in and of itself—otherwise,
she might stop liking being the submissive!

If, however, she starts performing demonstrations of dominance on you, immediately slap her ass. Eventually fuck her hard.
Don't worry—she will enjoy that you take this action. Nothing is
more flattering to a woman than being with a real man whom she
can't dominate[6], as long as he treats her well.

---

6 If you feel your partner gets extremely excited by doing demonstrations of dominance, I still recommend that you don't allow her to do it on you. Instead, read my other
book "Inside her Mind", where you can learn how to channel those wishes in a better way.

While she is on top of you, you will be able to feel how much pressure she puts on your tongue—which may be a lot of pressure! Learn how much pressure she enjoys and how she moves... then mimic it when you are going down on her.

Talking about heavy stuff, some girls enjoy having your teeth on their clits. I, however, do not describe any techniques involving teeth because the mix of tiny clits, teeth, and orgasmic contractions sounds like a recipe to disaster. Maybe I am being over-cautious here, but if you try it, do it carefully.

## Other Techniques

There are, of course, plenty of other techniques that you can try. You can explore the neighboring areas on her vulva. Quickly flicking your tongue in the inside of her vagina can be quite exciting, as can just lightly fucking her with your tongue. Licking her anus, or all the way from her anus to her clit, can also be quite exciting.

## Giving a Hand

While you are focused on using your tongue to make her clitoris crazy with pleasure, you can get some help from your hands. They can do a lot of things, such as the following:

1. Grab her boobs;
2. Caress her thighs;
3. Grab her buttocks;
4. Grab her thighs with your arms around them;
5. Grab her wrists hard while using your arms to push her thighs against the bed, pinning her down;
6. Hold her hands and slightly caress her fingers;
7. Push your fingers against the labia majora (her clitoris continues beneath the labia majora, in the same way your penis continues a long way into your body);
8. Play with your fingers over her labia majora, labia minora, the fourchette, perineum, and anus; and
9. Scratch her labia majora with your nails. (It should feel similar to when a woman scratches your balls with her nails—that is, extremely good.)

It is also very important to show her how much you are enjoying yourself by going down on her, by making appropriate sounds in key moments, tasting her juices and complementing her on her pussy.

## FINGER TECHNIQUES ON THE CLITORIS

Finger techniques are great to use together with oral sex, with penetration, or by themselves. Finger techniques alone are the best for less comfortable environments like buses, planes, taxis, bars, discos, cinemas, theaters, or even at home, when she is washing the dishes.

Finger techniques can be naturally divided into two groups: the clitoral ones and the vaginal ones, or the outside and the inside techniques (this chapter and next chapter, respectively).

The techniques involving your fingers on her clitoris are not very complex to describe but they are somehow difficult to apply correctly. They all aim at ensuring the right pressure at the right place of her clitoris, with proper speed and pressure, and these vary a lot from woman to woman. That is exactly why they are not easy to perform.

### Middle Finger Touching the Clitoris

Rest the palm of your hand on her belly, with your fingers pointing towards her feet. With your middle finger, touch her clitoris through the hood. You can move horizontally, vertically (in an extremely soft "come-hither" motion), or in circles. You can keep all the fingers together (in case your middle finger slips, one of the others will touch her clitoris instead), but is usually easier to use just the middle finger. Try different kinds of touch with each new partner. Basically, you should try a lot of them until you find the one she uses to masturbate. And yes, it is a good idea to see how she does it herself.

This is one of the techniques where your adaptation skills are paramount (don't miss Chapter 10). One of the many ways you can try is to move your finger(s) horizontally, making your middle finger travel all the way from one side of the clitoris to the other, over the hood with plenty of pressure.

If you want to move faster, lift your hand from her belly and use your wrist to make the swinging motion.

## Middle Finger Flicking her Clitoris

If you want to move your fingers very quickly on her clitoris, try this: Rest your right hand's index finger and thumb on her stomach. Point your remaining fingers towards her feet. Your hand should be resting sideways, with the top of your hand facing towards her head. Position your hand so that the side of the tip of your middle finger touches her clitoris. Now rock your finger back and forth (meaning

Fig. 6.3 Middle finger flicking her clitoris.Your hand rests on her belly, supported by your thumb and index finger. Your middle finger is now free to move extremely quickly.

sideways on her clitoris).

Notice how you can do this movement extremely quickly? Is that cool or what? When you get the gist of this movement, you can cause some women to start having a weird pseudo-orgasm that involves very quick and involuntary contractions of the uterus. Their belly starts shaking in a way that would make any belly dancer envious—very surprising and sexy to watch.

## Thumb Pressing Down the Clitoris

While your middle finger can easily become your magical clitoris wand, when you are having intercourse on top of your partner, face-to-face, there are fewer things worse than trying to rub her clitoris with your middle finger. To avoid damaging your wrist, I recommend that you use your thumb.

This technique is particularly helpful as a last resort during intercourse, when it seems that despite all your efforts, she is not heading to an orgasm soon—but you are. If that happens, you can stop penetrating her (while keeping your penis inside her) and use this technique on her clitoris, as you look her in the eyes and confess to her how horny and on the verge of exploding you are. It is a joy watching as she comes instead of you!

### Back of the Fingers Pressing the Clitoris

There is, however, a way you can use your middle finger during frontal intercourse. You should use the back of your fingers. Use both your middle and your index finger and move them up and down (towards her face, towards her feet) as you penetrate her and look her in her eyes.

### Several Fingers Rubbing Her Clitoris

Let's say you and your partner are having intercourse. She is lying on her stomach and you are lying on top of her. To better stimulate her clitoris, you can still use your hand, but remember that you are going to have the weight of two adult bodies on it. The best way to do this is to just put your hand under her crotch, so that you rest the back of your hand against the mattress, floor, picnic towel[7] or whatever, and she lies with her belly on your palm. This way you keep some mobility on your fingers. Keep them all together and use whichever comes handier to touch her clitoris. You can try very different things. As you are already putting a lot of pressure against her clitoris (your weight combined), you don't need to make very incisive movements with your fingers.

When you are not putting a lot of weight on it (as, for instance, in doggy-style), try using your fingers on the lower side of her clito-

---

7 Women love to have sex in different places.

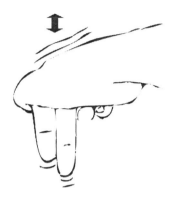

Fig. 6.4. Back of the fingers pressing the clitoris. This is how you see your hand when you look at it while using the back of your fingers on her clitoris, during face-to-face intercourse.

ris.

## Techniques for Big-clit Ladies

Where clitoral stimulation is concerned, it is really important to distinguish between small clits and big clits. As un-sexy as it sounds, the clitoris is the female version of the penis, which, in fact, develops from a hermaphrodite clitoris when exposed to androgenic hormones, present in male fetuses.[8]

I don't know exactly how the development from clitoris to penis happens, and where along that road the clit starts feeling more like a penis. Maybe a large clitoris is just that, a larger clitoris—but perhaps it is somehow more closely related to a penis. (Or perhaps a clitoris is just a miniature penis?)

What I know is that you can get the most effect from stimulating a large clitoris as if it were a penis. Imagine you are dealing with a tiny penis and try to masturbate it. Hold it between your thumb and index fingers and masturbate it gently. Place either one finger on each side or one finger below and one on top. Also, try to surround

---

8 Androgenic hormones are often taken by female bodybuilders, causing their clitoris to grow to impressive sizes.

the clitoris with the tips of the two indexes and two thumbs and gently perform a stroking motion. Give it a little help with your tongue to check if she gets even more turned on.

When you perform oral sex on a big clit, either suck it whole into your mouth or focus on the lower side of it.

Chapter 7:

# Touching the Woman's Inside

*A female view on this chapter:*

*She lies in bed as you play with your fingers inside her. She can't see what you are doing, but she can feel that you are doing it very well.*
*She starts feeling another orgasm on the rise. She swears some very nasty words and a few seconds later she grabs the sheets for another wave of violent orgasmic contractions. After all the yelling has stopped, and she lies catching her breath, she thinks: "It was so good! How the hell does he do that?"*

*

*"Pearls lie not on the seashore. If thou desirest one thou must dive for it."*
—*Chinese Proverb*

## ANATOMY OF THE VAGINA

We will start this chapter by taking an inside look at the vagina, where we will study in detail the extremely powerful magic spots it contains.

For some wonderful reason, Evolution hid these magic spots inside the vagina, perhaps to be stimulated during penetration, giving pleasure to women. And, as usual, Evolution did a great job: Women can gain enormous pleasure when these magic spots are touched.

Nature has evolved these magic spots to generate pleasure when stimulated bluntly by the penis. In this chapter you are going to read how to do better than that. You are going to read how to explore the full potential of these spots with your fingers. Unlike the penis, the finger can feel its way around until it finds the right spot, and then apply an incisive pressure on it. You will be manipulating Evolution's buttons to generate more pleasure than they were ever meant to.

One of the best parts of using your fingers is that, quite probably, your partner won't know all the magic spots herself. And her puzzled expression when you show them to her can be very sweet...

The drawback of fingering is that is not the most sensual or emotional thing to do. So, I recommend you take that into account when fingering. To mitigate this issue, I am providing, later in this chapter, a detailed description on how to start fingering while keeping a nice emotional and sensual mood.

We will now take a look inside the vagina. To better visualize it, please imagine you are the tip of your middle finger—this is a good way to describe a vagina because that is exactly how you "see" it. So close your eyes for a second and imagine you are the tip of your middle finger. Done? Good. Let's move on. As a precaution: throughout this visualization exercise, abstain from picking your nose—it could be a traumatizing experience.

## Diving into the Vagina

You—as the tip of your middle finger—approach the vagina through the vaginal opening. It is a pretty tight opening with an ability to enlarge. (The same thing goes for the vagina). When the woman is not excited, her vagina and its opening are closed. When she is excited, her vagina opens and broadens.

You slide into an excited vagina. It becomes roomier after you pass through the opening. The vagina looks like a tube that becomes larger at the far end. The far end has a wall, but it is not a plain wall. In its center, and occupying most of it, lies the cervix, which is the opening to the uterus. Two of the vagina walls are more pleasurable: the anterior wall (to the belly) and the posterior wall (to the back). So we will focus on these two walls and disregard the side walls.

You start by progressing along the top of the vagina, that is, the anterior wall. This wall goes markedly up from the vagina opening. In that upwards-curved region, two to three inches from the entrance, you will notice that in a small area, its tissue feels spongy. That is the G-spot and you will probably only feel it if the woman is already excited (more about this later).

If you continue moving inwards along that wall, you will find another particularly sensitive spot, called the A-spot. Contrary to the remaining magic spots, there is no special tactile sensation on the vagina wall that can tell you "it's here." This fact, together with being distant from the vaginal entrance, makes it the hardest spot to find.

Continuing moving inward from the A-spot, you will reach the end of her vagina. The end feels like a pocket (called the anterior fornix) because the cervix comes outwards from the inner end of the vagina.

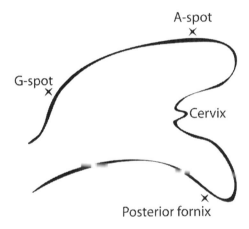

Fig. 7.1. The vagina. A side-view including the G-spot, the A-spot, and the posterior fornix.

As you have reached the end of the vagina from the anterior side, you will now move towards the back of your partner, along the inner wall. As you progress along this wall, you will feel the protruding surface of the cervix. The central part of it feels hard. You go over the cervix and proceed towards the back. After the cervix comes the posterior fornix. If you press against the posterior wall of the vagina here you will be able to feel your partner's rectum across the wall. You can feel its ring-like surface (it feels as if you are touching the Michelin Man). By pressing it very gently, you can feel that it is very flexible.

From the posterior fornix, you start moving back towards the entrance of the vagina. Still very close to the posterior fornix you will find the posterior fornix spot. When your finger first passes over it, it feels like nothing special. But it reacts to stimulation. When stimulated, the wall moves inward, creating a small "hole." This area is extremely sensitive and powerful (more about it later). That is the last erogenous spot on this trip. You can then pull your right-hand middle finger back, climbing outwards along the posterior wall.

## Your Fingers inside Her Vagina

As we said before, your fingers can stimulate her vagina in a very powerful manner. You can easily give her amazing orgasms from pressing and rubbing these magic points.

However, fingering her is not that exciting from the psychological point of view. It does not have the same sensuality and emotional charge as penetration nor the same kindness and lightness as oral sex. While some women do find it very exciting, others will suspect that you might be compensating for an ensuing "below par" penetration. Others feel that it is too invasive and yet others feel that is just not sexy—they have their own fingers, so this time they want a penis!

So, before you start applying these techniques during your first times with a girl, it is safer to take some "precautions." Use these techniques together with oral sex and do a proper introduction. Get your girl excited enough that she will ask for you to finger her. Will she ask verbally? No, but she will ask for it using her body language.

### How to Kick-start Fingering

Let's imagine you are giving oral sex to a girl you recently met. It is your first time together. She is loving it. Your hands move around her thighs, grab her ass, squeeze her boobs. She gets hornier and hornier. Then, you slowly slide your hand towards her vaginal opening.

She might think: "Hum... He is going there, that is exciting... but I hope he doesn't start fingering me hard, that is so intrusive..."

You close your hand into a fist and softly touch her entire vulva, perineum, and anus region with the knuckles of your fist. You apply a light pressure in that entire area.

"Oh, that feels good. That feels cozy, that feels safe... Good guy..."

You continue doing your oral sex technique with the light pressure of your knuckles. You slightly rock your wrist.

She will probably think something like: "Oh, that pressure on me is making my pussy really wanting to be fucked right now... but I love the way his tongue feels on my clit...."

You take back your closed wrist, open it and secretly lick your finger to get it wet. Very lightly, you position your finger to enter her pussy, but you don't enter yet. The tip of your finger should be touching the inner side of her small labia, just for her to feel that you are there—you are knocking on the door, not opening the door.

"Oh fuck, I want to feel him inside my pussy so bad. He has his finger right there; he is just waiting for me to let him in. Oh yes, I want him to continue, I trust him, I want him to make me come really bad..."

So she moves her hips towards you, pulling your finger slightly in. That means, "Come in please!"

You oblige. Slowly, your finger enters...

## Simplest Technique

The simplest of techniques is just to slowly move your fingers straight, back and forth, inside her vagina. You can use one or more fingers. One finger is the appropriate choice to start with, eventually adding a second finger when she is hotter.

Pleasure from the vagina comes from either touching the inner vagina walls or from passing through the vaginal opening. As fingers are pretty inadequate at passing through the vaginal opening (a rounder shape does better), just sliding your fingers in and out is not particularly stimulating for your partner. Still, it is quite a nice way to slowly start using your fingers inside her. When you start, use only the tip. That is enough to stimulate the walls around the opening of her vagina and is not so intrusive.

## Stimulating the Vaginal Walls

Much more interesting than moving your fingers back and forth inside her vagina is to also stimulate her vagina walls. I suggest you do this in four different ways:

1. Hitting a particular spot with your fingers when moving back and forth;
2. Sliding your fingers along a wall when moving back and forth;
3. Using a come-hither motion, either when moving back and forth or just standing still; or
4. Using a rotational motion on your fingers.

### Hitting

When hitting a particular spot with your fingers, if you want to be perfect, arch your longest finger so that the tips of your fingers hit the spot simultaneously.

To hit the right spot with your fingers, you need to aim. You can aim at a spot in two different ways: (a) you change the curvature of your fingers, until you find the right one that hits the spot when moving in and out, or (b) you change the angle at which your fingers enter the vagina.

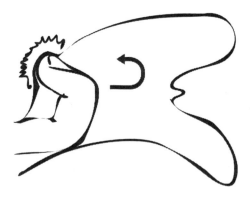

Fig. 7.2. The middle finger is hitting the G-spot. By adjusting the curvature of the finger(s), you take aim on where it hits. If you only want to hit, not slide, the movement of your hand should be rotational, as shown by the arrow.

Fig. 7.3. Changing angle to aim. Another way to change your aim is to change the entrance angle into the vagina. Again aiming at the G-spot, you will have better results if your fingers enter the vagina at a smaller angle (measured vertically, meaning the finger on the left side).

## Sliding

You can slide the tip of your fingers along the area of the wall close to the spot you are stimulating. You can also combine the

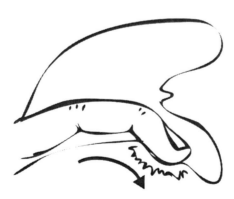

Fig. 7.4. Sliding motion on the posterior fornix. The sliding technique being exemplified on the posterior fornix. As the vagina wall is curved in that region, it is suited to a sliding plus hitting motion. In the sliding motion, the finger keeps permanent contact with the vagina wall.

sliding motion with the hitting motion—just carve some pressure against the wall at the end of the sliding motion.

### Come-hither

The come-hither motion can be used to apply continuous pressure in a small region (for instance, the A-spot), or to drag the underlying tissue (as in the G-spot).

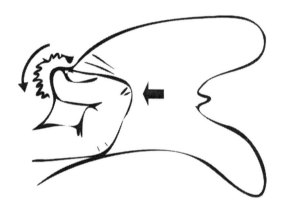

Fig. 7.5. Come-hither on the G-spot. The come-hither motion exemplified again on the G-spot. In the G-spot, try using the come-hither motion to drag the underlying tissue, not just rubbing over it.

### Rotational Motion

Finally, the rotational motion is self-explanatory. Rotate your fingers on the surface of her vagina, from left to right. It is usually not as powerful as the other motions, but is very helpful in finding the right spot.

## Precautions

Unlike a boneless, blunt, nailess, and not-always-hard-as-a-rock penis, fingers have bones, nails, and muscular strength, and are relatively pointy. They have the potential to generate a lot of pleasure but also to injure and annoy. So, be careful when using your fingers inside the vagina or moving them in and out. Do not use them with a roughness comparable to that of a penis. Be very gentle.

## Naming Conventions

To avoid describing every time for every technique what "up" and "down" means, let's make some conventions here.

I will always assume that your partner is lying on her back, tummy facing the ceiling. By "up" I mean towards the ceiling, by "down" towards the mattress. By "north" I mean towards her head, "south" towards her feet.

When I write a "finger facing upwards" I mean that the finger is stretched in the south–north axis, pointing northwards, with the nail facing down. Unless stated otherwise, whenever I say "two fingers," I mean "index finger plus the middle finger."

Now that we've got all that settled, let's move on. Bring your compass!

## Hitting the G-spot

Use the simplest technique (back and forth) while aiming at the G-spot. Do that by having the palm of your hand facing up, and insert your fingers with a strong upwards movement (30 degrees from the vertical line). Your fingers should slide slightly along the anterior wall before hitting the G-spot. When on the G-spot, and depending on the details of your partner's anatomy, you can just hit it, you can slide along it, you can drag it, or you can strongly press against it.

## Stimulating the A-spot

If you go beyond the G-spot, but stop a bit before the end of your partner's vagina, you might find the A-spot. Try using the come-hither motion with a one-inch amplitude. If your fingers are not long enough to do that so deep in her vagina, get her on her knees, resting her head on the bed, and try again. If you still can't find it, don't worry—there are plenty more fish in the sea and this one is the harder to fish.

## Stimulating the Posterior Fornix

This technique stimulates another spot deep in her vagina, this time on the posterior wall. To some women, this is an amazing hotspot, and can easily trigger an orgasm. It thus becomes especially interesting to women who don't orgasm easily from the more common erotic regions.

Use your middle finger facing downwards to reach this deep area of her vagina. Then apply the come-hither motion, as you did in the anterior fornix. When you stimulate the right spot for a while, most vaginas, just loving it, are going to dig a little hole in the vagina wall. Once that happens, you are home safe. Keep on stimulating that little hole—she will come soon!

A little caveat: as you can imagine, applying this technique will seem weird for your partner at first, especially if you don't find the right spot immediately. She might start thinking: "Why is he keeping a finger stuck inside me and scratching me? Is that a request for samples from my gynecologist?" So start doing it together with oral sex so that she does not worry about it.

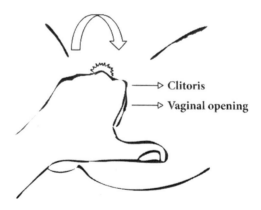

Fig. 7.6. Stimulating the posterior fornix. The entire hand rotates as shown in the arrow so that the middle finger stimulates the posterior fornix while its knuckle hits the clitoris on the way out.

Besides that, there is yet another variant of this technique you can use if the girl does not have a deep vagina. Almost as good as the one described above, this variant looks much less ridiculous. Use two fingers and perform the sliding motion along the posterior wall, hitting the posterior fornix. Use an entrance angle close to the vertical, thus sacrificing a bit of the sliding motion but keeping an equally stimulating hitting motion on the posterior fornix. Now—and this is the coolest part—make your middle knuckle pressure her clitoris on your finger's way out. Very cool. Very efficient.

After a girl comes from posterior fornix stimulation, her most common reaction is to stare bogged-eye at you and say, "I don't know how the hell you did that! How did you make me come that fast?" or, "Do you work as a male escort?"

## Stimulating the G-spot—Soft Versions

Contrary to the posterior fornix that conveniently digs that little hole to tell you where to press, the G-spot gets bigger. You can stimulate it in different ways: by hitting it straight-on, as described earlier; by using a come-hither motion; by using a rotational motion; or by squeezing it.

As a first shot, I recommend the come-hither motion with a strong dragging component. That means that you don't just "scratch" the wall, as in the posterior fornix. Push a bit deeper in order to actually stimulate the soft tissue underneath. Some girls also react very positively to a squeeze of the G-spot, that is, compression against the anterior wall. Some women, however, do not like to be stimulated in the G-spot. It makes them feel like they need to pee (more on that later), which is not exciting for them.

When you apply quite a lot of stimulation to the G-spot, you can sometimes hear a sound, somewhat related the sound of a pressure cooker when it has to release steam. No kidding. Nature is poetic.

If you have tried finding her G-spot without success, try again when she is more excited. Without excitement, no G-spot!

## Stimulating the G-spot to Provoke the Female Ejaculation

A recent trend is to make your partner ejaculate. This ejaculation probably derives from an expulsion of the liquid produced at the Skene's glands, which happen to be located at the G-spot, and which are homologous to the male prostate (where the liquid phase of sperm is produced). By provoking the ejaculation of this liquid, you will cause your partner to possibly soak your bed. This ejaculation is not to be mistaken with another phenomenon, which is "ejaculation" of lubricant fluid from inside your partner's vagina. This fluid is what makes the vagina wet when excited. Some women, during orgasm, produce much more of this fluid. So it just squirts out. Sometimes in gushes. Beautiful, but very dependent on the woman.[1]

These are two very different phenomena that can be called "female ejaculation." Let's go back to the first one—the ejaculation of the fluid of the Skene's glands—and tell you how to do it.

Your partner should be lying in bed, belly up. You should rest on your knees by the side of your partner's belly, facing her. Open your hand with the four fingers stretched together keeping the thumb apart. Fold the middle and ring fingers to approximately 60 degrees

Fig. 7.7. Hand for female ejaculation. The middle and ring fingers are bent back in order to stimulate the G-spot. Only these two fingers enter the vagina.

with your palm. Insert these two fingers in her vagina and reach for her G-spot (the index and pinky should be between her buttocks

---

1 Some people can also use their salivary glands to produce far-reaching gushes of saliva. Both groups are a minority, though....

now, but that is not so relevant).

Now use mostly your shoulder muscle to pull your hand up, pressuring against the G-spot. That's right, the shoulder muscle. Pull your shoulder, that pulls your arm, that pulls your hand, that pulls your fingers. You should also use the biceps, but do not neglect the shoulder muscle.

So, pull upwards and then relax. Repeat. Repeat again. Every

Fig. 7.8. Arm movement for female ejaculation. The keys to successfully applying this technique are: a very excited frame of mind, and empty bladder, a comfortable fit of your hand inside her before starting, a compound movement of your biceps and shoulder muscles and... physical fitness!

time, your two fingers should be pressuring hard on her G-spot. Oh... by the way, in all these three repetitions—this is the tricky part—do them all in less than one second. Yes. That quick. That is why you need the shoulder muscle. The movement is not only quick; it is also quite brutal. So start slowly on your first attempts until you really get the hang of it. The G-spot can withstand quite rough stimulation, but proceed step by step. People have hypothesized that the function of the G-spot is to provide some pleasure or relief during childbirth. That could be a good explanation for why the G-spot needs this sort of violent stimulation.

What will happen when you perform this technique?

She will feel a need to urinate. (It isn't a real need to urinate, but it feels that way to her.) If she lets go, she will start squirting. If not, nothing will happen. So it is all up to her. Tell her in advance what your plans are and make sure she visits the toilet before, to increase the chances of success in "letting go without fear of peeing."

## Touching the Cervix

While you make your exploratory journeys inside her vagina, pay a visit to the cervix. Touch it with your finger around its opening, or on the surface facing the posterior fornix. She might enjoy it a lot! I say might: It does vary from woman to woman. In case you can't reach it, make her sit in crouching position and try again.

If a gynecologist friend of yours tells you that the cervix has no sensitivity, don't worry—there is a reason why women love great lovers and hate gynecologists.

While this technique can provide immense fun, it is awfully intrusive—not a very good icebreaker, if you know what I mean. Still, there are worse techniques for that. Check out the next one...

## Fisting

It can be very exciting for a woman if you happen to insert a "few" extra fingers inside her, especially if you introduce the event with an appropriately spicy conversation. It is not for everyone, but for the ones who enjoy it, it can make for some romantic evenings.

To do so, make your hand as narrow as possible. If you had to escape from a slightly loose handcuff, what would you do? Do just that: twist your hand so that your thumb lies against your ring finger.

As always, progress gradually. This time, be particularly careful and slow—and generous on the lube. The goal should not be to insert your entire hand, but to give her pleasure as you add fingers, one by one. Move the fingers already inside to stimulate what you can. If it so happens that you insert your entire hand, amazing. Otherwise, equally amazing! The goal is that she feels as "full" as she possibly can.

## Synergize your Tongue and Fingers

Synergy is when the whole is larger than the sum of its parts. Isn't it a great example of synergy pleasing your partner with your fingers and tongue?

### Simple Oral Sex + Hitting the G-spot

The simplest technique for oral sex gets really powerful when done together with the G-spot technique. Try moving both your tongue and your fingers very quickly. It is an amazing bundle.

### Combos

In the example above, we combined stimulation of the clitoris and the G-spot. That is only one of the many possible combinations. In fact, you can try to combine any of the techniques from the present and previous chapters. It gets really tricky to stimulate simultaneously the A-spot, the G-spot, and the clitoris... and why not adding a bit of anal stimulation? After all, combining vaginal and anal fingering with oral sex is very pleasurable. It is tricky to combine all these together, but not impossible. Progressively try adding one more erotic area after the other.

Still, I recommend you not to try this regularly and especially not on first dates! It is too invasive, too tricky for you to put many eggs in that basket, and it can get a bit clinical, too.

A final tip: Let's say you are running out of hands and you would still like to stimulate her anal region. What to do? Bring one of your knees close to her, to lightly press against her anus. You may look like a hunchback, but she won't mind...

### The Fabulous Half-hour-long Orgasm Technique

The technique I am about to tell you is so fantastic that I don't expect you to believe it without trying. I had some doubts when I first read about it (in the ESO book mentioned in the "Sources" section, by Brauer and Brauer). But it works, so you definitely must try this one. In case it doesn't work (and I believe it does not work on every woman), try reading the original book. Their 283-page explanation is surely better than this one.

Basically, the technique consists of the following. Make your partner orgasm by giving oral sex to her clitoris. Just after she comes, start stimulating her G-spot. Do that until she comes from G-spot stimulation alone. After that orgasm, stimulate her clitoris alone until she orgasms.

Repeat. Successively switch between G-spot and clitoric orgasms.

The magic behind this technique is that the time between orgasms gets progressively shorter. Shorter and shorter, until an orgasm fuses with the next one in a non-stopping orgasm. I have seen twenty-minute-long orgasms being stopped by "tap out" of the girl... "Please stop, stop, I need to breathe..."

Chapter 8:

# Penetration

*A female view on this chapter:*

*Even before intercourse began, she was already so glad to have decided to take you home—she came so hard, thanks to all the foreplay. She was obviously very curious on how intercourse would be. As you started, she just loved how you turned intercourse into such a romantic and sweet experience. Besides that, you moved in and out of her in a way that allowed her to feel your entire penis pressuring against her. Even looking at you was exciting, you seemed so fluid and relaxed—as if sex was in your nature.*
*Very smoothly, you ask her if you can fuck her really hard. "Oh yes, please," she answers. So you start—much harder than she imagined.*
*Your pelvis makes a loud sound when it hits hers and sends shock waves through her body. She feels ravished—an exciting experience that touches her feminine soul directly. Sex never felt this intense before. She just loves it... "Oh my god, fuck, a real man, fuck!" she thinks, as she comes intensely in your arms...*

\*

*"Knowledge comes through practice" —Celtic proverb*

## THE POWERFUL PENETRATION MOVEMENT

We are now moving from manual and oral sex to intercourse. Buckle your seat belts; we are going for a ride...

### What Really Matters in Intercourse

In my view, the four factors behind a fantastic intercourse, full of female orgasms, are the following:
1.   Her excitement before the penetration begins;

2. Her excitement during penetration;
3. The movement applied for penetration; and
4. The duration of the penetration.

The first two elements are developed in different areas of this book. In this chapter we will focus on the third factor, the movement applied for penetration. The fourth factor, duration of penetration, will not be mentioned at all. Despite being the least important of the four factors, it is the one people mostly focus on, so there are millions of tips out there. Besides, I do not want you to be focusing on yourself. Focusing on yourself—on your pleasure, on your fantasies, but especially on your abilities, on how you look, or on your insecurities—is the key to terrible sex. In sex, don't think about you. Focus on her. Only on her.

## Introduction to the Movement

What I will explain in the following pages is extremely powerful. Despite being the difference between OK intercourse and amazing intercourse, few men perform the powerful penetration movement correctly. It is like most hidden gems—because most people think they instinctively know how to penetrate, no one actually bothers studying and improving the movement. Well, better for those who bother!

The problem with the instinctive movement is that it is perfect for your own pleasure but inadequate for hers—in fact, that makes two serious problems! Fortunately, using the powerful penetration movement conscientiously will take care of that.

It takes a while to learn how to perform this movement correctly and it requires some effort before you are able to do it. To shorten that time, I will make analogies to simpler movements, suggest exercises for you to practice, and explain all the details that you need to know in order to perform this movement correctly. At first blush, it might seem the ultimate nerdiness: to analyze how to fuck?! But get over that prejudice, and it will pay back with dividends.

One of the reasons for the complexity of the powerful penetration movement is that it is composed of three sub-movements that have to be combined in perfect coordination. When you master that, you will be able to penetrate in an extremely powerful, pleasurable, and fluid manner without getting tired. Your partner will feel it as a sign of powerful domination, strong desire, and strength—it separates the men from the boys. You can also use any of the three sub-movements independently, allowing you to have sex in many different positions—one of your three movements will surely be appropriate for even the oddest position.

The powerful penetration movement is a compound movement. Weird as it might seem, the simplest example I can think of a compound movement is the Nunchaku movement (the Nunchaku is a traditional Asian weapon). So, we will start by looking at the movement of the Nunchaku, thus explaining the fundamentals of movement composition. Once that is in place, we will move on to the powerful penetration movement itself.

The Nunchaku is an Asian weapon made of two wooden sticks joined by a chain. The martial artist holds one of the sticks with his

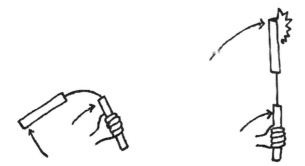

Fig. 8.1. The Nunchaku. The hit is powerful if it occurs in the instant when the outside rod and the inside rod are traveling in the exact same direction. If it hits before or after, it becomes much weaker. The same happens with compound body movements. In both cases, coordination is fundamental.

hand, and the other stick is dragged by the chain, reaching amazing speeds, as its movement results from the composition of two movements: the rotating movement of the second stick and the movement of both sticks together. If the Nunchaku hits its target when these movements are in synchrony, the hit is very powerful.

This composition of movements applies to all sorts of movements. Correctly composing many movements is the key for peak performance in sports and dance. Performing a powerful tennis serve, a powerful punch, or a powerful soccer shot is more about composing movements in total synchrony than it is about absolute muscular strength. When using many muscles in your body to perform sub movements in perfect coordination, the general movement becomes powerful and fluid. It becomes powerful because you have the strength of many muscles combined. It becomes fluid because, as you use many muscles, you can adapt the movement, control it much better in several dimensions, and make your body do exactly what you want it to do.

Now let's come back to the penetration movement. For starters, let's give you some motivation: It is unbelievably exciting for a woman to experience or watch the powerful penetration movement. You will see for yourself.

Before we move on, we also need a few words about safety. I believe that a correctly performed movement, yet powerful, is safe and presents no hazard. While I cannot be certain of that, many years of practice never resulted in any accident or injury. However, an incorrect powerful movement is surely dangerous because it is all about powerful movements with some of the most cherished and fragile areas of the human body. And a correct powerful penetration movement is hard to achieve. So you need to always follow the safety rules presented below, to ensure that you never injure yourself or your partner. These are more than mere disclaimers. These are real safety rules that you need to follow.

### Safety Rules for the Powerful Penetration Movement

* Be extremely careful not to let your penis slide away while moving inwards into the vagina. A large share of accidents on either penis or vaginas happens due to incorrect insertions. This can be extremely dangerous. Penises can break and vaginas can get cut. To be sure that your penis will not slide away when you move it inwards, never pull

it out too much. Always leave a fair share of your penis inside her vagina when pulling back. If you feel that you took it out too much, stop and put it back in smoothly and slowly before you resume your powerful penetration.

- Be sure that your partner is enjoying your penetration at every moment.

- In the event of pain or discomfort, immediately stop.

- Increase the intensity gradually. Do that every time you change position.

- Ensure that, for every position, the maximum depth penetration is not painful for your partner before you start the powerful penetration. In case it is, she will probably rotate her hips slightly or not bend over so clearly. You should either control your penetration by not going too deep, or use something that prevents reaching maximum depth while penetrating—such as placing your hands between you and her.

- Only penetrate powerfully after her vagina is fully dilated.

- Only penetrate powerfully while in perfect control. Be sure you are in control of your movement, support, and balance. Be careful when you are in acrobatic positions.

- Never use any kind of anesthetics while penetrating powerfully (for instance, condoms with lidocaine that help you last longer). You need to feel everything you are doing.

**Analyzing the Powerful Penetration Movement**

The powerful penetration movement is the composition of three sub-movements, applied in perfect coordination. The most important of these is the pelvic movement. The second one is a trunk-swing having your shoulders as the axis. The third movement is a chest swing having your waist as the axis.

Let's start by looking at each of these movements individually, step-by-step. Remember, you can use them together to form the powerful penetration movement or you can use each of them separately for different purposes.

The following exercises will seem a bit silly, but please trust me on this: Try them. The benefits might be huge.

## Sub-movement 1: The Pelvic Movement

If you stand sideways in front of a mirror, the pelvic movement will seem like a pendulum. Your pelvis swings back and forth, rotating around an imaginary axis that should be some eight fingers above your coccyx.

### *Step-by-step Rules for the Pelvic Movement*

1.  Stand sideways in front of a mirror. Your back should be relaxed, having its normal curvature.

2.  Keeping all of your body above your belly button perfectly still, pull your pelvis as far back as you can. Your thighs will also move, but only slightly. Your back will now present a much larger curvature (from your belly button down). During intercourse, this backwards movement works as the "pull of a gun's hammer."

3.  Move your pelvis forward in the swinging movement described above. Your back will now be totally flat, without any curvature. During intercourse, this movement is like "firing your gun." Firing the gun should be done with more intensity than pulling back the hammer.

To perform this movement you use your gluteal, abdominal, and back muscles.

Both ends of the sub-movement should be decisive, with a clear and abrupt stop, not a gradual slowdown (this applies to all three sub-movements). Focus on performing a perfect movement where only your pelvis moves, with as much fluidity and amplitude as you can. Practice moving like a pendulum, back and forth, back and forth, in a perfectly fluid movement, moving your body only from the belly button down.

In the pelvic movement, by describing a "circular" path, your penis pushes against and along the vagina wall. That is *extremely important*. Vaginal penetration is not pleasurable only by sliding in and out, but mostly by stimulating the vaginal walls.

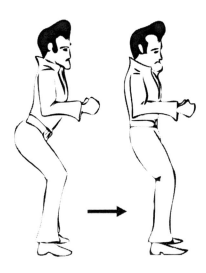

Fig. 8.2. Sub-movement 1. Look at our friend Elvis the Pelvis (who else to show us the pelvic movement?) He pulls his pelvis all the way behind before starting the penetration movement. His torso does not move. Imagine his penis moving as he swings—you will notice that it will press along the walls of the vagina as it moves inward.

## Sub-movement 2: The Trunk Movement

This movement is broader than Sub-movement 1: Your entire trunk moves in a swinging motion around your shoulder line.

*Step-by-step Rules for the Trunk Movement*

1. Stand sideways in front of a mirror. To better separate this sub-movement from Sub-movement 1, keep your pelvis in its most forward position (at the end of Step

3 of the previous list, after you have "fired your gun"). Keep it like that all throughout this exercise. Your arms should be bent 90 degrees at the elbow, forearms horizontal. Rest one or both hands on a surface at the appropriate height, to ensure that your hands stay still during the entire movement. (In real life, a female buttocks usually serves this role.)

2. Pull your buttocks backwards without any pelvic movement. Do this by moving your shoulders forward and stretching your legs. Your elbows should now be ahead of your trunk (when seen in the mirror). This movement, of course, is the gun-hammer-pulling movement.

3. Now move your buttocks forward ("fire your gun"), swinging your entire trunk using your shoulders as an axis. Keep your shoulders and arms still while letting your knees move forward. Your elbows should now be behind your trunk.

Fig. 8.3. Sub-movement 2. Now Elvis pulls back his entire trunk before starting. This translates into a back-and-forth movement of his penis, not stimulating the vagina walls that much.

To perform this sub-movement you use many different muscles in your legs and trunk.

## Sub-movement 3: The Upwards Movement

The third sub-movement, the upward movement, is useful in different situations. Together with the other sub-movements, it increases the power in the movement and channels it against the fornices in her vagina walls. You only start performing it when the other sub-movements are about to finish, that is, when the penis is already deeply inside the vagina. Done alone, with your penis stuck deeply inside her vagina, the upward movement allows for a very deep yet slow and short penetration, aimed at stimulating solely the fornices or the cervix. Done in this way, your penis is always fully inside her vagina—the movement just pressures it deeper against the vagina walls. It can be very exciting and stimulating.

*Step-by-step Rules for the Upwards Movement*

1. Stand sideways in front of a mirror, in the position in which you finished the previous exercise, that is, having your "gun fired" in both Sub-movements 1 and 2. You should have your waist and pelvis forward, with your elbows behind your trunk.

2. Now push your pelvis further forward and up. You can do that by slightly lifting your heels from the ground and pulling your shoulders further back. Without moving your hands, imagine you are pulling something with them.

This movement is performed with the abdominal and gluteal muscles.

## Practicing the Sub-movements

Practice these three sub-movements many times, with and without having the pelvis in the "fired gun position," that is, totally forward. Do it slowly and very slowly, trying to ensure the smoothest movement you can. See the path that your penis would do inside her vagina. Make it smooth.

Do it a bit quicker, focusing on getting a very abrupt end. You want your pelvis to hit hard against your partner's body, with a bang. You want to bang hard against her pelvis or butt, but you don't want to push her against the bedroom wall. So your movement should stop, abruptly, after your pelvis hits her.

Fig. 8.4. Sub-movement 3. Our friend Elvis is again going for the vagina walls. He applies this movement when his penis is almost fully inserted, to specifically hit the fornices (posterior or anterior, depending on his partner's position).

When you feel comfortable performing these sub-movements, try doing them in different positions (mostly lying in bed). Ensure that you are only contracting the muscles you need and no others.

## Putting the Three Movements Together

After you can perform the three sub-movements without any difficulties, it is time to focus on putting them all together.

To do so, follow the next two exercises:

*Conjugation Exercise 1*

1.  Stand sideways in front of a mirror. Assume the position described for initiating the trunk movement. Now relax your pelvis, so it takes a neutral position.

2.  Very slowly, perform Step 2 of the pelvic and trunk movements simultaneously. That is, pull your buttocks back using both a pelvic and a trunk movement.

3.  Pause when your buttocks are in the back-end position.

4.  Slowly, perform Step 3 from the pelvic and trunk movements simultaneously. Watch your movements in the mirror to ensure that both sub-movements progress and finish simultaneously.

Repeat this exercise many times until you feel it flowing without any difficulty. Achieve precise coordination, an abrupt finish, and some power. While you do this, ensure that you relax all muscles that are not being used.

*Conjugation Exercise 2*

Choose a song with a rhythm you find appropriate for these movements. Then, play that song while you practice Sub-movements 1 and 2 and follow its rhythm doing the exercise.

When you are already familiar with the rhythm, use it to make the conjugation exercise of the two sub-movements.

After you have no troubles conjugating both movements, add the third sub-movement to the conjugation exercise.

After you feel comfortable with the coordination of all your sub-movements, add more power. Practice until you can reach an impressive power—more than you will need to use in real life. When your muscular control allows you to do the movement with extreme power, by using only a small share of your muscular strength, you can perform the movement strongly, steadily, and without getting tired.

When you are proficient with power, add more speed. Try to make it really quick. For some women, a very fast and powerful penetration is an instant orgasm trigger. Because of that, the final step in this exercise list is to make it quick, powerful—and not get tired doing it. Of course, sooner or later you will get tired, but better later than sooner...

During your practice, you will notice that even a slight delay in one of the sub-movements (lack of coordination) seriously reduces the intensity of the powerful penetration movement. That is one of the secrets for a great movement: a perfect coordination of the sub-movements. The other secrets are perfect rhythm and totally predictable and repeated movements—this is so important!

Our brains are physiologically built to enjoy patterns. We like music because it has regular patterns. We enjoy a song if we can guess what we will hear next, and the song matches our guess. Very complex music is usually not appreciated the first time one listens to it, because the brain can't find the pattern. When it does, then we start enjoying it! It is the same with sex. Perfectly rhythmic and repeatable movements are bliss. Your partner's brain gets the pattern and just drives her crazy with pleasure. If you do your movements out of pace or with jerky movements, her brain will just be annoyed. And, as a rule of thumb, don't annoy her brain. Keep your rhythm. Keep doing the same movement in the same way. Practice Conjugation Exercise 2 until your penis can play the drums at the Berlin Orchestra.

This does not mean that you should keep the same rhythm throughout the entire intercourse. That would be terrible! But at each interval in which you don't deliberately change the rhythm, or that you are doing a very slow, romantic and therefore more variable penetration, keep it a rhythm, not a random in-and-out penetration.

Having read all you need to know to become a human jackhammer, it is now time to focus on the positions in which you can apply these penetrative abilities.

POSITIONS FOR VAGINAL SEX

## A Few Words about Sex Positions

Between porn movies and sex position books, you have probably seen hundreds of positions already. However, both sources are not focused on giving you the most accurate information. Instead, they are focused on showing positions that are exciting to watch. As you will realize by looking at the ugly clumsy figures of this book, that is not my goal here. In fact, my figures look like conglomerations of human arms and legs. These ugly positions, however, are very exciting for your partner, as she can feel more contact with your body.

In previous chapters, I said that the techniques described were to be regarded as frameworks: All need to be adapted to suit your individual partner. (There is a chapter on adapting techniques later on—don't worry). The same goes for the sex positions that I am about to describe.

## Changing Positions

Before moving on the positions themselves, let's talk about how to change between them. Changing between positions is the moment where the magic is broken, where the thinking mind takes control, and where the stimulation stops. Staying in the same position, however, might become boring. So, changing between positions has to be done with care. I recommend that you do one of two things: Either smoothly transit between positions, or verbally entice your partner to desire a new position.

To smoothly transit, you should switch to neighboring positions. For instance, starting in the missionary, you can pull her legs up and your torso back so that her legs now are up in the air, and after a while move her legs to the side, to sort of a spoon position. She can later stretch her lower leg, and after a while you can hop on top of her, as she lies flat on her stomach. Later on, you can move back and bring her back with you, so that she is on her knees. In this way, by always changing to a "nearby" position, and never interrupting your lovemaking, you can change between positions without breaking the spell. Plus, by slowly sliding between positions, you get to try numerous variants of each position. Sooner or later, you and your partner will find one that just clicks with how your anatomies fit. A wonderful moment.

Or you can use your words. Telling her how much her ass drives you crazy and how much you would love to watch it is a nice way to anticipate a switch to doggy-style. Keeping your complements to her ass as you resume your penetration in the new position keeps her excitement high, preventing the switch to create a downturn.

To do none of the above, and just stop what you are doing to say, "Hey, how about changing position?," or changing positions just for the sake of changing positions, is definitely a break in the sexual magic. Not recommended.

## Missionary Position and Its Neighbors

Almost everyone knows almost everything there is to know about the missionary position. One of its advantages is its romantic component, which you should explore by holding hands, kissing, saying sweet words, hugging close, etc. If your partner is very excited and in a very romantic mood, the missionary position goes well with applying the Sub-movement 3 alone—it is an efficient orgasm trigger. When doing so, give her some freedom of movement. She needs to move her hips so as to ensure that your penis hits her exactly on her favorite spot.

### Variant 1

You can try a variant of the missionary position by moving your pelvis around to the sides, not just back and forth. Seen from the

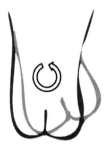

Fig. 8.5. Missionary Variant 1. Viewed from behind, the man in the missionary position (yes, that is a butt). While you are in a romantic mood, and feeling really close to your partner, slowly rotate your pelvis around. Allow her to move easily, so that you can, by trial and error, discover the way you best fit together.

back, your pelvis will perform circles. She will probably also try to adjust and play along. For a few girls, this can be quite stimulating. For most, it is just exciting to feel your pelvis moving so loosely.

*Variant 2*

You can pull her legs all the way up, so that her thighs are between your body and hers. This allows for a much deeper penetration (not always pleasurable—so be careful and don't do it at the initial stages of penetration). This also allows for her to watch your penis as it moves in and out of her. That is exciting. Call her attention to it and then move slowly, for her to watch.

Another tip: For this and other man-on-top positions, try pressing the side of your wrists against her body, slightly squeezing her between your hands.

Fig 8.6. Missionary Variant 2. View from the side. The advantage of this position is that she can look at you and grab you.

*Variant 3*

Coming from Variant 2, pull your trunk back and rest on your shins and knees. Her pelvis is now way off the bed, resting on your thighs or being held by your hands. Penetrating her like this deeply stimulates her anterior wall but is extremely exhausting and quite "unsustainable." A pillow comes in handy, allowing you to have a free

Fig. 8.7. Missionary Variant 3. It is quite a sexy position, and good for anterior wall stimulation.

hand to play with her clitoris.

### Variant 4

Coming back again to the traditional missionary position, you can improve it slightly by placing a pillow under her butt. However, you can do better than just placing a pillow. You can do the Turbo missionary position!

### Turbo Missionary Position

Starting from the missionary position, pass your arms around your partner's torso, placing your hands under her butt. Grab her butt and lift it off the bed. Now, penetration is easier, and the entrance angle makes it more prone to hit the anterior fornix. You can apply an intense powerful penetration movement (ppm from now on), as your penis now enters straight into her vagina, pushing against it its posterior wall, but without friction at the entrance (unlike in regular missionary sex). On the other hand, the woman has now less control over you and the penetration, so proceed with caution.

Fig 8.8. Turbo missionary. It allows close contact between the two bodies, ability to perform the ppm with ease, faces next to each other, able to kiss or talk in her ear...

To make it easier on your arms, close your wrists, placing the pinky finger side on the bed, and rest your partner's butt on the thumb side of your wrist. In this way you can keep her butt lifted without your getting tired. When you apply the ppm in this position, if the length of your penis and her vagina allow for a full penetration without pain or discomfort, the impact of your pelvis on hers will make a loud sound. Really loud, really exciting. Extra tip: Later on, you can use your fingers to play with her anus, as you softly tell her in her ear what you are doing.

Fig. 8.9. Turbo missionary, seen from the man's feet, showing the pelvis. Look at how the hands, between her booty and the bed, support her during the turbo missionary position. In this way, her weight is on your hand bones, without you having to perform any muscular activity.

## Doggy-Style

Being on all fours is usually psychologically very exciting for the woman. It leaves her very vulnerable to you and it suggests sex for pure pleasure, not for romance. Both the vulnerability and the search for pleasure are traits of submission. So play along!

In every sexual position, use its psychological charge to make your partner feel stronger emotions. So while you can be extra cuddly on some other positions, be dominant in doggy-style. Very dominant. Talk dominantly. Grab her shoulders and pull her upwards. Or push her upper back down until her upper torso is flat on the

Fig. 8.10. Doggy-style. The girl is lying on the bed in a more submissive attitude and allowing a deeper penetration.

bed. Or just let her be on her fours and pull her hair (make a ponytail using all her hair, and be sure to pull the hair that grows out of the nape and not from the top of her head). Grab her hips strongly. Slap her ass. Penetrate her very powerfully (but with care). Be very dominant. Start by assuming the dominance stance, and as she positively reacts, increase it.

But, what if she doesn't react positively? What should you do if being on all fours is as much submission as she is willing to take at that moment? That is fine, too. Doggy-style can be quite romantic as well. You can massage or kiss her back; you can grab her boobs or play with her clitoris (you can also insert your penis totally, stop penetrating her, be very cuddly, and rub her clit). You can grab her butt in your hands and describe in detail to her why you find her butt so incredibly exciting. Keep the conversation going. It is not easy to feel her reactions while doing doggy-style, so keeping a vocal communication can be helpful.

After a while, try moving your partner's torso up or down, in search of an entrance angle that increases her stimulation. You can also try placing some pillows under her belly, so that she can move forward. If you are in shape and don't have an enormous dick, try this: place your feet on the bed, by her knees. Rise while keeping

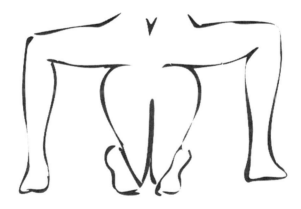

Fig. 8.11. Doggy-style with feet on the side. Seen from the back, he has now "climbed" on top of her. He keeps his legs spread and penetrates by moving his pelvis. While a bit tiring, this position is great for achieving a deep penetration.

your knees bent 90 degrees. In this position you will be able to apply a deeper penetration. You can also use this position to move to the next position on this list...

## On Her Tummy

With the girl lying on her tummy, you will have plenty of options. You can be the sweetest and most romantic lover ever, or a hardcore one. The best part of this position is that your penis will strongly press against the anterior wall of her vagina during its entire course, touching all erogenous zones there.

In the most romantic version, you lie on top of her, really close, placing your head just next to hers. By placing one of your elbows and knees directly on the bed and moving your weight there, you will be able to stay on top of her while not feeling heavy for her.

You can kiss her ears, neck, mouth, or you can talk in her ear. You can use one or two hands to stimulate her clitoris. The penetration should be slow and deep, pressuring the anterior wall and stopping at the deepest reach of her vagina. You can also try to move in circles, so that your penis also moves sideways inside her. Very often you will end up moving in synchrony, both of you performing slow but decisive movements.

Fig. 8.12. On her tummy. A really sweet romantic position. Maximize the contact between your two bodies, hold hands, and kiss her earlobe or neck. The connection between the two of you will be fantastic.

For the woman to feel you so close and in such connected slow harmony, plus the heavy pressure on her clitoris is usually extremely exciting and romantic. Spiced up with sweet sexy talk, this position will bring very sweet and emotional orgasms.

*Variant 1*

Some girls love when they can cross their legs and, in that way, compress the clitoris. While on her tummy, allow her to cross her legs by moving slightly to her side.

*Variant 2*

To do the powerful, non-romantic version of this position, you should straighten your back, place your knees on the bed, outside of her legs, and place your feet as hooks around her legs. Sitting like that, you are prepared to apply the ppm in all its might. Tip: By moving forward, towards the girl's head, your penetration will be deeper.

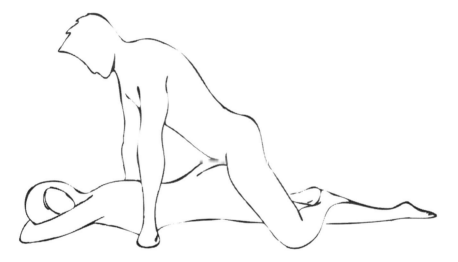

Fig. 8.13. On her tummy, Variant 2. Not romantic, but very stimulating and dominant. Apply a strong pelvic movement to strongly stimulate her entire anterior wall. Squeeze her body between your arms.

## She as a Spoon, You on Your Knees

Lay the girl on her side (by rolling her over from the previous position, for instance), with her buttocks facing slightly upwards. Kneel with open knees, so that your penis is at the appropriate height to enter her. In this position, she can have the advantages of the spoon position while you are allowed much more mobility than if you were in a spoon. Besides, in this position you can stimulate very strongly the anterior wall of her vagina, which is extremely pleasurable. Move around slightly in your position, in search for the best entrance angle and direction—some of them can be very pleasurable, but others can easily become painful, so be very careful as you move around in this position.

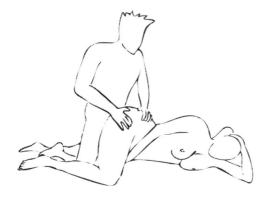

Fig. 8.14. Spoon. While she gets all the rest from the spoon position, you are still able to move and to admire her boobs, booty, and her face. Notice how your leg lies between hers.

## Variant

She can also pull her legs towards her head, to a fetal position. While this becomes harder for the man, some women love it.

Fig. 8.15. Spoon, variant. Not very different from the previous one except that you are at a different angle to her. Your legs are outside hers and she has pulled her legs closer to the body. This is not an easy position for you, but I recommend that you try it, as some women love it.

## Standing, Holding Her Forearms

Having sex while standing has some advantages. Not only can you apply the ppm exactly as you practiced in front of the mirror, as you can do it anywhere, in restrooms, elevators, living rooms, offices, etc. You start by penetrating your partner very slowly while both of you are standing. After you have carefully inserted your penis, slowly and sweetly bend your partner over, so that her torso becomes almost horizontal, at some 110 degrees with her legs. It looks like doggy-style with stretched legs. Grab her forearms with your hands—that will prevent her from falling. In this dominant stance, you can control her position by moving her forearms around. It is very dominant, which can be very exciting...

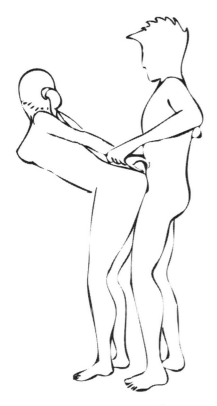

Fig. 8.16. Standing holding her forearms. The only tricky part here is inserting your penis. Lower your body so you can do that. Then it is very easy. Grip her tightly so she is totally sure she won't fall flat on the ground.

This position allows you to achieve high-intensity penetration, as you can freely use your leg muscles. The height difference between you and your partner should be compensated by opening the legs and flexing the knees.

A sexy variant of this technique is when your partner places her hands on the ground. Another is to pull her upwards and using a "shallow" penetration that hits her G-spot.

## The Nun and Her Cat

This position is counterintuitive but surprisingly pleasurable. The girl should lie on her back with her legs slightly open. After you start penetrating her, she should close her legs and keep them stretched out and still (that is why I called it "the nun"). To keep a romantic interaction, just keep close to her. To perform the movement in perfection, place your hands on the bed and stretch your arms so you curve your back (like a cat). Penetrate her with a strong emphasis on Sub-movement 3. Your pelvis should be pressuring hard—but slowly—against hers. You, your penis, and her legs—everyone is getting together to put some strong pressure on her clitoris and making the entrance of her vagina tighter—which is great, and she will love it!

Fig. 8.17. The nun and her cat. The trick here is to start with her legs open, before closing them as depicted. Be careful not to slide out during the penetration. Go slowly and with pressure.

### Variant 1

She can also slightly open her legs while keeping them flat on the bed and use her feet as hooks on your almost-straight legs.

### Variant 2

You can then move one of your legs to the outside of her legs and try a different kind of penetrative movement: Grab her shoulders or the bed frame for support and then pull your entire body North (towards her head) instead of using your pelvis. You only move North and South (that is, towards her head, towards her feet), not up or down.

## Girl on Top

Here, the girl sits on top of you. This is not a single position, of course, but a whole bunch of positions. They are favorable for the woman's orgasm, as she controls her own movements and can maximize her pleasure. Despite this advantage, however, I recommend that you don't start sex or reach your own orgasm in any of these positions—except for an occasional treat—but that you use them when your partner is already very excited and close to orgasm. Being on top, she can orgasm quickly and make her orgasm feel great—and you can see exactly how she moves when she is orgasming, so that you can mimic that motion later.

Fig 8.18. Woman on top, standard. The standard woman-on-top position. She can now do whatever she feels like. Just watch...

And now, the positions. In the first one, the girl sits facing you, with her knees placed on each side of your trunk. She has her back stretched, and her movements are not so focused on moving your penis in and out of her, but rather in keeping your penis inside her while she makes it hit her favorite spots on the vaginal walls. You can relax and enjoy the show! Of course, you can excite her with your hands, eventually playing with her clitoris or her boobs. By the way, as you enjoy the show, learn how she does it to touch her favorite spots...

## Variant 1

If the girl then moves a bit more forward, bending towards you, you can now plant your feet on the bed to get some support and start penetrating her. While this can tire you pretty easily, it has some advantages to it: You can suck a nipple with your mouth, play with her clitoris with one hand, and massage her anus with the other, while penetrating her gently. She will love it! This variant gets even better if you have some pillows behind your back.

Fig. 8.19. Woman on top, Variant 1. While you can't see in this figure, his left hand is playing with her clitoris, his right hand with her anus and he is kissing her right nipple. When kissing nipples, try different variations until you discover her favorite. Just don't suck on them like a newborn unless you want to trigger her dominant, maternal side.

## Variant 2

If she moves even closer to you, you can embrace her strongly while penetrate her deeply, using Sub-movement 3. Combining deep penetration with an extremely tight embrace is powerful. You are not forcing dominance on her by insisting on being on top. Instead, you are just giving, doing your very best to please her, despite being under her.

The second thing to do is to squeeze her very hard in your arms. The position probably echoes some sensation from her childhood, lying on her parents who were 10 times stronger than her. Now, she is lying over her dominant; she is not being forced under him, but instead is voluntarily on top of him. Still, she feels a very tight embrace that perhaps brings deep, vague memories of feeling protected. Try it. It is magical.

Some girls enjoy stretching their legs when they are on top, so that they can contract the gluteus and press harder on their clitoris. If your girl hasn't tried that, use your hands to push her legs towards that position to see if she enjoys it.

Fig. 8.20. Woman on top, Variant 2. There are two tricks to this position. To be able to make a penetration movement, you need to have your feet well planted on the bed. As you penetrate her, give her a mega-squeezing embrace.

### Variant 3

Your partner can also turn her back to you while she is on top. If you enjoy watching her butt moving against you, you will welcome this one. For plenty of women, this position is both physically and psychologically exciting, as it has a strong female dominant and a "sex-for-pleasure" components: She doesn't even see you.

### Variant 4

Starting from Variant 3, bring one of your legs to the outside of hers. Bend that leg so that you can plant the foot on the bed. You can then use that foot for support and perform a penetrative movement.

### Furniture trick

There is a furniture trick that will make your woman on top positions work much better: Place your bed some three or four feet away from a wall (depending on your height). While this destroys any Feng Shui aspirations you might have for your bedroom, you will be able to support your lower back on the edge of the bed and place your feet against the wall. Both you and your partner will then be able to move freely. It's really helpful.

Fig. 8.21. Woman on top, Variant 3. There she is, with her booty to you. Time for her to show her booty-shaking skills!

### Variant 5

Coming out of bed, you can take a nearby chair and just sit normally. She can then sit on top of you, facing you and keeping her body close to yours. This position is great for her to both regulate the penetration and the clitoris rubbing against your body.

### Other Positions

There are many other positions you can try. Some of them are exciting while others allow for a stronger stimulation of particular areas of your partner's vagina or vulva, such as, for instance, the spoon position with a leg crossed over her vulva. While I don't think there is any other position that will bring huge benefits compared to the ones presented here, you have nothing to lose in trying them all.

Always keep your focus on your penetrative movement and adapt it to each position in order to please your partner the most.

With the three sub-movements shown here, you can adapt your penetrative movement in different ways to different positions: You can use more of a particular sub-movement (be it 1, 2 or 3), use a higher entrance (bringing a deeper penetration), use a different angle, or apply a rotational movement.

## Why Women Enjoy the Powerful Penetration Movement

Many men resist the idea of applying the powerful penetration movement. This is understandable: They were taught, since little boys, that women are fragile and naive beings. They were taught that they should always be honest about their intentions, considerate, and gentle, as sex can be painful for the fragile female body. Sex was something that women would only grant out of love in return for the man's chivalry, or if fooled by the evil, manipulative, and powerful man.

This inaccurate picture made sense when sexual discretion was important for a woman's future and when educating boys to have sex with virgins. In fact, the above description was quite accurate: young, single girls, without sexual experience, raised in repressive, conservative homes were indeed fragile and naive beings that needed to be treated with extreme care.

However, most adult women of the twenty-first century are neither naive nor fragile. But many men still believe that the world is divided into whores and proper women (who happen to be fragile). That wrong belief seriously hampers their sex lives. Every woman has desires you could attribute to "whores." Most women try to look as proper as they can.

Yet most men believe sex is something offensive or dangerous to a proper woman if not done with a lot of care and respect. They believe that by having hard sex with a woman they are either physically harming her or they are treating her like a sexual object, and therefore offending her or harming their relationship.

But they are not.

When women experience hard sex with a man, properly done, they don't feel abused, objectified, or hurt. They feel desired, they feel powerful, they feel attraction, they feel excitement, and they feel pleasure.

Women feel great when they make a man "lose control." So men should just set themselves loose of their restrictions when having sex, so that they and their women can enjoy it. They should enjoy the fact that they are having sex with a woman, that they can touch her, that they can grab her, and that they can fuck her.

What they should not do is what some men do: slowly enjoy the physical pleasure on their penises while keeping their eyes closed, have sex non-stop with the explicit goal of making the woman have an orgasm, or have sex non-stop in weird positions to show how fit and hard and cool they are. All these are turn-offs for women. Women want to be fucked hard because they want to feel a powerful man totally crazy for them, due to their looks and sensuality. They want to feel a man orgasm because that is the proof of their power.

They want to feel Queens of a King in bed.

Finally, for simple physical reasons, ppm is great because harder and quicker sex is just more stimulating when things get really hot.

## When to Go Harder and When to Go Lighter

After practicing the ppm, you have a key to great sex. After that, it's time to start thinking about when to apply a harder or lighter penetration, a deeper or a not-so-deep penetration. There are four factors that I think are worth considering:

1. Emotional state;

2. Excitement level of your partner;

3. Your physical condition; and

4. The teasing factor.

### 1. Emotional State

Sex is a unique experience. When two people are into each other, even if they just met, they can become strongly emotionally attached by having sex. It is only required that sex is done with an emotional component. Choosing when to penetrate harder or lighter is part of that emotional component. Usually, you should start slowly. Sure, there are plenty of exceptions: the quickies, the times you want to show her how uncontrollably horny you feel for her, the times you are role playing, or when you just want to be really rough, for variety sake. But, generally speaking, you should start slowly. In fact, the beginning of intercourse is one of the most emotionally charged moments of the entire sexual experience. The look in a woman's eyes as you fuse with her for the first time is something unique. Make that moment special—do it very slowly, even dramatically.

As sex progresses, there will be different moments, different tensions. When romance is in the air, it can be savored by a lighter penetration. When doing so, try to find a common rhythm and movement, as when two people slowly dance or when they kiss. To achieve this, "listen" very attentively to her movements, and as soon as she moves her hips, adapt your movement to match hers.

In other moments, when a more crude excitement dominates, it is time for the harder, deeper, or quicker penetration.

### 2. Excitement Level of Your Partner

There is a stairway to an orgasm. Your partner needs a certain time before she orgasms. However, doing the same thing for a lot of time eventually becomes boring. So, the simplest road to orgasm is providing increasingly stronger stimulation, either physically or psychologically. Start with lighter penetration before putting in the pressure and speed. Besides that, it is advisable to have her vagina well lubricated and open before applying the ppm.

### 3. Your Physical Condition

Even an athlete will have problems performing the ppm quickly and powerfully for very long periods. So, obviously, you have to take your physical condition into consideration when you decide to apply the ppm. As in any "sport," manage your effort not to get tired too early. I recommend taking it easy on the speed, as it is the speed, not the power, that gets you tired…

### 4. The Teasing Factor

Have you seen aroused men "suffering" a lap dance in a strip club? Many of them look like they are on the verge of exploding and, in fact, they are. If the stripper would start having sex with them, most of them wouldn't take long before having a very strong orgasm.

You should cause the same effect on your partner. Tease her. Use different games to do it.

A very simple game to tease her is to penetrate her only with the tip of your penis. Use just the tip and while you do it, talk with your partner about it. Make her crave for your full penis. Make her lose control. Steadily penetrate her only with the tip of your penis. She will go nuts. She will pull you. She will grab you harder. She might even jump around in bed trying to pull you in. Don't let her succeed. Be dominant and hold her still as you use only the tip of your penis.

When the time is right, tell her that you will stick your entire dick into her. She will be so excited when that happens that she might orgasm on the spot. After a lot of teasing, some women only require two or three insertions to orgasm.

Teasing is very powerful. Find out what she craves for and tease her before she gets it. However, tease her seldom. Teasing shows sexual power over the other, the kind of sexual power that women usually have. Your woman won't feel like a Queen if she is the one usually being teased—that is, if you demonstrate the kind of sexual power that she should have over you. So tease her while respecting her Queen status.

Chapter 9:

# Anal Penetration

*A female view on this chapter:*

*As you have sex with your partner, she is getting more and more excited. You seize that excitement by running your finger around her anus. You tell something very naughty in her ear, something that brings memories of how good she felt last time you did it. She can't help but begging: "Yes, oh please, fuck my ass pleaaase...." You obey. She loves it and comes really hard, yelling as she grabs the sheets.*

\*

*"An iron rod bends while it is hot." —Greek proverb*

*"Don't shake the tree when the pears fall off themselves."—Slovakian proverb*

## ANAL SEX TECHNIQUES

### From Vaginal to Anal Penetration

The techniques for anal sex are not very different from those for vaginal sex, given the obvious similarities between the rectum and the vagina. There are, however, some key differences that you have to keep in mind when switching from vaginal to anal sex:

1. Anal sex has a different psychological context;
2. Anal sex requires some practice on the receiving end;
3. The rectum only has one pleasurable wall;
4. The anus is much tighter and longer than the vaginal entrance.

These differences translate into some changes in the penetrative movements you'll use during anal sex.

As said above, the rectum is only pleasurable in its anterior wall, that is, the one separating it from the vagina. Somewhere along this wall lies the underside of the posterior fornix, that very pleasurable area. That area is one of the reasons why anal sex is so pleasurable to women, together with the stimulation of the anus and the "filling feeling." As these last two predominate, however, there is no need to push your penis against the walls, as you do in vaginal sex. Besides, as you want the penetration to be pleasurable and comfortable at the anus, and the anus is quite deep, when performing anal sex, do not use a marked pelvic movement (Sub-movement 1) as in vaginal sex. A movement closer to the plain "back and forth" Sub-movement 2 is better suited for anal with most partners, and Sub-movement 3 is pretty worthless in most positions. Besides, choose positions where you stimulate the anterior wall, or none, rather than the posterior wall.

Despite these differences, the keys for success are the same as vaginal sex: relaxation and excitement. Anal sex usually occurs just after vaginal sex, which allows for a build-up of excitement before starting. The heavy psychological charge of anal sex increases that excitement, especially if catalyzed by adequate words.

Relaxation is usually the key issue. There are three main obstacles to her relaxation that you have to overcome:
1. Hygiene concerns;
2. Religious or social repression; and
3. Fear of feeling pain or getting hurt.

A couple of pages further down we will deal with the hygiene concerns. The second bullet point, religious and social repression, is addressed in Chapter 12. What about her fear of feeling pain or getting hurt?

Contrary to the other two points, her fear of getting hurt is extremely well justified. It should not be dismissed, but deeply respected. The way you ensure her that you will not hurt her is by doing everything extremely slowly, moving millimeter by millimeter, giving her full control, following the appropriate techniques and by *telling her that it will hurt.*

Since she learned how to speak, everyone who has told her, "It won't hurt," was lying: nurses, dentists, gynecologists, you name it. You don't want to be in that gang, do you? So tell her it will hurt. It will hurt in the beginning, when she doesn't have experience, and it will hurt every time you are not careful enough. But, in the end, it will be very pleasurable. And, as women demonstrate all the time, pain is never an obstacle for them to achieve the things they want to achieve.

## The Beginning

The most important difference between anal and vaginal sex is that anal sex requires patience, tranquility, and softness in the beginning. Not only her first time, but every time you perform anal sex. You have to let the girl accommodate your penis. That takes some time, and you definitely have to wait for her. You can do this with your penis, with toys, or with a couple of fingers (both toys and fingers have the big advantage of not losing their rigidity if you make them wait for minutes while your partner slowly lets them slide in). Be it a toy, a finger, or a penis, focus on being gentle. Allow her to relax, while at the same time make her more and more excited, using your words and your hands.

While some women prefer that you do move slightly, back and forth, during this relaxation/initiation period, others prefer that you stay absolutely still and let her control the penetration. If you are moving and she says, "Stop!" do exactly that: stop where you are, not moving in or out. Play statue. It is really necessary to wait for her anus to relax before she is able to fully enjoy the pleasures of anal sex. A good way of letting her have exactly what she needs is to initiate anal sex in the spoon position, so that she can control the penetration easily.

Another key difference from vaginal sex is the need for lubrication. In some cases, just the carry-over from the vagina or a bit of spit are enough, but most of the time, a lot of lube is required. When putting on lube, put some in her anus and some on your penis—all along your penis, like toothpaste on a toothbrush, not only on the tip—because you don't want to make a "lube stop" later on.

## Losing Her Virginity

If you want to initiate your partner into anal sex, both of you will need calm, patience, and low expectations. Ideally, you should try several sessions with slim-shaped toys or fingers (whatever she finds more arousing) before moving to real penis penetration. The toys (e.g., anal plugs) can be left inside her while your hands remain free to tease and please her.

When inserting either fingers or the anal plug, don't push it in. Let her relax, accommodate, and slightly suck it inwards. Talk to her. Tell her how exciting it is, how well she is doing, and how great it will feel when she is able to receive real anal penetration.

Every time you do a session of anal initiation, be sure to give her orgasms from other sources, such as her clitoris or vagina. Don't depend on her feeling pleasure from the anal penetration to make the evening a great one. Anal sex can be amazingly pleasurable, but hardly ever during the first time. And you do want to make her feel good about anal sex and look back at your anal sessions as an escalation of pleasant successes, not as a series of painful failures.

## Hygiene Issues

A potential obstacle to anal sex is hygiene. While being great for sex, the anus has other functions that do raise some incompatibilities. If your partner is into anal sex, in the long run she will probably start doing enemas, which is the best way to ensure totally clean and relaxed anal sex.

But, if your partner is just starting, enemas are probably the last thing on her mind. She has probably seen how clean it is in the porn movies but doesn't realize that the actresses give themselves an enema before shooting. So, she probably has pretty high expectations regarding the cleanliness of anal sex and could become disappointed or embarrassed.

There are some things you can do to minimize her negative feelings. One is to have a lot of paper close by to wrap everything that you use on her anus (e.g., toys, condoms) so that, if any accident happens, she never notices it. Another thing you can do is try to assess if the session is a good time or a bad time to try anal. After meals is a bad time. After she has been to the toilet and taken a long shower is a good time.

In the long run, making her aware of the advantages of doing enemas is probably the best solution, despite being a very tricky subject to bring up. You really don't want to sound like you are criticizing her hygiene.

## The Great Lie of Anal Sex

A lot of young women in Western societies have tried anal sex. Some enjoyed it. However, they will not admit this to their new partners when they enter a new relationship. Why? Because they have no personal advantage in telling the truth. Look at what a woman has to gain if she tells her partner that she never tried anal or that she only had one painful experience:

1. He will respect her more;
2. He will be more patient when trying anal sex with her;
3. If he is not very skilled at performing anal sex, she will be allowed to avoid it without having to answer, "Why did you do it with him and not with me?"
4. She can set up an exciting anal pop-the-cherry scene;
5. She will keep it as a prize to offer him when he deserves it; and
6. She will make her partner feel fantastic in bed for being the first guy with whom she has enjoyed anal sex.

As you can see, there is plenty of motivation for a woman to feign ignorance. But this simple white lie has a dark side. Because of it, plenty of men believe they were the first to have anal sex with a bunch of women. They believe, therefore, that it is not painful or troublesome to "pop her anal cherry." After all, past partners were enjoying deep penetration after a few minutes! When meeting a real anal virgin, these men will be much less tolerant of her needs for accommodation and relaxation, thus giving her an unpleasant experience. So we should all be very careful with anal virgins—one might be for real!

This does not mean that if an anal virgin reacts very positively, she is a liar. People do differ, and anal sex is easier for some women than for others. Actually, it is totally counterproductive to find out whether she is lying or not. It is a sweet lie that makes the relationship more exciting. Why not live it as if it was true? See it as a chance to show how delicate and smooth you can be. If she is a true anal virgin, anal sex will be only pleasurable for her. If she is not, the worst that can happen is that she will regret that her true initiation was not as kind and pleasurable as the one you would have given her. Don't ever act like you suspect her. In case you are wrong, imagine how terrible it must feel for her: doing anal sex for her first time, giving you such a special gift, tolerating the pain bravely, and then being accused of being cheap because it was "too easy"? That is more than enough to destroy a relationship.

## Exciting Your Partner for Anal Sex

Your partner's extreme excitement and relaxation are prerequisites for anal sex. She needs to feel a strong desire and deep trust that you will not hurt her. It is worthless to debate the topic and rationally convince her to try it. You can convince her to give you her anus for penetration, but you cannot convince her to desire it—so, she will not have a pleasant experience. Bottom line is, you cannot persuade her to become an anal sex enthusiast—you have to make her so excited about the idea that she wants to try it.

If she has strong prejudice against anal sex, thanks to bad past experiences or a dominant personality, building that excitement can be quite difficult. However, I believe it is hardly ever impossible. The first step towards anal sex is to avoid rejections. In the future, you don't want to insist on something she already said no to, so the best thing to do is to prevent her from saying no. Don't touch her ass or mention the topic when rejection is probable—namely when she is not deeply excited, when she hasn't showered, etc.

The second step is to demonstrate your competence in bed. The more new things you show her, the more pleasure you give her without ever hurting her, and the more "you take care of her," the more she will trust that anal sex with you will be a positive experience. She is more likely to feel like doing it with you—giving herself to you—as she will see you as her dominant. So, keep anal for last in your bag of tricks.

The third step is to associate anal sensations with pleasure, and to show that you know that anal sex is pleasurable and exciting. So, when she is already extremely excited, start touching her anus. You can do that during oral sex just to trigger her curiosity, or during intercourse. The best position to do this is during Turbo Missionary; you can talk in her ear about how good it feels, playing with her cute asshole, as you touch it. The area surrounding the anus is quite sensitive, so it is a good idea to pass your fingers quickly and repetitively over her anus and perineum. If she is responding so-so, keep it at this level. If she responds very enthusiastically, however, you can eventually insert just the tip of a finger, and play a bit more—not yet with the intention of fucking her ass, just as pleasant play. Make her feel curious. Add how exciting it is for you to play with her asshole, and tell her how tight her ass is. This will sound like a compliment, and will make her feel secure that you are aware of the difficulties you would face if penetrating.

The fourth step is to give her some orgasms with a strong anal component. Try, for instance, to masturbate her clitoris as you lick her anus. Or play with your finger around her anus while she is getting close to orgasm and keep it there during orgasm, to associate it with pleasure.

The fifth step is to do the same as before but start inserting fingers or butt plugs. You should start with the fingers, as it is more spontaneous. After the fingers, you can then unveil the butt plug. Somewhere at this stage, she should be slightly annoyed that you haven't yet given her anal sex. She should be longing for it. When you are making her come with your finger playing in her anus, she should hopefully be thinking, "Please fuck my ass, for god's sake!"

So do it. The sixth step (but not a really necessary one for most cases) is to find a special motive, a special day. That motive can be symbolic or emotional—a particular sweet date, your first month together—or something practical. For instance, her period is a very good excuse to try anal sex.[1] Turn her on beyond any control. Then, if she wants to feel your dick, she has no other option than using her ass as a replacement. On that particular night make her more excited than ever.... Tell her a fantasy so exciting and so strong on anal that she just has to try it.

The final step, as weird as it might sound, is to back off. Play chicken. When she says, "I want you to fuck my ass," back off and suggest using a butt plug instead. Don't do this as a wimp who believes that anal sex is violent and that women are fragile flowers, but as a sexually experienced man who believes that she is still at "beginner's level" and yet not able to perform anal sex. That will play with her female pride.[2] She will want to show you how wrong you are and how great she is in bed. And, as most managers will tell you, motivation is the most important key to success.

On one hand, you will be telling her fantasies about how great it will be when she can fully perform anal sex. On the other hand, you will tell her that you should move slowly and use yet another butt plug instead of going straight for your dick. Listening to these two lines of argument, she will force you to fuck her ass.

Be careful, however, and continue proceeding slowly. All that motivation will evaporate if the pain is too strong!

**Alternatives**

If you have tried everything and failed, then it might be a good idea to understand what is her view on the topic of anal sex. Whenever you have sexual conversations, choose an extremely sweet environment, like walking in a park hand-in-hand. Don't blame her; just try to understand her heart. Only then can you do what it takes to address her fears or wishes.

---

1 However, you won't be able to have vaginal sex before anal sex, which lowers the excitement.

2 Playing with her pride is extremely powerful. For instance, try telling a partner (especially if you are not in a monogamous relationship) that you don't want to orgasm that particular night with her, despite having sex. Use a silly excuse. She will do everything in her reach to make you orgasm—including things she wouldn't normally do.

On the other hand, introducing anal sex can be much simpler than the seven-step procedure described above. If this seems to be the case, don't force yourself to stick to the plan—just move ahead. As I said, for some women it can be quite easy from day one.

## POSITIONS FOR ANAL SEX

The positions for anal sex are the same as for vaginal sex, with some modifications. The exceptions are "the nun and her cat" position, which is inappropriate for anal sex; and the inclusion of the spoon position, which is particularly suited for anal.

### Spoon

The spoon position (with you also laying behind her, forming a spoon) is not very good for intercourse—because you don't have anywhere to support your legs—but is great for initiating anal sex.

In this position, the woman can freely maneuver her hips to slowly and in a controlled manner let your penis enter her in the exact "amount," and then move as much—or as little—as she wants. When you start moving, move very slowly and be predictable and obedient.

### On Her Tummy

This position is the same as in vaginal sex. It is really good due to its stimulation of the anterior wall and its romanticism. You can have anal sex while talking in her ear: "My dick is slowly entering your cute asshole. It is soooo tight! Sweetie, will you be able to open your tight little asshole enough so that my entire dick slides inside you?... Wow, you are so impressive!" In this position she feels like you have total control over her. That is very exciting. But she needs to trust you!

### Doggy-style

Doggy-style is very exciting, too, because it allows for wild sex, exploring the psychological charge of anal sex. It is a very fitting position for calling her bad names, slapping, etc., but also for some sweet talk describing everything you are watching from your privileged position. As doggy-style is the best position for her to stimulate her clitoris until she orgasms, suggest that to her. She might be shy of doing it without you telling her to.

### She as a Spoon, You on Your Knees

This position is just super for anterior wall stimulation and you can use it in the same way as the spoon position—that is, to initiate penetration while remaining totally still and letting her control.

### Standing

The standing position where you hold her forearms can be modified for anal sex. For instance, it can be very exciting to put your partner in a more obviously submissive position, such as standing against the wall—either flat against the wall, or at a distance with her hands against the wall. Another interesting alternative is for her to place her hands on the ground while keeping her legs stretched, having anal sex. Not for everyone, but very sensual.

### Missionary Position with Spread Legs

This is the anal equivalent of the missionary position. To stimulate the anterior wall, use a strong Sub-movement 3, while slightly falling on your back. As she is spreading her legs like that, be sure not to miss the chance to explore her vulva's exposition and to play with her clitoris.

### Facing the Mirror

In case you have a mirror in your bedroom, try yet another position: Keep the girl in the same position as the one before, but move to her side, keeping yourself slightly below her, while raising her butt with your hands. Have her butt face the mirror so that she can see in detail your dick sliding in and out of her while also observing her open pussy. Very exciting...

Fig. 9.1.
Facing the mirror. We are seeing this couple from behind the mirror. Both of them can look at the mirror and see the details of their anatomies as they slowly perform anal sex. Spice this up better than a movie scene by describing to her exactly what she is watching.

## Double Penetration

If the anterior wall feels really good in anal, and if the posterior wall of her vagina feels so great, imagine how wonderful it is to feel both being stimulated simultaneously!

Besides the huge physical pleasure, the psychological charge of double penetration is extreme. It is a mix of being extremely sexual and being extremely able. She will feel proud of having the courage and the ability to do it. So you can use your words to increase her emotions: "You are fucking unbelievable. So hot, a real woman! It is so amazing to see how you can take two whole dicks all inside your cute tight ass and your sweet little pussy... You are so amazing!"

To go for double penetration, if you don't want to share your partner, you need a dildo. There are many different kinds of dildos. For double penetration, choose one that is soft and flexible—it will be more comfortable for her—and which doesn't have a lot of stuff sticking out, because you don't want to torture your balls by smashing them against it. The best ones for her vagina should vibrate and have something that she can grab on to, so that she can move it in and out as you penetrate her ass. If you want something for her butt, then a butt plug is probably the best choice. Go for the soft ones.

When performing a double-penetration on your girl, be very careful. With strong orgasmic push-outs, the vaginal dildo can come flying out of her pussy. You'd better not be in its way...

## Conclusion

In these four chapters you have acquired techniques that will allow you to be extremely good in bed. As women are so different from each other in how they perceive touch and experience pleasure, the next chapter will go over what you need to know in order to apply these techniques—in short, how to adapt them to each different partner.

Chapter 10:

# How to Adapt to Each Partner

*A female view on this chapter:*

*He really knows how to touch me. He does it so well. He can touch me very hard yet never hurting me. He can touch me very softly yet without tickling me.*
*What is he trying now? Yes, I like that... mmm, yes... oh yes, like that, oh yes, exactly like that, yes, oh my god that is so great, that is so perfect, I am going to come again!*

\*

*"Half a word is enough for a wise man"* —Portuguese proverb

*"A woman can say more in a sigh than a man can say in a sermon."*
—Arnold Haultain

## ADAPTING TO YOUR PARTNER

Despite women sharing a lot of characteristics, they are not all alike. They have different sensitivities, preferences, and backgrounds. To give your partner enormous pleasure, you have to adapt to her. This adaptation should be done in different dimensions: the way of touching her body, the words to use, the context in which to frame the sexual act, etc. Everything should be adapted to suit the partner. In this chapter, I will focus on adapting the physical stimulation. The adaptation of psychological stimulation comes in later chapters.

I have been quite persistent about the man taking the lead during the sexual act. That leadership can only be successful if the man adapts to his partner, optimizing the sexual act for her. Leading without tuning in to her preferences can yield some nasty results.

Imagine how will a woman feel if she is having sex with a man who totally leads the action without trying to adapt to her, and does so in a way that is inadequate for her sensitivity.

First of all, she will not feel as much pleasure as she could otherwise feel—that breeds frustration and disappointment.

Secondly, while she tries to "communicate" with him, he doesn't listen—that breeds irritation.

Finally, she feels she has no control to how he touches her. That breeds lack of trust. All and all, she feels frustrated, disappointed, irritated and without trust.

On the contrary, a partner who picks up every little sign she sends, adapting his performance to her preferences, can give her much more pleasure and allow her to relax. This is not a minor detail. There is a lot to adapt in sex, as girls' preferences vary quite a lot. The amount of pressure perfect for a particular girl might feel like an itch to another girl and be painful to a third girl. To successfully apply the techniques described in the previous chapters, you need to adapt them along these three major dimensions:

1.   Listening to her;
2.   Finding the right spot; and
3.   Finding the right pressure and movement.

**Listening to Her**

Being able to listen to her is of paramount importance. She sends signals all the time. You just have to pick them up.

The way she moans, the way she breathes, the way she stops breathing, the way she moves her hips, the way she moves her hands, the way her skin changes, the way her pussy changes, the way she looks at you and, of course, what she says, all give you the indications you need to tune in to her preferences. Be attentive to all these signs as you adjust your techniques. You might even invite these signs by, for instance, holding hands as you perform oral sex on her.

**Finding the Right Spot**

Make predictable screening movements when searching for a spot. That is, move slowly in one direction. This allows her to feel whether it is becoming "hotter" or "colder" and then to express that to you (usually by moaning louder). If you move randomly or too quickly, she can't feel properly. Stay in each point you are testing long enough for her to feel it and get used to it. Use references to memorize the exact location of every interesting spot you find—and no, marking them with a pen is not allowed! The substitute for marking them with a pen is to memorize how the spot feels when you touch it. It is quite easy to do this with your tongue and fingers. Both give you a lot of indications on where you are touching.

With your penis, however, things are not so simple. You have to memorize her position and yours. Sometimes, just bending your back can make a big difference!

### Finding the Right Pressure and Movement

To find the right pressure, start lightly and progressively increase the pressure. I don't recommend using lots of pressure unless she explicitly wishes it (by pushing herself against you or even asking for it). Besides, it is usually a good idea to keep a bit of extra pressure in the bag to add in the last few seconds before her orgasm.

It is also a good idea, during sex and foreplay, to start with the techniques that are lighter and less direct before moving to heavier handling. There are two reasons for this: Not only do you progressively find how roughly she likes to be touched, but you also allow her desire for harder stimulation to grow with her excitement.

### Why You Should Have an Adaptation Strategy

Adapting techniques to a partner is not straightforward. On top of it, while you should adapt each technique as much as you can, you don't want to look like you are adapting a technique to her. You want to come across as a mighty King who knows all about sex due to your superior genetic talent and mystical connection to her, helped along by your long experience with women. You don't want to come across as a guy who read about techniques in a book—book knowledge is just not respected nowadays!

To adapt your techniques in a way that seems like natural talent, you need an adaptation strategy and a relaxed attitude. The relaxed attitude will disguise your technical side. (I know your secret—you are reading this book!) So, despite your being deeply concerned about how much she is enjoying the techniques, act and talk like you are only driven by attraction and tenderness towards her, not even slightly concerned about adapting techniques.

Before I describe the full adaptation strategy, let's look at the rules for adaptation. I think it is a good idea to keep them in mind at all times.

## Adaptation Rules

*Rule 1: "Keep her excitement rising."*

The main goal during sex is to make your partner increasingly more excited. Sound too obvious? Just don't forget about it when you are focusing too much on a technique that was just the best on your previous partner—even though this partner is not reacting all that positively. No girl enjoys every single technique described in this book. So, if one technique is not working, move on to the next one. Don't jeopardize the escalation of excitement.

The only exception to this rule is if you want to slow down her excitement in order to postpone her orgasm, thereby making it stronger—or just to tease her. When you do this, I advise you to show her explicitly that you are preventing her from coming, like, "Today you can't come against my mouth, only with my dick," or, "No, you are not allowed to come yet," or just pausing with the stimulation altogether—that can be exciting, too. In fact, you can even make her come quicker by stopping once in a while. Some women get so eager for more that they come quicker. Cool.

But, if you stop for no apparent reason, bringing her to peaks of excitation and then slowing down or changing to a less pleasurable technique, you can become quite annoying.

*Rule 2: "Play it safe."*

No, this rule is not about condoms. It is about blackjack, the card game. In blackjack, the higher your hand, the better—as long as you don't go over twenty-one points. If you do, you blow it. Applying techniques is more or less the same. You add more pressure and she likes it more and more, until… KABOOM!

Can you remember how annoyed you were with the last woman who squeezed your dick too hard? You definitely don't want your partner to feel the same about you! You don't need twenty-one to win at blackjack, so don't use too much pressure (but do get close to twenty-one, because you don't win with a ten, either).

### Rule 3: "Go step by step."

As you know, excitement is a crescendo that makes her desire harder and quicker techniques. Excitement is a hunger. Don't satisfy her hunger too soon or she won't be hungry anymore. Don't touch her hard or quickly in the beginning. Make her always feel a bit "hungry."

If you apply too much speed in genital stimulation or penetration early on, her excitement will stall.

Besides that, it is hard to pick up her signs when you do a lot of new techniques simultaneously. So it is always better to increase your stimulation step by step, so that you can take your time to properly evaluate her reactions.

### Rule 4: "Keep a steady channel of nonverbal communication open."

You need to have an open communication with your partner. Without it, you can't adapt. If the music is too loud or it's too dark or you guys have to be totally silent not to wake up her mother or children sleeping in the next room, solve these issues before you proceed. You can't adapt if you can't get her feedback.

### Rule 5: "Have a shelter."

A "shelter" technique is one that works well on the girl. From it, you can always try new techniques. If they don't work as well as you expected, you can go back to your "shelter" technique and keep her excitement rising.

### Rule 6: "Try everything."

The only way of being sure that you find exactly what your partner prefers is if you try plenty of different things. If you just stick to one way of lovemaking, you might miss out on something she would really enjoy.

Try stuff. Try everything. Try opposites. Not only is variation good for its own sake, but it is the only way to be sure to find what she enjoys.

### Rule 7: "Trust her opinion more than this book."

This book is written based on my experience about what most women enjoy. However, some women are very far from average. Some women orgasm when fingers stop moving in and out of them. Others prefer oral sex at the U-spot rather than the clitoris. There are no absolute rules. If your partner gives you any hint that she prefers something different, no matter how absurd it might seem, just follow her hint or lead and forget about what you read here.

It is of critical importance that you stay open for communication so that you pick up on all her directions—in fact, this is the most important rule of all.

## Adaptation Strategy

### Step 1: Use Anticipation

To ensure that a girl is receptive to whatever you are about to do, nothing is better than start teasing her in advance using the power of *anticipation*. Make her guess what you will do next by suggesting it with your words and gestures. Before a French kiss, kiss her mouth corner. Before oral sex, pass your tongue somewhere else along her body as though performing oral sex, or kiss her slowly towards her vulva. Before intercourse, grind her, simulating sex while still having your clothes on—all of this is exciting and makes her ready and eager for the next step.

Suggesting with your words is even more exciting: Telling her exactly what you will do to her leaves her eager to feel it. Imagine how she must feel when listening to you saying, "Can't wait to feel the tip of my dick entering your tight pussy, then my entire dick sliding inside you, pushing against that soft pussy." Wouldn't you love to hear a sweet and sexual sentence like that before intercourse?

These suggestions, mostly the ones with gestures, can be made more exciting by slightly postponing the fulfillment of the expectation: for instance, by kissing around her pussy when she expected you to go straight for her clitoris. However, don't postpone the fulfillment for too long. Doing so is a demonstration of sexual power over your partner that can bring irritation and frustration.

There is also another interesting form of anticipation (to be applied sparsely): Negative anticipation. You don't keep her anxiously waiting; you make her think that she won't have it at all. When she feels disappointed, then you give it to her, out of the blue. For instance, after some wonderful foreplay, when she is expecting and eager to feel your tongue in her pussy, put on a condom. She will feel disappointed that you skipped oral sex. Let her think so, act as if you are about to start penetration. And then, instead of penetrating her, give her oral sex. Oral sex will then be a wonderful surprise.

### Step 2: Seize the Excitement Peak

When you initiate a new stage of lovemaking (for instance, initiating oral sex or intercourse), she will feel an excitement peak. Seize that peak. Make it last longer. Initiate the new stage very smoothly, and be more focused on exciting her than on stimulating her.

Add a spiritual connection twist to a new stage. For instance, start oral sex almost without moving your tongue, like if you are savoring something sacred. Start intercourse ultra-slowly, feeling and letting her feel every new first millimeter. Many times she will be eager to fulfill her desire, so she will push you to be quicker. Don't obey—you don't want to give her some relief now; you want her to come harder later on.

### Step 3: Find a Shelter

As discussed above, when you are not yet familiar with your partner, it is important to find a technique she enjoys and which keeps her excitement rising—a shelter. From that technique, you can try all sorts of other techniques. In case you are not very successful, you can quickly return to your safe shelter and make her feel more pleasure again. Candidates for shelter are techniques that most girls enjoy without requiring a lot of adaptation. In oral sex, for instance, a good candidate for a shelter is the simplest technique.

Your first goal should not be to make her come quickly—that is risky and not very sexy. Your first goal should be to find a shelter from where you can take some chances and come back without risking loosing her excitement crescendo.

### Step 4: Try Different Techniques

Once you have found a shelter, you can try the more creative techniques. If she reacts positively, keep on going for a while. If she doesn't, then return to your shelter and do the shelter technique for a while more before trying out another technique.

### Step 5: Make Her Come Really Hard

After you tuned in to some techniques that please your partner, and you have build up her excitement, you can start thinking about giving her a very strong orgasm. You don't want to make her come just because you kept on licking her for a long time and she managed to focus enough to come. You want to give her as much pleasure as possible and make her come when you increase your stimulation to make her come. Besides that, focusing on orgasm is just not very sexy. Imagine it on yourself: what would you prefer?

1.  A lover that stimulates you properly and with the clear goal of making you come, in the name of saying, "I did my job!"
2.  A lover that gives you pleasure for a longer time, teases you a bit, does several different things, focuses on finding what you enjoy the most, and makes you psychologically excited; and who keeps you away from orgasm until you can't take it any longer, and then does something special that makes you come in a fantastic way?

So, when you feel that she is getting really hot, put many exciting things together to make the orgasm a very exciting one. That means performing whatever technique you are doing at its best, perhaps with a bit more intensity, and adding psychological and extra physical stimulation. For example, if you are doing oral sex, adding stimulation can be done by grabbing her legs stronger, using your fingers more, playing with her anus or her pussy, etc. During intercourse, that can be done by penetrating harder and faster, talking to her differently, slapping her, holding her tighter, playing with her clitoris or her anus or using a vibrator on her clitoris. Whatever feels most appropriate.

When she is reaching the orgasm, don't relax. What you do and say in those final seconds have a large impact on the power of her orgasm. This is the moment you have been waiting for, so give it all you got. Do everything in your reach to make her even more excited, compliment her, and be extraordinarily attentive to her signs and body language. Follow the rhythm of her hip movements, stay close to her, but give her room to push you or pull you so that she can "perfect" her orgasmic experience. For instance, if she is coming through oral sex, she probably wants you to stop the clitoral stimulation pretty soon, but no need to back off. Staying very close to her allows her to push herself against your mouth again, if she feels like doing so.

## How to Ask

I have been a pain repeating over and over that it is a lousy idea to ask your partner what she enjoys or wishes for, especially if it is your first time together. This might seem silly if your goal is to apply the best possible physical stimulation, but if your goal is to make her feel as excited as possible, it makes total sense.

However, that does not mean that you should neglect her opinion or not be open to feedback—quite the contrary. Every piece of information she gives you is precious. Make her feel free to talk about it and give information—and as soon as she does, act on it.

To avoid the problems of asking directly, there are ways of asking that are not so problematic. One of them is to give herself the power to do whatever activity and watch in detail how she does it. This applies to masturbation, oral sex (no, you won't make her lick herself), and penetration. In oral sex, place her on top of you and feel how she rubs herself on your tongue. For penetration, watch carefully where she is hitting your penis inside her while she is on top. And for masturbation, watch her touching herself, without her noticing that you are doing that. To do so, place one of her hands on top of her clitoris while you are busy doing something else. As she doesn't suspect that your goal is to watch her touching herself, she will feel free to touch her clitoris the way she likes it, neither feeling watched nor that she has to teach you. Orders like, "Rub that clit, sweetie," or, "I want to see you rubbing your clit, horny girl," works fine, too.

But if you really want to ask, I recommend that you do it in a sexy way. Use the tone in your voice to mark the difference between asking for directions or a rhetorical question to make her excited, expressing how careful you are with her (and use the second). For instance, let's say you want to ask whether to use two or three fingers in her vagina. You can ask directly, "Do you prefer two or three fingers?" which I definitely do not recommend; or you can use two fingers on her, and wait until she is obviously enjoying it, going wild, and then ask, with an ironic, sweet, innocent voice: "Do you enjoy having my two fingers slowly fucking your sweet and tight pussy?" She will of course reply, "Yes," so you can then ask back: "Hmm, how about three? Will that be even better or will it hurt this sweet pussy?," to what she will probably reply, "I don't know," so you finish with: "Let's try, really slowly... oh, three fingers inside your horny pussy! Does this feel good or I am hurting you?"

As your concern was to avoid hurting her while doing something uncommon and experimental, it is OK to ask. Plus, the conversation was sexy. But asking clinical, technical or objective questions as a way to adapt regular techniques is not OK, because it is not sexy. I know that a lot of book authors and sex educators will tell you otherwise, but listen: There are rules you follow to be OK; and there are rules you follow to excel. They are just not always the same rules. So, if you are still inexperienced, go ahead and ask until you learn more. But once you reach a higher level of sexual competence, asking is not very sexy. Your goal is to give her something new, better than she has ever felt before. So stop asking questions. Use your empathy instead. Want to know how? Turn the page.

Chapter 11:

# Empathy Is the Thread of Perfect Sex

*A female view on this chapter:*

*I feel so close to him. Seems like I have known him for years. He really understands me. He knows how to look into my eyes and always say the right thing. We communicate like I never thought it would be possible. We were made for each other.*

\*

*"Women speak two languages—one of which is verbal."*
—*William Shakespeare*

*"I would rather trust a woman's instinct than a man's reason.*
—*Stanley Baldwin*
*(Former Prime Minister of the United Kingdom)*

## ABOUT EMPATHY

Empathy is the ability to understand, on the fly, the thoughts and feelings of others. Unlike the cold mind-reading manipulation techniques of some salespeople, empathy is fueled by kindness and openness. It is powerful because human beings have a huge potential for connecting to each other and forming strong intuitive bonds.

With empathy, a relationship becomes smooth and harmonious. We can sense how the other person is feeling and what he or she would enjoy next—and then act accordingly.

Moreover, we can read in others how our actions are perceived. This allows an empathic person to quickly learn how to behave in order to cause an appropriate effect in another person.

Women love being with men who have this ability. For some women, this is the most important quality about a man. Women don't call these men empathic men, though; they call them sensitive men. Sensitive men are not called "sensitive" because they are fragile (as a few men imagine). They are called sensitive because they have the power to sense. They have that power because they use the right side of their brains to interact with others and the world—as women do. The reason women love sensitive men is because they are easier to communicate with. For most women, to date a non-sensitive man feels like going on a date with a guy who hardly speaks English. Not very attractive, isn't it? That guy might be great in a lot of things, but as she has to make a conscious effort to communicate, he will always feel distant. So you see, empathy is extremely important in relationships and sex.

So where does one get this empathy from?

Empathy is a natural animal ability. Newborn babies, unable to see most of the world around them, show the ability to understand the emotional state of their mothers. Some social animals do that, too, as most pet owners can testify. There is nothing mystical about it. It is just very important for social animals to be able to understant how the others are feeling. The only remarkable thing is how our overly literate society managed to amputate such a basic talent from so many of us. We all have an objective, language-based side and a subjective, nonverbal side. Growing up in societies founded upon clear, objective, written rules pushes us to disregard that second side. School is the epitome of the first side—sensual relations are the epitome of the second.

While formal schooling prevents all of us from fully developing our subjective skills, there is a huge difference between the genders: It's in the way each plays. In boys' world, play follows rules. There are winners and losers according to rules. Worse than losing is to cheat or to twist the rules. It is a totally objective play, having the enormous advantage of allowing boys to permanently develop their physical abilities and to compete directly without getting into serious fights. It is all advantages... except for in the development of boy's subjective abilities.

Girls play in a totally different way. They play subjectively. They play games where you can't tell what the goal is and what the rules are. Still, they fiercely compete with each other for beauty and status—subjectively. This allows girls to develop social skills, beauty skills, and subjective abilities—the so-called female intuition.

In other words, while boys develop their physical abilities and their abilities to act together as a group, girls develop the ability to read other people and to act in ways that influence their behavior.

The end result of boys growing up in rule-based schools and with rule-based play is that many men grow up totally unaware of the subjectivity of life and human relations, especially with women.[1] These men struggle in communicating with women because they do not use the same language. On top of it, that subjective language does not come in manuals that these men can read and learn from.

This subjective language is often perceived with the unconscious mind, not the language-based one. Because these thoughts are not constructed as words, we describe this language as "feelings" and "intuitions," as opposed to logically constructed, language-based thoughts.[2] But they are not feelings, like love or hatred. They are thoughts. Thoughts from areas of the brain that don't work based on language.

Fortunately, this subjective language is not rocket science. It is easy to learn once you know it is out there. So, for the rest of this chapter, I will describe exactly what you can do to understand these thoughts and improve your empathy. It is described for the conscious mind to understand: objectively, logically and clearly.

SEVEN POINTS TO INCREASE YOUR EMPATHY

1.  Step into other people's shoes;

---

1 Surely there are innate differences that drive girls and boys to play differently or that offer women a superior command of intuition. However, if boys were more exposed to subjective play, they would develop their skills much more than they do.

2 This is actually not totally accurate. While most women do use their intuitive side to generate these thoughts, the more analytical/manipulative/political people of either gender are very conscious about this subjective communication.

2.  Get to know the female mind;
3.  Practice reading body language;
4.  Believe she is predictable;
5.  Respect your partner;
6.  Set her free to communicate; and
7.  Communicate nonverbally.

## 1. Step into other people's shoes

To increase your ability to intuitively feel what other people feel, nothing better than starting by imagining you are the other person.

People are not all born alike; they have very different circumstances and problems to deal with. Nevertheless, we often ignore all this when interacting with others. A good way to avoid ignoring these differences is to sit down in your living room and imagine you are someone else.

Let's say you are a single guy, very interested in spending a great night of mutual satisfactory sex with a woman, and you have just politely approached a potential candidate whom, not so politely, rejected you. Before developing any bad feelings, place yourself in her shoes.

But do it properly.

Just imagining that if you were an attractive woman, you could choose most people from the opposite sex to sleep with and how you would use that to sleep with lots of women is not an accurate way of putting yourself in her shoes, because most women don't act like that. So, probably, that is not how they are feeling. You could alternatively say to yourself that women are from Venus and have different priorities. That still does not make you feel like women feel like. So, try harder. Try imagining a reality where you could exactly feel like a woman.

Here goes my suggestion: Imagine that you rubbed a lamp, a genie came out and, out of gratitude, gave you a super power: Every woman now has a strong desire to have sex with you. Unfortunately, after a first round of sex, your powers stop working on that woman. To make things worse, every time you have sex with a new partner and other people hear about it, you become a lot less powerful.

Cherry on the cake, even if you don't have sex, your super power will fade as you grow old.

That is more like an attractive woman, wouldn't you say? Now, how would you act in that reality? Sit in your living room and imagine living that reality.

Imagine that an average woman approached you. She looked OK, even better than you, and she seemed interesting, attractive and kind. You know she is attracted to you because your super power works on every woman. Still, would you even consider sleeping with her? After all, you will be loosing power any time you take any new partners. Wouldn't you rather use that power to get something special?

Planning as you sit down in your couch, you might instead decide to attend the next Playboy gathering (or wherever you find women attractive) and bed the most attractive woman. That would be a great sexual experience that would leave you fascinated with your new partner. As soon as sex ended, however, the playmate would be free from your super power. Probably, she would quickly show you the door. Wouldn't you be heartbroken? You would feel like you were good for nothing, except for that super power the genie gave you, right? On top of that, imagine all you had lost. Before sex, you had a playmate chasing you, totally fascinated. After sex, she even despised you. The only reason she ever noticed you was because of your super power, which, by the way, had just become weaker by sleeping with her...

As you sit in your couch imagining what would it be like to live like that, how would you act, what would your priorities be, and so on, you will start feeling like a woman. You will fear the same things they fear and you will develop the same strategies they use.

When you are done imagining, you will probably feel a stronger empathy for women. And, if you are interested in developing the skill, you can do similar thought experiments to empathize with your employees, your bosses, elder people, teenagers, people from other groups, and so on.

## 2. Get to Know the Female Mind

Beyond the circumstantial I just mentioned, there are some real differences between men and women. If you know about these, if you know how their mind works, you don't have to deduce every time how a particular girl is reacting to something you say or do, because you will have a pretty good guess as to what that reaction will be. Knowing the female mind, you will know what they value, how they think and what they enjoy. You can then do things that would seem absurd and impossible to most men.

From the Queen & King fantasy, you already have a primer on how their mind works. To develop your skills, I advise that you read women's magazines and watch Sex and the City. Read a romance book from the Harlequin collection. Better even: instead of reading these magazines and books, analyze them. These are great sources to understand the female instinct because they are basic and over-simplified, aiming exactly at the unsatisfied sexual instinct. Besides, they are stripped of any content that can be interesting to men, so everything you observe is material to be analyzed instead of enjoyed. So, when you review these sources, seek to understand the images being conveyed. Understand how the central characters are built so that women identify with them and how the other characters usually express some exaggerated negative characteristics. Understand how the female reader/viewer sees the world for all this to make sense to her.

Making a parallel, the male equivalent of the Harlequin books and Sex and the City are porn movies and blockbusters like Braveheart (or The Patriot, Rocky IV, etc..). The plot is always the same: The main character is either a leader or an independent man. He is brave and strong and dislikes violence. But an enemy cruelly attacks someone from his family or pushes the hero beyond an acceptable limit. Given the need to protect or just to avenge, the hero then has a moral justification to beat the crap out of his enemy—sometimes killing hundreds of his enemy's employees or friends in the process. This happens only after a serious struggle, where the hero uses all his strength and abilities to defeat the impressive enemy. The movie ends with a crowd applauding the hero.

Now, am I saying that this is all there is to men? No. What I am saying is that, for a woman who is interested in exciting her man during sex and in understanding the dynamics of male bonding and male interaction, with the intent on making her partner happier, porn movies and Braveheart are useful sources of inspiration. She will have a very good idea of the male instinct, understand her partner's choices better and be more sympathetic with his dissatisfactions. She can then sit down and ask herself: "How can I make him feel those things that he, deep inside, craves for?"

After learning the core of his desires, she can then try to perfect her understanding by reading more elaborate, male-oriented publications, listening more accurately to the things he says and paying attention to the differences between her and her partner.

So, when learning about women, the Harlequin books and Sex and the City are the equivalent to porn and Braveheart for men. They will give you access to the core. After the core being well mapped, there are more elaborate sources of information, such as female talk shows, books, blogs, etcetera. Also, in case you haven't read them yet, I find it extremely useful to read seduction books, such as the ones from David deAngelo, Mystery, Neil Strauss and Robert Greene, mentioned in the "Sources" section.

My favorite, however, is to listen when women talk to each other. Don't dismiss it as "girl-talk" and go find a guy to talk with, but instead open your ears and your mind, listen carefully, analyze what you hear and understand what their goals are and how they communicate (and compete). Pay special attention to everything that sounds or looks foolish. When something looks really foolish, it's because we are seeing it with the wrong glasses. No one is a fool. Seeing foolishness in others means we do not understand something. It's exactly the stuff that seems foolish or weird that deserves the most attention and analysis.

Plus, you should try to gain access to the real thing, that is, how women talk to each other when there are no men around and when they are not socially competing with other women. When they remove their masks. This mostly happens when they are in pairs. So, I advise you to sit next to pairs of women in cafés, etc., holding a book and having earphones in your ears (without playing any music). Listen to how they really think and talk about men (that is what they mostly talk about when in pairs). You might be shocked...

My last advice is not to take women's opinion about themselves literally, as they are very focused on their image. Always read it through. Focus only on their deeds and on the subtle cues they leave in their words—never on their professed motivations.

### 3. Practice reading body language

Words are but a small part of human communication. Even when we depend totally on our words to communicate (as in emailing) we communicate poorly. We need the personal interaction, because we communicate with facial expressions, intonations and body language.

I advise that you practice these skills by sitting in public places and just observe people interacting from the distance; that you watch TV without sound and, when in a group, stop thinking about whatever topic is being discussed and look around, inspecting each of your friends and trying to understand what is going on in their minds.

### 4. Believe She Is Predictable

A key requirement for your empathy to progress is that you believe that your partner is predictable. Believe that her mood and her thoughts control her actions, not some random "female weirdness." If she reacts in a totally different way than what you expected, it's because you are not seeing the full picture. Don't worry; as you know more of the unconscious mind and get better at reading its signs, the coherent whole will emerge.

### 5. Respect Your Partner

Whenever we feel respect for someone and we believe we have the power to change their mood (be it our boss, our friend, or our child), we become extraordinarily attentive to their expressions of mood. So, be sure to feel respect for your partner so that you feel a permanent interest in understanding her mood.

Don't ask her all the time about her mood—that is boring, almost like psychological stalking. Just keep your interest. If you have no respect, or feel indifferent to her reactions, you will be unconsciously blocked from having an empathic relationship with her.

Respect her deeply as a person and as your partner, but don't give her any extra respect for being a woman—that is a no-go and the first step on the road to be abused by women.

## 6. Set Her Free to Communicate

If your partner feels totally free, she will communicate with you in order to make your sex the best possible. If she is worried about your feelings, your prejudices, or, in general, how you will interpret her, she won't communicate honestly.

Questions like, "Was it good for you?" are ridiculous because they are pseudo-questions, with two alternative answers: "yes" or "break my heart." While this question is the extreme example of looking for validation instead of honest communication, you might try minor versions of it without noticing. If you show how proud you are of your sexual abilities or show a serious concern about doing the right thing, you will be pushing her to pretend she is enjoying it, which is not good; especially if she would rather be giving you some important tips on how to actually improve.

So how should you behave?

Naturally. With self-reliance. If you have some difficulties being self-reliant in bed (which is extremely normal), try to hide them, as well as hiding that your partner's reaction matters so much to you.[3]

In case you want to ask questions, (something I do not recommend), ask them neutrally, without a "right answer".

Finally, the other key component for her to feel free to communicate is that she trusts you and knows that you will not be judgmental.

---

3 Put yourself in her shoes: What is more exciting to you, a woman giving you a blowjob who is deeply enjoying herself and enjoying the pleasure she is giving you, or an insecure woman suffering from performance anxiety and asking questions?

## 7. Communicate Nonverbally

Communicating nonverbally means that, by having a permanent communication through your gestures, moans and expressions, the two of you can communicate your feelings and desires without talking. You need to open that channel of communication. You need to nonverbally "talk" a lot and then listen when she talks back. Be expressive during sex. Make facial expressions, communicate. Whenever she does something that you enjoy, express it. Don't be a Clint Eastwood in bed. Share your joy. Look her in the eyes. Let your pleasure and desire for her be visible on your face.

To "listen" to her nonverbal communication, be very attentive to her movements, facial expressions, and breathing. During sex, every sound and every sigh has a meaning. Listen with an open mind. Don't listen in order to validate your pre-conceptions. Just listen. Grab her in different ways, expressing different feelings, and see how she reacts. Pay attention to her movements, to the changes in her skin, or to her lack of movements. When you are doing well, she opens herself to you, exposing herself, bending over, and assuming more sexual postures, more abandonment attitudes—she exposes her neck, opens her legs, pulls her hips back, relaxes most muscles, and grinds you. From the entire body, the part that talks the most is surely her vagina. Her vagina—who is, after all, female—talks the whole time. Listen to it.

Chapter 12:

# How to Talk Her to Wonderful Orgasms

*As you have sex with your partner, you talk to her in a very exciting and relaxing way. She feels closer to you, intimate, and yet very excited. You keep saying naughty things to her, getting naughtier and naughtier. The combination of your lovemaking and your words is such that she just starts coming... and coming... and coming...*

\*

*"For women the best aphrodisiacs are words. The G-spot is in the ears. He who looks for it below there is wasting his time." —Isabel Allende*

## THE FOUR FEELINGS

We will now focus on one of the most powerful ways to take a woman to orgasm as she lies naked in a bed. Exactly that one you are thinking about: talking!

It might just look a little bit surprising that you might give a woman orgasms just by talking to her. However, if you consider the hours that women spend just talking, not saying anything in particular, it becomes obvious that, for women, to talk is a totally different thing than it is for men.

For women, to talk is something special that is neither rational nor direct. It is a way to describe feelings, not information. Therefore, you have to talk in a way that transmits the right feelings to your partner. You do that by using the right words, intonation and facial expressions. The easiest way to do this is by feeling the appropriate feelings and then trying to express them as openly as possible.

The appropriate feelings to transmit are universal. Anywhere in the world, the feelings that make her sexual experience much more intense are the same. However, the way to transmit them (that is, the exact words to use, the intonation to apply and the facial expression to make) is very different across the globe. A marked facial expression is considered desirable in India but scary in Scandinavia. A strong intonation is considered exciting in the U.S., but phony and irritating in France. Strong and sweet words are considered exciting in Brazil but offensive and manipulative in Germany. These differences happen across countries, but also across regions of a country, age groups, social classes, and even across "urban tribes." Therefore, as we progress in this chapter, focus on the concepts, not on the exact words. Feel free to adapt the wording to one better suited for your tribe, age, country, language, and sensitivity. Taking care of using the proper words, expression and intonation for your group, let's then move on to the feelings that should be transmitted during sex. Not surprisingly, they are the feelings that result from the Queen & King fantasy:

1. Admiration;
2. Dominance;
3. Horniness; and
4. Tenderness.

To understand how important each of these four feelings is, imagine your lover communicating the opposite of three of the four feelings to you[1]: contempt, no sexual interest, and coldness. That would be a nightmare, right? Well, if you don't express the four feelings, she has no way to know whether you are feeling the good feelings or the bad ones—so be very expressive...

**Admiration**

You can show your admiration about lots of different aspects of your partner: her looks in general, her looks in particular (her skin, her boobs, etc.), how good she is in bed, how good her kisses feel like, etc. You can also express admiration for other things outside the bedroom, but which still belong to the Queen & King context.

---

1 Submission, the opposite of dominance, is not a bad feeling.

For instance, how she dresses well, how charming she is, etc. Don't only mention how good she is; mention how she is the best.[2] Of course, unless she is really amazing, it is improbable that she is really the best in the world. So, lower your sampling group. For instance, tell her in her ear how she was the most beautiful women in the place you guys met or in a nice party you attended. How she stood out in the middle of the other women and how everyone in the room admired her… "And none of them dreamt that you look that much better naked." Describing admiration in a way that makes her feel like a Queen is extremely positive.

Before we move on to the next feeling, let's give a little example of a short sentence that expresses only admiration and none of the remaining three feelings. It is a very poetic example: "Your ass is so amazingly beautiful."

Now let's move on to the other three feelings, as admiration by itself is not enough: You can admire her because she is a real Queen (which is great), or you can admire her because you have never seen a naked ass before (which is not so great). The other three feelings will help getting that straightened out.

## Dominance

To express dominance, you should use sexual topics and match your words with appropriate gestures. Use your hands to move her body around as well as the other gestures I mentioned earlier, in Chapter 4. Be straight to the point. Don't insinuate with shyness that you would like her to do something.

Talk in a way that shows you understand what she enjoys and that you are calling the shots. For instance, tell her what you will do next. Building on the previous example: "Your ass is so amazingly beautiful," with dominance added to it, becomes, "Your ass is so amazingly beautiful, I will fuck you really hard." This sentence doesn't sound very good yet. That's because there are still two ingredients missing. Let's move on…

---

2 The best among the women she is competing against—other women of present time. Don't mention or compare to your past partners.

## Horniness

Expressing horniness is quite easy and it should come naturally if you are not trying to hide it. You can express horniness by swearing abstractly—that is, using plenty of swear words not directed at her—and by admitting how horny she makes you.

Taking our test sentence, "Your ass is so amazingly beautiful, I will fuck you really hard," and adding some horniness, we get, "Fuck, your ass is so amazingly beautiful, I want so much to fuck you really hard."

## Tenderness

Being tender is about projecting the positive and caring feelings you have for the other person. Don't be confused by being tender and dominant simultaneously. Being dominant is not the opposite of being sweet, lovable, and tender. Being dominant is the opposite of being submissive. Being tender is the opposite of being cold or harsh. Submission–dominance and tenderness–coldness/harshness are totally independent. So, tenderness and dominance go extremely well together.

To express tenderness, sprinkle your sentences with those small magical adjectives like "sweet," "cute" or "soft," and call her "sweetheart," "sweetie," or "baby." Change some of your orders to rhetorical questions, such as switching from "I will fuck you right now," to, "You want me to fuck you right now, don't you?" While you are taking the lead in both sentences, the second sentence shows respect. Said with a sweet smile and voice, it shows tenderness. Use your genuine smile, be sweet, and show you care.[3] Unless you really overdo it, you won't look dorky, as your tenderness is backed up by horniness and dominance—a velvet glove on an iron fist.

Let's look again at our test phrase. Adding tenderness to, "Fuck, your ass is so amazingly beautiful, I want so much to fuck you really hard," we get, "Fuck! Baby, this sweet ass of yours—"(gently pass your hand on her butt—"is so amazingly beautiful, I want so much

---

3 I don't know about you, but I always feel extreme tenderness for a woman that chose me to have sex with her.

to fuck you really hard."

## MAKE IT LAST LONGER

While the sentence above already expresses the four feelings, it can be greatly improved. After all, you want to keep on talking. As you talk, she gets excited. There is not much to gain in being overly succinct.[4] This does not mean you should talk the entire time, absolutely not. But once in a while, telling a few sentences is a very good idea.

Let's imagine your partner is lying on her stomach. You can start from a basic idea: "great ass/makes me horny/will fuck you" and turn it into an exciting one-minute long poem. Watch:

*"Fuck! Baby, this sweet ass of yours is so amazingly beautiful... I get so horny just by looking at it. When I grab it in my hands—"(gently grab it)—"and I feel how _____ it feels [here choose an adjective that describes her ass and a beautiful ass in your social group: hard/soft/big/cute, whatever], I get shivers down my spine and my dick just feels so hard (grab her ass harder). What an amazing ass you have! You look so good lying there—"(pass your hands over her body) —"I feel so horny I just want to fuck your cute tight sweet pussy really hard. It's already feeling so good to slowly slide my dick into you, like this. Feels so wonderful... I'm trying hard to hold back and not just start fucking you so hard right now... "(Play with her ass, open it a bit apart)—"It is so beautiful... Oh my god, seeing your sweet little pussy like this... She is so beautiful."*

Can you find the four feelings all over that sentence?

You need to put them all in, because without them, the sentences will not work well. Without admiration, the woman will feel underestimated, "cheap," just one more in your hands. Without horniness, the whole thing gets too romantic and undercuts her ex-

---

4 Unless, of course, she is from the minority that prefers silence during sex—remember, nothing works on 100 percent of women. Your empathy and adaptation will tell you if you meet one of these.... or maybe she will!

citement. Without tenderness, you will sound aggressive and she will not relax. She will not empathically communicate with you and your emotional connection will not develop. Without dominance, you might sound dorky. She might hear, "You are so admirable, my goddess, how lucky I was to get you into bed." She might agree and not let you see her again. So, put all the four feelings in.

As you noticed, I finished off with some compliments on her pussy. That is because women over-evaluate their pussies. While most men don't actively evaluate a woman for how her pussy looks[5], women believe they do (some women nowadays even do plastic surgeries on their pussies). So, give her pussy the respect and aesthetic appreciation she (wrongly) expects. Don't hold back on compliments. Lick her pussy as if you are compelled to savor such a beautiful and seductive part of her. To understand this better, put yourself in her shoes and imagine how fascinating a woman would be if she would adore your dick as a work of art and feel compelled to suck it for her own pleasure. Mmmmm...

## WHAT TO TALK ABOUT IN BED

What topics should you talk about in bed? Well, mostly about sex. Being more specific, here are some interesting topics:
1. Describing feelings she is already experiencing (induction);
2. Describing what you are going to do next (anticipation);
3. Describing things that make her excited; and
4. Describing sex from the Queen & King point of view.

Let's now go over each one of these four topics in detail.

### Feelings She Is Already Experiencing (Induction)

To describe something she is already experiencing might seem like a terrible waste of time. Why bother, if she is already experiencing it?

The answer is: because we are not always paying attention to our sensations and because we are inducible. Let me give you some

---

5 We do evaluate how it smells and tastes like, however....

firsthand demonstration on how we don't pay attention to our sensations.

I am writing this book sitting on a couch with my feet on a nearby table. When my mobile rang a few minutes ago, I experienced a lot of pain on my knees. They had been stretched for hours in a row so they should feel painful! But why did they only become painful when the mobile rang? Because I was focusing on the writing. I was in the state of Flow, so some part of my brain acting like a bouncer didn't bother my attention with sensations like pain (or pleasure). This happens when we write, watch a movie, play videogames, or even when we have sex. We are performing, focusing on what we are doing, and not on what we are feeling. During sex, this probably also happens to you and to your partner—your minds are not always totally focused on feeling the sensations. Your partner is probably thinking about her performance, anxieties, worries, etc.[6]

By describing to her in detail what she is actually feeling, you are increasing her ability to feel her own sensations. Besides, it is also very erotic for her to hear you talk about what you are doing to her pussy. It invites the conscious and language-based parts of her brain to think about the exciting things happening down there. Finally, it is also good to describe what you are doing because we are inducible. By describing something to us, we in fact start feeling it. Induction is so important that deserves an entire chapter, Chapter 15. To increase the effectiveness of your description of what she is feeling, you should describe what she is feeling from her point of view. Let's see an example:

*Are you feeling how great it feels on your pussy's entrance, when my dick slides in [slide it in] and out [take it out] from your pussy? Now... deep in your sweet pussy, are you feeling how good it feels as my dick bangs against it? [Do appropriate motion.] It feels really good, doesn't it? It feels good to have my dick all inside you, making you feel your entire pussy, all pushed by my dick, all inside you, all for you...*

---

6 Unless she is totally tied up, unable to move or to perform in any way. In this book, however, we only mention those kinds of play superficially.

Yep, she will feel your dick much more. If you want to make it a bit more hardcore, you can add the following sentence...

*Your pussy becomes so full, with my dick inside of you. It feels so good, doesn't it? You really like to feel a hard dick in your pussy, don't you? Especially when you are on your fours, right? With your butt up, like an animal, feeling me fucking you hard and like an animal, don't you?*

If, on the other hand, you want to add something more suave and sweet, you can try something like:

*It is so wonderful when I am all inside you and we hug like this. We get so close together, in and out...*

## What You Will Do Next (Anticipation)

In sex, what comes next is usually better from what came before, all the way until orgasm. Therefore, what comes next is usually more exciting. So, it is a good idea to talk about it, because it will get her excited by hearing it. As she is not yet feeling those sensations, it is better to describe it more visually. The previous example would then become:

*In a while, I will stick my dick inside you... I will start by only sliding the tip in, so you can feel your pussy opening up for it. Then, my dick will slide into your pussy, slowly, pushing her from the inside... until it will be all inside you, and you will feel your pussy totally opening for my dick. You love it when you have my dick all inside you, don't you?*

## Things That Make Her Excited

Let's start this third topic by asking you, the reader, a very personal question. When you masturbate, does your orgasm occur when you imagine something particularly exciting, or is it only due to the physical stimulation?

I will guess you went for the first option. Not only do you orgasm when you imagine something particularly exciting, but you do feel a stronger orgasm by imagining (or watching) more exciting situations, right? So, that is exactly what you should create for your partner. Describe the things that she finds particularly exciting to trigger a stronger orgasm, in the same way you do to yourself during masturbation.

In the next chapter, I will mention how to tell her exciting stories and fantasies—but let's leave that for later. Now I will focus on how to tell her exciting stuff that relates to the sex you are having with her at that exact moment. You will make her hornier if you mention stuff that is usually exciting for women. When she is closer to orgasm, doing so will make her come harder. The stuff women usually enjoy are:

- Her being naughty;
- Her being skilled in bed;
- Things that are pleasurable to her;
- Her orgasm;
- A penis;
- Other parts of the male body (shoulders, chest, butt, balls, etc.);
- Close contact to the male body;
- Male orgasm;
- Male horniness;
- You finding her beautiful; and
- Her giving herself to her King and being dominated.

This is not an exhaustive list, of course. By building sentences with these elements, you create a very interesting conversation for her. Let's look at an example:

*You make my dick so hard! Can you feel how hard it is? It is this hard because it is totally horny for you. It is your way of being such a beautiful, serious woman on the outside, and such a sweet naughty little slut in bed. With an amazing body. Oh my god, you really know how to squeeze my dick in that soft tight pussy... It is so hard not to come. It is so good when I just stick it all in... Feel how hard I am pushing into you. [Place her hands over your butt so that she grabs it. Then contract your butt, as you push into her.] And my balls, can you feel how my balls hit against your pussy? Can you feel how hard they are? Can you feel how they are so full of cum for you? See what you do to me? You make me so crazy for you, so full of cum, I just want to come in your pussy and fill your pussy with cum, keep on fucking you, fucking your pussy totally flooded with cum.*

From now on you don't need to keep on talking, because she probably already came.

If you are practicing safe sex, the story above won't exactly come true. Tops you will get a condom full of sperm. She will never feel that "flooded vagina." However, that's OK. In her imagination, there is no condom, your orgasm will flood her vagina, and that is all that matters.

This ability to believe in a convenient and imaginative story (for a while) has a technical name: "suspended disbelief," a concept used in filmmaking. When we watch a movie, we are not puzzled to see Rocky Balboa being punched one hundred times while his opponents are knocked down after a couple. We don't find it ridiculous that Indiana Jones jumps around hanging by a whip and finds lost civilizations all the time. We believe these unbelievable things because we were built into believing them in the beginning of the movie: Rocky is shown to be really tough and Jones to be an archeological genius. The whole sequence of events keeps its logic and the fantasy increases step by step, so there is nothing that brings us out of the "reality" we want to believe in. We suspend our skepticism because we know that doing so is good for us. It allows us to dive into the movie and enjoy it as if it was true.

However, our suspension of disbelief has its limits. If something out-of-context or too fantasist happens (such as, for instance, Rocky Balboa suddenly finding a lost civilization), our disbelief ends, and we become annoyed with the movie director.

So, use the suspended disbelief, but don't overuse it.

Coming back to our example above, there is no problem whatsoever with your not flooding her pussy with your sperm while you tell her you are, because you want to avoid pregnancy or disease. Those are good reasons, so she will suspend her disbelief. If, however, you were unable to sustain your erection, using the previous speech would be harmful. The speech is all based on how horny you are for her and how hard you feel. So stating that you are hard while not being that hard would not allow her to suspend her disbelief even for a second[7], and you would look pretty bad...

I would like to stress that every woman is different and that you can always adapt stuff to better suit your partner. Let's say, for instance, that your partner is too afraid of getting pregnant. Then you can add to the description the magic sentence: "If it weren't for this condom, I would..." There is always a way around. If she doesn't find some of the points above exciting, there will be others she craves.

**Sex from the Queen & King Point of View**

As I mentioned before, the woman craves to live out her Queen & King fantasy. Therefore, nothing is more appropriate than using words that stress the Queen & King fantasy. To do so, more than just using the four key feelings, you should explicitly detail some of the points necessary for the Queen & King fantasy: the woman's sexual openness, your desire for her, your dominance during sex and, indirectly, how good you are in bed.

To refer to her sexual openness, you can praise her anytime she shows some sexual openness. That is very different from suggesting that she would be better if she would be more open, which is, in fact, a criticism. An example of a compliment on her sexual openness (in this case, literally) is this: "It is so hot seeing how you open your ass like that..."

To express your strong desire for her, there are plenty of alternatives. Give her compliments on her body, her sexual performance, etc. For instance: "You are so amazing. I get so hot seeing how you open your beautiful ass like that..."

This is still not very different from the examples for the four feelings presented above. Now let's add some explicit dominance: "You are so amazing. I get so hot seeing how you open your beauti-

---

7 That can be easily achieved, actually. But you will have to wait until chapter 15 for that. It is not by talking to her conscious mind as we are doing here, but to her unconscious mind.

ful ass like that…You just love when I shove my dick into you, don't you?"

To spice it up, slap her ass. If she approves it, slap it harder. Finishing off this sentence, you can add some self-compliments: "You are so amazing. I get so hot seeing how you open your beautiful ass like that…You just love when I shove my dick into you, don't you? Fuck, with all the horniness we have together, we can't resist fucking, can we?"

This sentence above is still well-behaved. Depending on your partner's reactions to these sentences, you can keep on "lowering the level." Increase the intensity of your fucking, of your slapping, pull her hair (from the nape), and add a bit more swearing to your words. If you feel insecure whether she likes it, you can ask, "You are such a sweet little slut, aren't you? You really love getting that ass slapped, don't you? You like it hard, don't you?" If she doesn't answer or answers something like, "Yes…" "Kind of…" or, "A bit lighter, actually," it is better to take it easy! You have probably exceeded the level she was willing to go to. If she answers with something enthusiastic like, "Yes! Yes! Yes! Slap your little slut!!" you are on the right track and should keep on going.

Always testing your waters, keep on lowering your level, swear harder, and slap her harder. As you become increasingly more aggressive, she might become increasingly more enthusiastic about it. Let her pull you to do these things, rather than trying to push her to accept them.

In some women—a minority—their desire to be dominated by a King is strong and craves for more than slapping her butt or calling her a few bad names. With these girls, you can move on to symbolically slap her face. I repeat: symbolically. These are slaps to the face that do not cause pain, but symbolize your dominance. Try one and see how she reacts. Repeat only if she shows plenty of enthusiasm. If she is clearly enjoying this and pulls you to continue, you can take yet another step forward and spit on her. I recommend that you start by doing that on her back, not on her face. This is so charged with symbolism that the girl will probably come when you do that to her (seriously). But remember, that will only happen with girls that enjoy this kind of play, which are a minority.

If you have given your girl a hard submission experience, using the level of dominance she finds adequate, she will love it and say that you are "a real man" (that means a King, in our context). If, on the other hand, you were way below her adequate dominance level, she might feel a bit incomplete, and maybe next time she will give some hints that you can be more dominant.

If you have blown her adequate dominance level, she will probably think you are a jerk and will be pissed at you, as you would be if she started slapping you for no reason. It is not because you have sex with her that you are allowed to slap her—it is by triggering her Queen & King fantasy that she allows you to do so. Allowing you to have sex with her is just the first of a series of power transfers she will eventually enjoy doing.

Surprisingly—or not—the women who enjoy the most submission are the most powerful ones. Women in high positions, very beautiful women, muscular women, tall women—all these women, without wanting to, dominate men in their daily life. Remember, they want to dominate women but to be desired by the attractive men. Except when other women can see it, they don't want to dominate men... but they do. More appropriately, men decide to submit to them. Men look at them with deep respect, feel intimidated, pay them loads of attention, follow their whims and submit in some-times-pathetic ways. They treat them as underlings treat a Queen. So, these women see them as underlings. They long for a man they can't dominate, a King. They crave for the day when that King dominates them, showing how different he is from her underlings[8]. Most importantly, when a man treats her like other women get treated, without excessive respect. She misses that. Besides, as these women perform so much during the day and receive compliments all the time, to perform or dominate during sex is the last thing they want. To relax, they want submission, an empty head, demonstrations of affection and care, a non-intimidated partner and lots of pleasure.

When you perform this type of domination, be aware that is just

---

8 Therefore, this eagerness for a King becomes stronger in societies where men act submissively to women.

a game for sexual arousal. What you do then does not translate to "real life" after sex is over...

DEALING WITH SEXUAL REPRESSION

Sexual repression exists in every society around the world, but at different levels, and acting on different steps of the sensual interaction and on different parts of people's minds. Sexual repression is not only the repression of sex by political, religious, and familial authorities. Actually, those sex-repressive systems are sometimes not very repressive of the mind—people might be afraid of being caught fulfilling their wishes, but their minds feel free to imagine. Other, more "permissive" systems that place pressure on what the individual should feel like are sometimes much worse for the mind—despite allowing for more regular sex.

Sexual repression works in such a way that no one believes they have a sexually repressed mind. For this reason, it is not by asking someone that you can spot how repressed they are. If in the place you live in, people don't spontaneously and frequently kiss, do not confess how they are sexually attracted to other people, do not admit frequently to feeling like touching and having sex with other people, or only behave like this when drunk or using drugs, then your fellow men and women's minds are repressed. Don't feel bad about it; things used to be much worse.

In case you have a strongly repressed or shy partner, you should adapt your way of talking to avoid offending her. Stop saying the "bad words," switch to more technical, sweet, or esoteric words, but do keep on using the four feelings and the descriptions.

## Putting Repression into Play

Despite repression being an obstacle to female pleasure, it can be manipulated to work for you.

I know two strategies to do just that. One of them hits the sorcerer with his own spell—you use spirituality to reformat sexual repression. The other strategy explores the excitement that comes from breaking the rules. Repression can then become an endless source of rules to break and ways to excite your partner. Few things are as fun as breaking the rules others impose on us.

What you should not do is to respect her repression: To praise her for being pure and then want to have sex with her is a no-go.

## Using the Spell Against the Sorcerer—Spirituality

When someone is being repressed by society, peers, religion, or family, that person is rewarded. The exchange is like making a bargain.[9] The repressed person gives up the pleasures of sex for the acceptance of others, the respect of others and, especially, respect for him or herself.

It is instinctive that we want to feel superior to other people. Some people do that by competing in sports, in school, at work, in beauty, in the money they make, the art events they attend, etc. Other people, usually with fewer chances of success in these more objective competitions, use morality. Morality is highly flexible and is adjustable to our own needs. Adapting the moral code for his personal traits, or using a moral code that fits him nicely, the moralist feels better than other people. This is so powerful and important that people go a long way to feel morally superior to others.[10] They give up on a lot of things they would rather do as long as they get their return: respect from others and respect from themselves.

To prevent sexual repression from destroying the woman's sexual life, you need to give her a replacement for the respect she acquired by not having sex. You do that by inviting her feel respect for sex, inviting her feel that sex with you has something religious, sublime, heavenly, and that by having sex with you, she is, in fact, becoming a better person, more spiritual and deserving more respect.

To do so, use spirituality talk during sex. Instead of seeing sex as sex, talk about energy connection between the souls when the bodies meet and similar stuff. Spirituality talk circumvents sexual repression by using the same instruments: the divine, the pure, the soul. When a very repressed woman is in bed with you, she might

---

9 In reasonably free societies—not in countries where sexual acts are still punishable by law, of course.

10 All ideologies and religions have a moral code. "I am better than them,'" is at their root.

appreciate believing that her horniness derives from the fusion of two twin souls and that the "energy" invading her is making her a more enlightened person. She would hate to admit that horniness is an animal instinct to ensure offspring, and that she feels much better after sex due to a hormonal switch that alleviated her symptoms of lack of sex.

Talking spiritually makes the woman feel even more special than just expressing tenderness and admiration. Spirituality is so important for women that many sex books talk only about spirituality.

Besides its powers in fighting sexual repression, spirituality has yet another virtue—it fits perfectly with the most basic female instinct. As we saw in Chapter 2, women do an instinctive search for the best man available to be the father of their children. That implies seducing and having regular sex with the King, and avoiding sleeping around with other men. To manage this ambivalence (wanting sex with a top man, but disliking sex with other men), all the sexual programming of women is wired to have disproportionate responses. If sex is "so-so," she does not enjoy the experience and doesn't feel like doing it again. If sex is really good, she feels in Heaven and wants to repeat it all the time. The reason for these extreme reactions is not only about the real differences in the way sex was performed by her lover, but also by her "interpretation" of his stimulus. It is this interpretation that can cause her to feel either extreme pleasure or extreme dislike in sex (both quite hard to understand for men).[11] This enormous difference is created by her female mind.

For the woman experiencing these antagonistic feelings, it is hard to explain them using reason. As I said before, this part of her mind is controlled by the unconscious, the irrational, the "heart." Her thoughts are not formulated in words. She perceives them as feelings. So, the woman looks for other explanations for what she feels. Spirituality meets this need. For her, an explanation involving

---

11 One of the worse things a woman can feel is rape. Heterosexual rape is a terrible feeling incomprehensible to men. This feeling will occur even if the rapist has sex in a tender way. Being forced to have sex against her will is evolutionarily terrible for women, so they have genetically programmed mechanisms to dislike it. Many men will find it worse to have consensual sex with an ugly woman than to have forced sex with an attractive woman. Women are very different from men in this regard.

complementary energies, twin souls meeting, etc., can be pleasant and believable. To learn more about this, I invite you to read some of the hundreds of spiritual books about sex out there. Lots of inspiration for you!

### Breaking Rules as an Antidote for Repression

When we break rules, we feel free. When we break rules without harming anyone and do something pleasurable, the transgression is utterly exciting. If there is a realm of life full of rules to break, it is sex. Especially for women, it is rules over rules. What she should do, how she should do it, with whom she should do it, where, and when. It is an entire life receiving orders, guidance and advice, more or less explicit, on what her sex should be like.

But... what happens during sex no one knows and no one can see. If she trusts her partner, sex is perfect for breaking rules. The more rules others impose on her, the more exciting it is to break them. Few things are as exciting for a woman as hearing, during sex, how she is breaking all those unfair rules imposed on her. If not done in a derogative manner, few things are as exciting as being called a hooker[12], a whore, and a slut. It is exactly what she has been told not to be!

To increase the effect, you can try to understand how your partner was repressed and thus make her transgressions sweeter. Sometimes, it is exciting for her to hear that she is a slut who enjoys sex too much; that she is a submissive who enjoys being ravaged during sex; that she is a sinner and specifically mention religion[13]; that she is naughty, enjoying mostly kinky sex; that she is a sexual animal that pulls loose from the chains that restrain her; or just that she is

---

12 You need to be careful in translating "hooker" to different languages and cultures. In some places, by hearing "hooker," a woman will think of the powerful side of the prostitute: beautiful, desired, very good in bed and free of prejudices, someone who can fulfill her sexual fantasies and be very well paid for it, becoming more and more beautiful in a virtuous cycle. In other places, a woman will think of a hooker as a miserable woman with no other choice but to let herself be raped in order to survive. This last interpretation is obviously not exciting.

13 This is mostly for non-believers who are raised in religious environments, not for true believers, who could become quite offended and blocked.

a beautiful woman with a free mind who cares nothing about rules others try to impose on her.

Chapter 13:

# Jealousy

*Despite jealousy never disturbing your life together, she knows how much you value her; you show that through your jealousy.*

\*

*"When love is not madness, it is not love."—Spanish proverb*

## About female jealousy

We all know what jealousy is.

And we all know it brings a lot of problems.

Curiously, we do not always talk about the same thing when we talk about jealousy. To clear this point, let me present what I believe to be the five main reasons for a woman in a relationship to feel jealous:

1. Insecurity that her man will dump her for another woman;
2. Fear that other women are better than her;
3. Fear that the relationship with her man is fake, or that he is lying;
4. Fear of lowering her social status in front of other women; and
5. Believing that jealousy is the "correct" way to act.

As you see, and opposite to what you might have expected, her man having sex with other women is not on the list. The reason for it is that occurrence of sex, for women, is not a priority. And, looking logically at it, women are right about this. What sense does it make that the occurrence of a pleasurable event—sex—should damage a long-term relationship? The genesis of this weird idea comes from the male sexual instinct. Men are genetically programmed to abhor the idea of their partners having sex with other men. The reason for this is that to have his wife pregnant from another man is an evolutionary disaster. It is *evolutionarily* worse for a man to have his wife pregnant by other men than it is for women to be raped—she, at least, will have children; the cuckolded man won't. So, evolution took care that men avoid this at all costs—it created male jealousy, which peaks when his wife has sex with other men. It drives most men crazy.

Women, of course, don't share that instinct. Their husband having hidden children with other women is evolutionarily irrelevant. Their husband replacing them as Queens—that is definitely not irrelevant. So while male jealousy is triggered by the fear of his partner having sex with other men, her jealousy is triggered by the fear of losing her Queen status.

This idea is not new. It was investigated back in 1992 by David Buss, Randy Larsen, Drew Westen, and Jennifer Semmelroth at the University of Michigan. They asked men and women to imagine that their partners were being unfaithful. This would happen in two different ways. In the first one, they would be sexually unfaithful. In the second one, they would be emotionally unfaithful. Result: 60 percent of men reported feeling more distressed by the sexual unfaithfulness, compared with only 17 percent of women. The researchers then repeated the study measuring physiological distress instead of asking, and obtained similar results.

Not only should this interesting result make us reflect on what we generically call "jealousy," but it also helps us in understanding why couples fight so often about jealousy. Men and women are just not talking about the same thing when they feel jealous!

It is critical to understand this difference. You might think your partner is being silly by feeling jealous due to some innocent flirting—if you think in terms of male jealousy. But if you think in terms of female jealousy, she is not being silly at all.

To avoid female jealousy, you must be very careful in making your partner feel totally safe about her Queen status. She has to feel that she is special, superior and, in your eyes as well as in public eyes, more attractive than other women. Being her exclusive sexual partner is not enough (nor needed) to block her jealousy. To be seen as your Queen, both by you and by other people—that is what prevents jealousy. Don't fall for those modern deductions like "as long as I am being faithful she should not feel jealous," or "those women were just talking to me, she is just imagining things." In fact, do the exact opposite!

If other women give you extra attention at a party or similar, don't play their game while claiming that your partner is being paranoid. Do the opposite. If she claims that they were hitting on you, agree with her. You will look more like a King, both by having women hitting on you and by them not being able to manipulate you. In fact, seeing women hitting on you might even excite your partner, as long as you don't, in any way, put her royalty at stake. So, when someone gives you extra attention in front of your woman, look like you understand what is going on, don't look surprised, but perform a huge and public demonstration of affection and attraction for your woman. Show how your partner is better than the women hitting on you

The above assumes you don't want your partner to feel jealous. In monogamous relationships, however, some little bouts of jealousy are helpful once in a while to spice up the relationship... if you do that, I recommend doing it without sacrificing her status of Queen. That is paramount. You can mention attraction to other women—any man feels that—as long as you are even more attracted to your woman.

### Optimizing your own jealousy

In the same way that you should pay attention to her jealousy, you should pay attention to yours. Few things are as noxious to a relationship as a jealous husband/boyfriend. So please hear this: if your partner has decided to cheat on you, no matter how controlling you are, you will never be able to prevent it. The woman who, when single, required several dates and a romantic evening to have sex, will have quickies in the most extreme places when cheating on her husband/boyfriend. And, as you know, there are a lot of men out there who don't mind waiting for her, in previously arranged places, to meet her during the fifteen minutes she manages to escape. The more controlling you are, the sweeter it will be to cheat on you, if she decides to do it; or the more annoying you will become, if she is not planning to cheat on you. So drop it.

In case you have doubts about this, let me address a common concern: many men believe that they can actively seduce previously unwilling women to sleep with them; so, other men can do the same to their woman. To avoid that, they become controlling.

This is, however, a wrong belief. Women are permanently evaluating the guys around them as sex partners. In the seduction process, the woman decided from the start there was a possibility she would want to have sex with the seducer, so she lets herself be seduced. Sure, it might seem like you won her over, but she was available to start with, even though she did not show you that.

So, to avoid that she cheats on you, don't make her feel like cheating on you. Cheating is all about wanting to cheat, not about having opportunities to do so.

Now, I am telling you not to act in a controlling manner.

Does that mean you should never be jealous?

No.

When you are jealous in a smart way, she feels desired. She feels that you are aware that other men find her desirable and she feels that you are not taking her for granted. So, in clubs or not so intimate parties, it is perfectly fine to be slightly jealous; if someone is dancing with her, after a while you can go and get her to dance with you instead. Don't bend over to men who are hitting on her; intrude the conversation, be social skillful and fun, but clearly send the body language signs that she is *yours*. Don't reproach her, or accuse her, but don't be a wimp, be a King. It's not that she was doing anything wrong, it's that most men out there are attracted to her and you know that. Plus, in the same way that her Queen image is important, your King image is important as well. Of course, don't overdo it. Being always interrupting her conversations with men, not allowing her to socialize, preventing her from having friendships and even some flirts is terrible! Let her do all that. The goal is not to make her feel chained to you, always under watch, without any freedom. The goal is that she feels totally free but that she also feels that you care for her, that you protect her, that you find her very desirable and that you are not a sucker to be played with.

In private, never let your jealousy make you sour or insecure, or criticize her for talking to a particular guy. Even if she was not attracted to that guy, by telling her she was, you are saying you find him attractive—and that will make her feel attracted to him. Plus, she knows that in the future she will have to be overly distant to that particular guy and that gets in the framework of "forbidden love". And you don't want to do that! Also, don't talk about your rights as her partner and her duties. Rights? Duties? That is totally unattractive. You don't want her to see you as an obligation!

Another thing to remember is that women often make their partner jealous on purpose. They love that. If she does that, show her you are a King, don't let her play you.

The take away point is that you cannot physically or morally prevent her from cheating. Focus on winning her permanently and on using jealousy to improve your relationship, not destroying it.

Chapter 14:

# Creating Fantasies and Bringing Them to Life

*As you lie in bed, you start telling your partner a story on something most men don't even dare mention. Your story makes her extremely excited and brings her to the verge of orgasm. She is twitching of horniness in bed, not believing a man can be this sensual and honest. You add your final spicy details to the story, making her come really hard to the sound of your words.*

\*

*"Someday you will be old enough to start reading fairy tales again."*
*—C. S. Lewis*

FANTASY TELLING

### What is Fantasy-telling?

Fantasy-telling is about telling your partner goodnight stories for grown-ups. At night, as you lie together in bed, you can describe in detail situations that turn her on. These goodnight stories always have a happy ending—her orgasm. This orgasm can happen just from the excitement of hearing the story, or you can give her an orgasm on command. If not, you surely can give her "a hand," if she doesn't do it herself while you talk! You can also start having sex while you tell her the story... Whatever way she happens to come, she will sleep like a baby after a goodnight story. Women love reading erotica. To have their partner telling it to them feels even better.

## The Three Goals of Fantasy-telling

Telling a child a goodnight story serves three purposes: please the child, teach your child values, and make the bond between the two of you grow stronger. In the same way, goodnight stories for grown-ups have three purposes:
1. Excite and give your partner pleasure;
2. Understand what makes her horny; and
3. Introduce some new ideas before bringing them to life.

### Excite and Give Your Partner Pleasure

Listening to a goodnight story for grown-ups is extremely exciting as it has a lot of exciting ingredients: Visualizing the entire fantasy in her mind is exciting. Having you accepting her hidden fantasies is exciting. Listening to you talking about sex is exciting. Being close to your naked body is exciting. Imagining that maybe someday that fantasy might come true is exciting.

All together, it becomes extremely exciting.

### Understand What Makes Her Horny

The way to adapt to your partner is by testing and understanding what makes her horny—in touch, kissing, sex, but also mentally. By telling her fantasies, you can test her reactions much better than if you exposed her to these situations in real life—or if you asked. In fantasy-telling, you can feel what excites her the most and thus build a custom-made fantasy for her as you go along. When you are done, you have just found out what she is most hot about!

### Introduce Ideas before Bringing Them to Life

Telling fantasies is the way to introduce new realities into your life. After you have told her the fantasy, made her all excited about it and made her orgasm while imagining it, it is only natural that she wants to carry it out!

As sports coaches say: First you visualize yourself doing it. Visualize, visualize, visualize. Then you just do it—and it just comes naturally. It is also like that with fantasies and new sexual experiences.

Let us now go over a list of fantasies. In each fantasy we will see how they are useful for the three goals above. At the end of the chapter, one of these fantasies is written down ipsis verbis, so you can see how to do it in detail.

These are just a tiny fraction of the fantasies that can be told. They were selected because they are quite hardcore. Softer fantasies, like light bondage, role-playing, sex in exotic environments, etc. are more suited to be played directly in real life than to be told before hand.

Not these ones, though...

TELLING A FANTASY...

## Initiation

To tell her fantasies, lay in bed with her, get close with some sensuality... rest your leg over her pelvis, hold your hand in her ass, etc. and start telling, in her ear, the fantasy of that evening. As your first fantasy ever, I advise using a fantasy where it is obvious that your only goal is her excitement and that has a small risk of shocking her. A good option is, for instance, the fantasy of having sex in public. The exciting part of this fantasy is that other people admire the Queen's beauty, boldness, and sexual abilities and envy her for conquering you, the King, who is so hot for her and gives her so much pleasure. Let's look at it in more detail.

### Fantasy of Sex before an Audience

In this fantasy, both of you go out at night to a fancy place with fancy people. Choosing people with status is important, as your woman wants to be envied by people she considers of value. So, describe the setting around you as a very nice party or a very nice hotel, for instance. As a first fantasy, play innocent—tell her a story on how the two of you started having sex without knowing that people were watching. That could either be in the gardens of the party or in your hotel room. Unfortunately, some people came to the gardens without your noticing, or the curtains of your hotel room window were open or you forgot to close the room door.

The point is that some very attractive people spotted you having sex with your partner. Silently and full of curiosity, they gathered around to watch you. They became very excited. The men were very excited watching your partner, the women were very excited watching both of you, and they felt envious of your partner.

*Fulfilling the three goals:* While this fantasy is not very exciting, it gets her used to listening to fantasies. You can understand which parts of the fantasy make her hot (the men, the women, etc.). Finally, it is a fantasy that you can easily fulfill in real life.

## Fantasy of the Queen Having Sex with a Female Underling

Here is a statistic: "54 percent of women between the ages of 18 and 24 say they've kissed another girl" (Cosmo Poll, Dec. 2008)[1].

Being your partner, the Queen, ruler over other women, it is only natural that she is excited about having sex with them, in a format where it is clear that she is a Queen and the others Underlings.

While this might not sound so natural to you right now, you should act as if it does, because it will feel quite natural to your partner.

In this fantasy, you describe your partner having a sensual interaction and eventually sex with another woman (I am providing an example of this fantasy at the end of this chapter). Use a lot of time on foreplay. A lot of time. You shouldn't even mention real sex in the first fantasy: most women have no problems kissing another women. Doing oral sex to another woman is a different story. Getting their fingers inside another woman's vagina is usually even less appealing. So avoid getting that far in the first time you tell the fantasy. Kissing, nipple sucking—all that is OK for a safe first time.

Then, add a lot of power play to the girl's interaction. Probe your partner to see what she finds more exciting about being with a woman.

While you can include a particular girl in the fantasy if you suspect that your partner desires any of your common friends, it is better to ask her to imagine an attractive woman and then include that girl in the fantasy. Don't include yourself in the fantasy. The goal, for

---

1 Not a very reliable source, however.

now, is for her to consider sex with other women.

*Fulfilling the three goals:* This fantasy probably will excite your partner. It depends on how much her conscious blocks her unconscious, how she relates to other women, and what are her unconscious motivations. Making some variations on this fantasy will allow you to understand what excites her most about being with other women (or if nothing at all...). You can also talk about it afterwards. Here there is no problem in asking, as you are not asking about your performance but about her particular deep unconscious desires.

## Fantasy of Being Double-penetrated by You and Your Twin

In this fantasy, you introduce her to your twin brother. He is exactly like you. You both start having sex with her. She can't tell one from the other, as you are exactly alike. This makes her very horny as she gets twice the pleasure and she is sure she is not making you jealous—she is not desiring another man at all! Describe in deep detail how each of you kisses one of her earlobes, each of you sucks on a nipple, etc. Escalate your description of the excitement that the three of you are feeling until there is no other way to satisfy that desire then by double penetration. You and your twin brother double penetrate her. Describe in detail how good that feels. Have a dildo close by when you tell her this fantasy. You might probably need it.

*Fulfilling the three goals:* This is a very exciting fantasy that introduces a lot of new themes: anal sex, double penetration, multiple partners, and more than one man. It has a kind of magic to it—it takes away all the blame and choice. She had anal sex and double penetration because she did not want to be selfish. She did not have sex with another man, either, because she was always with you.

Of course, she will probably also find it very exciting to be with another man. It is up to you to know whether you feel comfortable with that. (And by the way, never ever tell this fantasy if your partner has a twin sister!)

## Fantasy of the Queen with Her Best Male Underlings

Tell her to recall the guys she most desired in her past and that never wanted her: she might recall the cool older guys at her high school, her girlfriend's boyfriends, etc. Don't ask her who they are. When she has already selected a fair number of these desirable guys (somewhere from four to eight), start telling her a fantasy...

Create a situation in which these guys meet her. They are all very much into her. Tell her how these underlings now bow to their Queen, how they adore her, etc. Tell her how much they try to please her as she lies there being pleased. Tell her how after all that exciting foreplay, she proceeds to have sex with each one of them, makes them totally crazy with desire and pleasure, and makes them all come really hard. She should also come very hard, but always in a clearly dominant stance.

*Fulfilling the three goals:* This is a super-exciting fantasy for women who, sometime in their lives, were unpopular or rejected—and there are plenty of women with a past like that. It can be almost therapeutic for them, and it is good for your relationship. It shows her that you understand her desires and frustrations, that you look at her desires as normal, and that you look at her as a Queen, no matter what. She feels that you admire her. She also feels that, next to you, she can improve and achieve what she wasn't able to achieve before. Of course, this fantasy introduces the idea of sex with a lot of men. Be careful if you don't want her to even think about it. But, very probably, she already does, as it is a very exciting and logical fantasy to have. Anyway, that should not be a worry for you—it is just a fantasy. In real life, most women focus on one man at a time. One of the reasons women love commitments is that, once they become hooked on a particular man, he is the man they fantasize about.

Besides, this fantasy is not so much about group sex. It is about her succeeding in getting all the men that rejected her, and being the absolute Queen.

## Fantasies to Break Taboos

This is a group of fantasies that excite your partner by breaking taboos. I mean harmless taboos, not laws made to protect innocent people. Examples are sex in her office, in her parents' bed, sex in her friend's bed; risking getting caught by her employees, her boss, her parents, etc. Another idea is to tell her how you will fuck her in her ass while she speaks on the phone with a client. All these are fantasies where she is "naughty" while others believe she is a well-behaved girl/woman. She will feel avenged on that undesired responsibility and she will feel the excitement of getting caught—the forbidden fruit is always the most desired.

*Fulfilling the three goals:* These are very simple and innocent fantasies. They might be helpful in understanding what is most exciting for her, and they are very easy to bring to reality.

## Other General Fantasies

There are many other fantasies that will make your partner really excited. You can try different kinds of fantasies, and then proceed along the lines of the ones she seems more interested about. For starters, build fantasies where you tell her how:

- Either you or she are different characters (have a different job, like a fireman, etc.);
- She will be penetrated by some large object;
- She will be given immense pleasure with large objects and toys simultaneously;
- She will penetrate her female underling with a huge strap-on;
- She will be in extremely dominant situations (not with you);
- She will be in extremely submissive situations;
- She will be raped[2];
- You will tie her up and fuck her;
- You will tie her up and use many toys on her; or
- She will tie a female underling up and fuck her.

## Fantasies to Break Mental Blocks

Besides getting her excited, fantasies are also extremely good at destroying mental blocks your partner eventually has. You should build custom-made fantasies to address each of her blocks—things you think she would enjoy but which she is reluctant to try. As an

---

2 Use a rapist whose face she cannot see. In case she starts reacting negatively to this fantasy, you can then "take the mask" of the rapist and tell her it was you in disguise, only intending to make her horny, and continue telling the fantasy.

example, let's go over a custom-made fantasy made to solve a particularly hard case.

### Custom-made Fantasy for a Girl Who Did Not Want Her Partner to Come in Her Mouth

This fantasy was created for a couple with a sexual dissonance: he was crazy about coming in women's mouths but she felt strongly against it. Surprisingly, she was sexually open in a number of other topics, just not on this one—his favorite. To solve this issue, it was required to understand a bit more of their sexual life. Despite being in a relationship with him, the girl was not on any contraceptive pill, so they always used condoms for vaginal penetration and he could not, in any case, ejaculate inside her. Being a think that is usually very exciting for a woman, she probably missed that. So, despite being totally lukewarm about her partner's male fantasy of coming in her mouth, she should be very hot about her female fantasy of him coming inside her vagina. So a fantasy was created to seize this. It went as follows:

Lying in bed while receiving a blowjob, the man closed his eyes and started talking. "Oh, it is so wonderful... I am imagining that my dick is feeling the naked skin of your pussy, on the inside... It is so wonderful feeling our skin touching. Nothing is more emotional, intimate and wonderful than feeling you, feeling your pussy directly on my dick. I feel shivers of emotion as I feel your skin on mine..." As he was telling a fantasy that made her really hot and which she approved as a good thing, she tried to fulfill that fantasy, sucking him in a way that would feel like a pussy. This went on for minutes, with her trying her best to mouth-pussy him, and him always adapting his talk to whatever action she was doing. (Can you guess what she did when he said, "Oh fuck it is so good to feel my entire dick inside your pussy!")

He never said a word about coming. When she started sucking for him to come (as she usually did just before taking his penis out of her mouth in the last moment), he said, in a very excited voice: "Damn, I can't resist to what your pussy is making my dick feel. It is so good, so good. Oh my god, I feel so much like just coming in your naked pussy, directly feel your skin against mine as I come in your beautiful pussy, coming really deep inside your body, holding you close to me, letting my cum flow inside your pussy, all for you..."— kind of a description of the night when daddy and mommy made their little baby...

In the last moment (the warning for her to take his dick out), he yelled: "Oh, I am going to come so hard on your pussy, I am coming, coming on your pussy, on your pussy, coming on your pussy!!" She took it all in her mouth, swallowed it and stood there smiling at him, feeling very happy as he still wriggled in bed.

By framing the situation in a context that she enjoyed, she loved giving him pleasure. Her block wasn't exactly on feeling sperm in her mouth. Probably it was something about "male oppression" or the like. By building a bridge between what she enjoyed and what he enjoyed, the idea no longer seemed negative. She overcame her block and became a strong enthusiast of making him come in her mouth, no longer pretending it was her pussy.

This fantasy was helpful in removing a mental block. Had he tried to talk her into it, it would have been a disaster. She would have felt pushed and unappreciated and he would have feel frustrated. If she would ever do it, it would have been with the feeling of sacrifice and a bit of humiliation. That fantasy would have been destroyed forever for that couple.

That is why it is so extremely important to never pressure your partner to do anything in bed.

Besides removing mental blocks, you can also use fantasies to remove physical blocks. For instance, by telling a very hot fantasy about anal sex while you use a tiny little finger up her ass. Or by telling her exactly how she feels in her vagina as you stimulate her...

## FULL-LENGTH EXAMPLE OF A FANTASY

I will now give you one full-length example of an important fantasy: the introduction to sex with another woman.

The fantasy I wrote here is a long and detailed one, told in a very soft manner. You normally don't have to be half as descriptive and soft as I am here, especially not if you are telling her a fantasy on a theme you don't consider problematic. Feel free to speed it up if you feel it is too long or to use more sexual words if you feel it is too mild.

As you will see, many of the sentences are put forward as questions. A lot of these questions are rhetorical, so you don't have to wait for a reply. By using questions, you are showing her that you are telling a fantasy to make her feel excited, not to make yourself feel excited. Having a sentence starting by, "Do you remember..." sounds a lot better than, "I want you to remember..." Sounds sweeter—and sweetness is just the sweetest thing in the whole world.

However, not all questions are rhetorical. Some key questions are there for a reason. These are probing fantasies, where you should ensure that your partner is enjoying the fantasy at every step of the way. To these key questions you should wait for her reply, to be sure you are going the right way. Sometimes she doesn't reply. That might be because she just wants you to take control and just stop asking questions, or because her answer is no but she doesn't want to ruin the play, or because the answer is yes but she is not brave enough to admit it—use your empathy to distinguish what is the case and don't repeat the question to pressure her to say yes. If you suspect she is leaning toward a no, try a different route and pose another question. If she is too embarrassed to say yes, try a lighter wording. If she just nods and the question is not so important, she probably just wants you to go on, so please do...

## Fantasy of the First Time with Another Woman

*—Sweetie, I want you to close your eyes now. It's time for a bedtime story...*
*—Mmm...*
*—I want you to imagine you are driving to this beautiful spa in the mountains. You will stay there for an entire evening. As you drive, you notice how beautiful the nature is there. Then you arrive. The spa is a beautiful brown house on a slope, two floors, in minimalistic style, with lots of glass windows. You park and walk to the reception.*
*As you walk in, one of the girls at the reception greets you with a big smile. She is called Jenna. She is Asian, petite,*

*young, and quite beautiful. You chat for a while, as she friendly explains how the spa works. You'll begin by having a quick tour, then some time for yourself alone in the inner swimming pool, where you can have a drink. You can then choose when to go to the baths, have a massage, or chitchat in the lounge. Later dinner will be served at the restaurant. For the guests to feel more relaxed and comfortable, all guests and workers are women. No men are allowed in the premises.*

*Jenna leads you around the spa. It is such an amazing place! To start with, the building itself is awesome. The architect created an extremely cozy and inspiring atmosphere, while paying huge attention to detail. Everything looks good here. And, as you look through the windows to the outside, you notice how beautiful the mountains look like, covered in snow.*

*The people here are also quite attractive. Women, several women, beautiful and cool women, looking relaxed, happy and laid-back, wearing the same robe and greeting you with relaxed friendliness.*

*Jenna takes you to the swimming pool. She leaves you at the dressing room. You change to a brown bikini and enter the swimming pool area. The water at the pool is perfect, so you enter the pool and just look around. There are three women already in the pool. All are attractive. One of them is a bit older, but hot, another is your age, and the last one a bit younger. All of them look great. You particularly notice the younger one, as she has such a beautiful face, with green eyes and a shy expression. She gives you a shy smile. Then, the older woman starts talking to you and soon the four of you are chitchatting about the spa and life in general. The conversation is relaxed and pure, without any bitching. Your drink arrives, some kind of Cosmopolitan with a ginger flavor. Interesting. You have one, then another. After a while, you talk a bit more with the shy beautiful girl. She is called Alice. She is a student of _____ [area your partner works in] so she is eager in learning from you. You talk about _____ and the conversation just flows wonderfully. She is so nice and sweet. You do feel a great synchrony with her, despite her being only twenty-one [adapt to be younger than your partner, but not so young that it would sound sinful or illegal]. And, despite the conversation being about work, you still manage to have fun and laugh! Much more interesting to talk about work when is this fun and looking at a beautiful face for a change, isn't it?*

*Soon, you ask Alice if she wants to go and check the rest of the premises with you. She happily agrees. You drink one more of their drinks and go. You let her out of the swimming pool ahead of you. She starts climbing the stairs and you follow. You look ahead and see her legs and behind, inches from your face, wet, full with water drops, making her skin even more shiny.*

*When you stand next to Alice, who is a bit shorter than you, you can't avoid noticing that she has an impressive body with beautiful boobs. Very beautiful, firm, and natural. [Here describe in a way that does not offend your girlfriend. If she has or plans of having implants, replace natural with "beautifully made." Also, describe something that attracts her. Maybe perky boobs is more her style?]*

*You look around, find where the bath area is, point it out to Alice and walk there. She follows. You open a door and walk in, with Alice behind you. Inside an attendant awaits, with towels in her hand. You stop and greet her. Not noticing, Alice bumps into you. You feel her wet, large breasts on your back.*

*The attendant hands you a towel and points at a basket to dispose your bikinis. She tells you that in the sauna and baths you will appreciate not having your bikini on you. Still, you feel a bit embarrassed. Alice, however, looks twice as embarrassed. You decide to take your towel and wrap it around you body. You then remove the bikini and place it in the basket. You turn around, ready to go and watch Alice*

*as she does the same. As she undresses her bikini, you give a curious look at her breasts, trying to see beyond the towel...
As you prepare to leave, a tall girl dressing like she works here enters the room. You notice how she is, like Alice, very attractive. But, except from that, she is quite the opposite from Alice. She is the sporty type, fit, tall and seems very comfortable and friendly. She is also a bit older than you. She smiles at you and presents herself as Sandra and explains that she is a masseur. She asks you if you want a massage.
What do you prefer sweetie? Having a massage with Sandra, or taking Alice to the baths?[3]
—Hmm... taking Alice to the baths.
—You open another door and enter a beautiful large room with a convoluted swimming pool in the middle. Water flows from one area of the pool to another, through a small waterfall. Three naked women lie under it, enjoying the water falling on their bodies.
You take Alice's hand and explore the rest of the baths with her. All the guests are either in the large room or in adjacent rooms. Instead, you take a narrow, badly lit corridor and discover a small room with no one inside. This room is different. It is perfectly decorated as an ancient Roman bath, its walls painted with figures of two bathing goddesses, wearing only their jewelry. They are drinking from large metal cups. The only light in the room comes from the large candles that hang from the walls. There is a large tub or small pool on the left side of the room. On the right side lies what looks like an ancient massage bed. At the far end of the room stands a wooden table. On top of it, you spot two sets of jewelry, with golden arm and leg bands, necklace and a wreath. They are exactly like the ones wore by the women in the painting. By the pool, you see two large metal cups. You show the jewelry to Alice, who gets really excited about it.*

---

3 Simple question: do you rather be submissive (take Sandra) or dominant (take Alice)?

*Turning your back to Alice, you put on the jewelry. It fits you perfectly. Then you turn around, and, as you look into Alice's eyes, you decide to tease her and impress her. You smile and slowly drop your towel to the ground. Momentarily, her eyes open wide and her chin drops. She regains control and says: "Oh my god, you look amazing, like a real goddess!" And you do, with your beautiful naked body adorned by that stylish, ancient jewelry. Isn't it great to see the excitement in Alice's eyes?*

*—Yes it is...*

*—So you walk past her and slowly enter the pool. You notice as she turns her head around as you walk by... Slowly, you feel the warm water touching your foot. It feels so nice... you then enter a bit more, until you totally immerse in the warm water. You reach the opposite wall and turn around. Sitting with your back to the wall, with your breasts appearing above the water and your wet hair, you look at Alice. Wearing the jewelry and the towel, she stands looking at you, admiring you...*

*So you ask her with a friendly smile: "Are you coming?"*

*"Yes," she answers, heading for the tub, but stopping at the border. She is shy of taking off her towel. So you tell her: "I will get you a dry towel later. Come on in with the towel." You walk to the border to help her enter the pool. You bring her to the end of the pool and lie next to her, floating in the warm, steamy water.*

*You then look at the paintings on the wall. In the first one, the two goddesses are talking to each other in the pool. You point it out to Alice. She smiles. In the second painting, further away, the goddesses are drinking from their cups.*

*So you rise, passing your naked body close to Alice, and bend over to fetch the cups. You notice how that makes her tremble. Still standing, naked in front of her, you hand her one of the cups. Inside the cups, there is red wine. You lower yourself to level with Alice and toast, "To the goddesses!" and take a sip. It tastes good... A very good red wine, Barolo*

*probably...*
*She agrees with you and says: "Mmmm... really good," and*
*then she continues: "I just don't know about that goddesses*
*part. You sure do look like a goddess, not me," she says, point-*
*ing at herself, wrapped in a wet immersed towel, and laughs*
*a nervous laughter. You look at her body and you notice*
*how beautiful and attractive she is...it would be great if she*
*would take that towel away...wouldn't it? So, do you want to*
*help her overcome her shyness and remove that towel?*
*—Yes, I do...*
*—So you tell her: "Why don't we solve that?" You then slowly*
*put down your cup as you look at her. Her big breasts are*
*compressed under the towel. She looks excited at what you*
*are doing. You rise slightly, just to let your own breasts again*
*come out of the water. You are now very close to her and you*
*notice how Alice looks at your breasts. You then use your*
*hands to touch her towel.*
*You tell her, "Let's make the second goddess appear..." and*
*calmly, you open her towel, slowly, exposing her beautiful*
*big breasts. They are underwater, but you can see how beau-*
*tiful they are, how they expanded out of the towel as soon as*
*you opened it. You look at the pink nipples and feel extreme-*
*ly eager to grab those big breasts, fondle them, caress them,*
*play with them... but you don't, as you want to feel closer to*
*Alice instead... So you carefully take the towel away from*
*Alice and place it at the border of the pool, while you avoid*
*looking at her body anymore.*
*"A goddess is born," you tell her as you lie next to her and*
*take another sip.*
*Then you look at the wall again. In the third painting, the*
*goddesses lie next to each other, embracing each other, in*
*what looks like cuddling. You point it out to her, as you*
*say: "Look at what goddesses do..." and then you laugh. She*
*laughs as well. As you laugh, you reach your right arm out*
*to her, and she lies on your shoulder. It feels so great to have*
*her relax close to you... To feel her soft beautiful face so close*

*to yours, and her arm resting on your chest. Under water,*
*you pull your body under hers, so that she is now floating on*
*top of you, lying on you. She wrapped one of her legs around*
*yours. It feels so cozy. You can feel her big soft boobs against*
*your belly. It feels so good to have her big boobies on top*
*of you while feeling her warm body on yours, immersed in*
*that warm tub... it feels so relaxing and so sweet... her skin*
*feels so soft against yours. You can really feel the difference*
*between the roughness of the male skin you are used to and*
*the wonderful, soft, young, female skin of Alice. And you can*
*feel how Alice touches you in your embrace. She definitely*
*feels like getting closer, so she hugs you tighter. You do the*
*same and let your hands roll around her body. You feel very*
*excited to touch her female and beautiful body.*

*Then you look at the fourth painting. In the fourth painting,*
*the two goddesses lie side by side as muscular slaves mas-*
*sage them. Hmm... and there is a massage bed next to the*
*tub...*

*Do you want to suggest Alice to lie in the massage bed for*
*you to give her a massage, or do you rather forget about the*
*painting and keep enjoying your underwater embrace!*
*—Let's go for the massage.*
*—So you show Alice the fourth painting and propose her*
*to try the massage. You get out of the pool, share your dry*
*towel, and then you tell her to lie in the massage bed, belly*
*down. You find some finely scented oil next to the bed and*
*start dropping it on Alice's legs.*

*You can see her entire body now, in detail. You look at her*
*beautiful legs, and at her attractive bottom. You feel like*
*touching her. So you start massaging her, from her feet up,*
*passing your legs in her thighs. It feels very exciting to pass*
*your hands on her thighs... first, because you have never*
*before touched another woman's thighs, but also because*
*you can feel how she is enjoying it even more than you are.*
*She is slowly rocking as you massage her. As you move your*
*hands more sensually in her thighs and reach for the in-*

*ner side, you see her getting goose-skin. She is getting hotter and hotter. Your hands move close to her butt, and then you move them back... you have never felt a woman's butt before and Alice's is perfect. Round, beautiful with a great skin, mmm... you just enjoy and move your hands so to grab her ass exactly as you feel like, feeling every little detail of her ass, as you hold it in your hands. [Check for your partner's reaction. If she gets more excited, proceed quicker with the fantasy, becoming more sexual. If not, continue at the slow pace, with massage, tenderness, smoothness, and then explore a bit more when Alice turns around and she gets to massage her breasts.]*

—*Mm...*

—*Mm, that is exciting for you, isn't it, to grab Alice's ass in your hands, and fondle it as you please, feeling her soft but big ass all in your hands...*

—*Yes...*

—*Alice moans as she rocks her ass, enjoying it even more than you do. Then you move to massaging her back. You do massage her back, but you tease her... you move your hands sensually on her skin, making her more and more excited... and then you come back to grab her ass some more. You enjoy that, and she enjoys that... She keeps pushing her hips outwards, exposing her ass and inner thighs... You move your hands from her ass downwards, to her inner thighs, and back. You look at her pussy, and you can see that she is totally hot for you!*

*So what do you do? Do you feel like gently start touching her pussy or do you feel like leave it for later and just keep on caressing her?*

—*Caressing her...*

—*So you pass your hands slowly upwards from the inner thighs, and as she rocks her hips towards you, you avoid her pussy and go over her back, slowly massaging her... then you reach her collarbone and grab it between your hands. You then bend over and start talking in her ear. You tell her how you love to massage her and that she should now turn around... which she does. Her breasts now lie totally free in front of you. As Alice has her eyes closed, when you gently pass your hands in her belly, your gaze is fixated on her big beautiful boobs, those boobs that you will soon feel in your hands. Alice can no longer keep away from you, so she stretches her arm to touch you as well. She slowly caresses your thigh, up and down, and that feels exciting... to know that she is totally hot for you makes you very excited... that she is loving your touch... she then opens her eyes and looks you in the eyes with a sweet look...to close them again in order to better have a feel for your magical hands.*

*You start again massaging her legs and feel her shaking when you move upwards. Again, you avoid touching her pussy. Instead, you slowly progress until you reach Alice's breasts. You can feel how excited and eager she now feels. You slowly move around her breasts, feeling them with care, evaluating them, and caressing them, while still avoiding the nipples. You feel so hot by having another woman's breasts in your hands. It is so exciting, you can feel your pussy totally wet by grabbing Alice's breasts. Her breasts are amazing, so it is twice as exciting...*

*Alice's eyes are closed, but her expression is open. She is enjoying your magic touch more than she has ever enjoyed any other touch. She is in bliss. She is moaning. You have not yet gone over her nipples. Alice is under your hands, moaning and moaning, totally hot for you... and those pink nipples just in front of you...*

*Do you want to grab her boobs in your hands and play with her nipples?*

*—Yes!*

*—So you take a pause to build tension and then slowly grab her boobs as you have felt like doing for the last hour. You grab her boobs to feel them, to feel them good, all in your hands, and Alice is moaning under you. You can feel those big soft beautiful boobs in your hands, and that makes your*

*pussy really wet, really wet. You play with those boobs, you grab them and then you just move closer and take a nipple in your mouth. You have never felt a real nipple before, and you take it in your mouth and you gently kiss and suck on it, as you grab the boobs with your hands. You suck on that nipple grabbing those big boobs in your hands, and that makes you soooo hot... sooo hot. Alice enjoys that sucking even more. She passes her hand over you, embracing you, petting you. She is pulling you closer, pulling your against her boobs, she wants to hold you closer and closer.*
*Do you want to get closer to her as well? Or do you want to tease her some more? Or do you want to start feeling her entire beautiful body with your hands, hmm?*
*— Closer... I want to get closer to her.*
*—So you place your hands on the massage bed, and slowly climb on top of Alice. You lie on top of Alice and look in her eyes. She holds you and looks at you with a deep romantic look. You move your head slowly towards her and feel her soft lips against yours. You kiss. It is such a great kiss. You can feel all your naked body touching hers, her soft skin, her boobs, her boobs in your hands. You place one of your legs between hers. Now you can feel her soft and already wet pussy against your thigh. Alice goes totally wild when you do that... She starts rubbing her pussy against your thigh, while kissing your more passionately than before. Yet, with a female softness...*
*The soft skin around her lips, her small and beautiful face... it feels so good to kiss such a beautiful face, feel your hands against the soft skin of her boobs, feel your body locking on hers, your thigh against her wet pussy, so wet, that is making you so horny, so horny, feeling that she is so hot for you, so hot for you...*
*You feel how your own pussy is getting wetter and wetter. So you move your hips so that you can also grind against her pussy, both of you rocking your hips together, having sex together, an intimate sex. You feel the softness of her thigh*

*against your pussy, her soft young skin, very soft, and you run your hands up and down her body, feeling every inch of her, passing over her breasts, holding them, squeezing them a little, but they are so hard and so big, that is so exciting, and you keep on running your hands over her body, feeling the curves in her body, her soft butt, you grab her soft butt again, feeling a female butt in your hands as you press your hips against her, so close to her, locked on a soft tongue kiss, feeling so connected to her, and feeling all her desire for you, how much she is overwhelmed by kissing you, feeling you, by being with a woman for the first time and choosing you for being the one to show her how it is, you can feel how she is losing emotional control, she just wants to grab you closer and closer...*

*She is so hot for you know, feeling your beautiful body against hers. She is holding your left breast with one hand and you notice how she moaned harder when she felt your beautiful breast in her hand, and now she has the other hand on your butt, and she became even hornier, she is passing her hand over your butt, feeling how beautiful it is. She is so horny now, you can feel how she started moving her hips stronger against yours and now she placed the other hand on your butt as well, no longer feeling it but now she is squeezing it, squeezing your butt in her hands, pushing you to fuck her pussy harder, she is moaning so hard now because she is starting to come and she is pulling you against her, she stopped breathing, she is screaming in your ear as she grabs your beautiful ass, pushing your pussy against hers, she is fucking coming now and she is screaming, she is scream-ing, "Oh my god! Oh my goddess! Oh my goddess!!!" and she is totally crazy for you coming so hard, you feel her pussy squeezing against yours, her spasms, pulsing in her orgasm, her yelling and you start coming together with her, that beautiful girl coming, so hot for you, under you, you start coming really hard feeling your pussy totally soaked start-ing to come, feel how your pussy rubs against hers and you are fucking coming together on her pussy as you grab her big boobies and she grabs your amazing ass, the two of you coming really hard on each other, really hard on each other, coming really hard on her beautiful shaved wet pussy, grabbing her boobies, feeling her entire body twitching in pleasure and holding you, totally hot for you, fucking amazing coming like that, together with her...*

*The End*

## Alternatives

She might as well have chosen Sandra instead of Alice. Or, on the contrary, she might have chosen to dominate Alice more clearly. She chose, and I created an appropriate story for her. As she chose Alice, I assumed she preferred the dominant position and developed the story accordingly, offering a few branching points where to opt for another kind of fantasy—more romantic or more dominant. She went for the romantic version. Had she chosen the dominant version, I would create a more dominant ending for this story; and perhaps in subsequent evenings I would increase the level of dominance steadily until I reached her limit.

If she had taken Sandra, you could tell her how Sandra was a great masseur, and then describe in detail the wonderful massage Sandra was giving her, not failing to stress all the dominant aspects of Sandra, and how Sandra was pushing it, despite your partner's "efforts" to resist her female charms. Sandra might have asked two other masseurs to help her, a total of six hands giving good feelings to your partner, in a way that no woman could resist, and these three expert masseurs would just skillfully rub your partner's body until she orgasmed (however, be gentle in this description, avoiding submitting your partner to any demonstrations of dominance from other women). Or, if she preferred something more intimate, Sandra could then ask the two other masseurs to leave and stay alone with your partner, in an erotic but more intimate manner. As long as she is choosing, you can rest assure that your story will have a happy ending.

Chapter 15:

# Giving Direct Orders to Her Unconscious Mind

*It does not matter where she is or what she is doing. If she hears or reads those two magic words, she will come. Such is the power of hypnosis.*
*You come to her place and offer her a bouquet of the finest red roses.*
*"That is so sweet of you!" she says with an open smile. "Oh, and there is a card! I'm curious!..." She quickly opens the envelope and pulls out the card. As she reads the two words you wrote on the card, her body starts contracting, a deep grunt leaves her lips and she rushes to hug you. Then her orgasm hits her, spasm after spasm, as she grabs you with all her strength and tries not to moan too loud—without much success.*
*Women just love roses, don't they?*

\*

*"Fear not the path of truth for the lack of people walking on it."*
*—Arabic proverb*

*"Those who dance are considered insane by those who cannot hear the music."—George Carlin*

### THE UNCONSCIOUS AND THE ORGASM

Up to now we have focused on how to give your woman orgasms by following her unconscious desires. We will now take one step forward: I will show you how to make your partner orgasm through direct orders to her unconscious mind.

The human brain has several layers of consciousness, resulting from different areas of the brain. The area we usually consider the "myself," the conscious, lies in the neocortex of the brain's left hemisphere. Through it we perform some of the exclusively human activities, such as rational thinking, talking, etc. All those things other animals don't do.

What other animals do, however, is have sex. Without being able to talk or think rationally, they have sex and experience orgasms. That is not surprising as the part of the brain involved in sex is not the conscious. It is the unconscious.

Somewhere inside ourselves, but out of our direct control and awareness, a part of us decides when to feel excited and when to trigger orgasms. It is inside our brain, but seems out of reach. If we could reach it, we could consciously decide when to have orgasms. We could perhaps even tell other people to have orgasms—that would be a lot of fun! But, unfortunately, we don't seem to be able to bypass the other person's conscious mind and talk directly to their unconscious... or can we?

Actually we can. We can bypass the other person conscious mind and communicate with their unconscious mind—through hypnosis.

## Why We Can Trigger Orgasms during Hypnosis

A lot of people are skeptical about hypnosis (but less skeptical about astrology). So I'll start by showing you why there is nothing weird or surprising about experiencing orgasms while in hypnotic trance. To do so, I need your honest answer on the following two questions.

### Have You Ever Had an Orgasm During an Erotic Dream?

Most people have experienced orgasms during sleep. That is a clear example of an orgasm obtained without physical stimulation. The excitement that builds that orgasm derives solely from images generated by the unconscious mind—the experience we simulate through hypnosis.

### Have You Ever Felt Weird Feelings Deriving from Your Previous Night's Dream?

Sometimes we spend a whole day feeling weird about something. Sometimes we feel suspicious about someone. Or we have some confusing thoughts.

Often, we can track these feelings to our latest dream. We dream with our unconscious mind and sometimes the entire dream is not deleted when we wake up (especially if we use an alarm clock). Sometimes what we were dreaming sticks to our mind and we carry it for a while, as memories. Even more extreme, sometimes we experience repeated dreams. That means that we do have some kind of memory for unconscious experiences, where we can store dreams.[1]

In the same manner as dreams do, you can leave triggers during the hypnotic sleep so that, during the waking state, your partner can remember what happened during that hypnotic sleep.

As you see, there is nothing weird or even unique about hypnosis. Just a lot of prejudice.

**Being Rational about Hypnosis**

Surprisingly for me, a common negative feedback for the draft version of this book was: "The powerful penetration movement does not apply to my wife/girlfriend and I don't believe the hypnosis section." I would answer with, "Have you tried either of the two?" and the reply would be, "No, but I don't need to. I already know."

Funnily, these people were convinced that they were being rational. But they weren't. The rational approach is to check for yourself and to collect data that allows you to build your own opinion rather than trusting mainstream opinion (which is hardly ever correct).

Plus, look at the expected returns: If it works, you have acquired a wonderful tool to bring pleasure to your partners. If it doesn't work, you wasted a couple of hours. So, why would anyone not try hypnosis?

Well, because we are prejudiced, we want to believe we know everything already, and because we are very afraid of looking foolish. However, being prejudiced, believing you know everything, and

---

1 Many of the hard-to-believe applications of hypnotherapy (such as regression and "past lives therapy") come from exploring these unconscious memories. Some hypnotherapists believe that the unconscious memories are trustworthy. I totally disagree with this view—if they can store dreams, they cannot be trustworthy!

fearing looking foolish are three common reasons for not improving in any area.

## GIVING ORGASMS THROUGH HYPNOSIS

It is very easy to give orgasms to your partner through hypnosis. It is a simple process of only a few steps. First, get your partner's permission to hypnotize her. Second, you place her under hypnotic trance, during which you talk directly to her unconscious mind. Third, you describe an extremely erotic scene that makes her very excited.[2] Fourth, you give her an order to come. She comes. Fifth (after she stopped coming), you tell her that she will not remember anything when she wakes up until you repeat that order. At the moment she hears the order, she should remember everything that happened under hypnosis and have an orgasm—exactly like the one she just experienced. Finally, you bring her out of the hypnotic trance.

From that moment on, you and your partner have a fantastic toy to play with. You just need to order her to come, and that she will. You can play, on average, for about thirteen days until the effect dies out.

### Convincing Your Partner to Be Hypnotized

The first step towards making your partner come at the drop of a single phrase is to convince her to let you hypnotize her. It can be quite difficult to convince someone to be hypnotized. Even when the person allows herself to be hypnotized she might keep up some resistance, making it harder for you to hypnotize her.

So it is important to do this step well.

The key for your partner to feel like being hypnotized by you is, again, excitement and relaxation. If you have already shown her a new world of sexual experiences, can you imagine how excited she will feel when you tell her: "I think you are now ready for the most surprising sexual experience I will ever give you."

However, she will only feel relaxed in doing something as scary

---

2 This third step is optional. You don't actually need to build an erotic scene, but it just makes the whole thing more interesting.

as hypnosis if she trusts you. That is all up to you and how trustworthy she perceives you to be. Even feeling excited and relaxed, she will probably have lots of doubts. Hypnosis has a terrible image, so it is only natural she feels like that. To clear her doubts, it is important that you learn about hypnosis, so that you can explain to her everything she needs to know and make her feel confident that you know what you are doing.

Finally, it is still scary and a bad idea to have someone controlling your unconscious mind and making you forget about it afterwards. So, there are two things you can do:

1.  Agree with your partner what you will induce her to do, before you start.
2.  Film the entire hypnosis session and show her the tape if she wants to.[3]

This way she will be sure to know everything that happened. She will feel increased trust, and there is no such thing as too much trust.

### Putting Your Partner under Hypnotic Trance

Start by sitting your partner in a very comfortable position. Comfortable enough that she can stay motionless for half an hour (which is not an easy thing to do). While she should be comfortable, don't let her lie down. She must be sitting in a position where she can't fall asleep easily, otherwise you risk that she will start snoring while you are pronouncing your magic hypnotic words.

Place an object in front of her where she can focus her gaze, or tell her to close her eyes. You can hypnotize her both ways. If you go for the object, take one that is reasonably shiny, like a metal. While using an object makes it easier for your subject to fall into a hypnotic trance, for a rookie hypnotist, it is easier to go for the closed-eyes version. You will be protected, feel less pressure, and you can even take your time to check what to do, in this book or in your notes, while she waits with closed eyes. (At the end of this chapter you will

---

3 Giving her the tape, however, might be a bad idea—she can misuse it later on if you split up.

have a complete script you can read out loud to hypnotize her.)

Using an extremely deep voice—not unlike Darth Vader from Star Wars—with a slow and extremely monotonic rhythm, start your induction. The voice is very important—practice it beforehand (and I will tell you later how to practice).

### Stage 1: Describing the Relaxation

Start your hypnotic session by describing how she is feeling a deep body and mind relaxation. Start by describing a relaxing setting that is easily understood by her conscious mind, such as, "It is late afternoon, you are lying in a sun bed, and the temperature is just absolutely perfect. You feel the sun smoothly warming your skin. It is so relaxing."

### Stage 2: Ordering the Relaxation

Besides just describing the relaxation, start ordering her to relax. For example, "Your legs are getting more and more soft, they are getting more and more relaxed," or, "You feel your mind to be totally empty, totally relaxed." Order each part of her body (starting at the feet and ending at her head) to become more and more relaxed. Use multipliers, such as, "When I snap my fingers, your body will become twice as relaxed."

### Stage 3: Testing the Hypnotic Level

This is the test phase, where you check how deep in hypnotic trance she is. The goal of these tests is to understand whether your subject is ready for the next stages. It is not strictly needed to go through this stage. If you don't, you only risk giving hypnotic orders to someone who is not hypnotized.

These tests consist of telling your subject she is unable to move a particular body part (the eyelids, an arm, etc.) and then checking if she complies. If she does, by being unable to move that body part, progress to the next stage. If she doesn't comply, do not show surprise with her lack of compliance; just keep doing Stage 2 for a while longer. Use plenty of multipliers to make her more relaxed. Do not repeat the same test again in the same session. Apply a different test or just go straight to Stage 4. Don't be afraid of jumping directly to Stage 4. Stage 4 will send your subject deeper into hypnosis anyway, and as you are not doing performance hypnosis, you don't need to filter out the less hypnotized individuals.

### Stage 4: Putting Her Under Deep Hypnotic Trance

Send her to the deepest hypnotic level you can. You do that by counting. You can count from 1 to 10 or decreasing from 20 to 1— or any other numbers you choose. The point is that each number you count, she will be one step deeper into hypnosis. When you finish counting (or before that) she will be deeply hypnotized. This relationship between the numbers and the hypnotic trance can be made directly or through an analogy. When it is direct, you order that her trance symptoms become increasingly more intense as your counting progresses: an emptier mind, a deeper relaxation, etc. In the analogy relationship, the counting is depicted visually as, for instance, the descent of several stories in a beautiful building. This beautiful, modern, and safe building was previously presented as your subject's mind[4], so going down several stories means getting into deeper levels of consciousness.

Either way, the important part is that you do a progression in that, at each increment, takes her deeper into hypnosis, knowing that she will end up in a very deep level of hypnosis.

## Erotic Induction

### Making Her Very Horny

When your partner is already in a deep state of hypnosis, you can introduce the erotic component. Describe a fantasy that makes her very horny. Speak only positive things and in a gentle manner—she is now in a very vulnerable situation. Don't try "risky" or dominant fantasies. Only positive and sweet fantasies. You can use your imagination. As in a dream, she is much more prone to believe different

---

4 This building example was taken from the book "Instant Self-hypnosis," by Forbes Robbins Blair, mentioned in the "Sources" section.

and original situations than when you talk to her conscious mind. She is also much more prone to obey orders on how she should feel like, such as, "You are feeling a lot of pleasure deep in your pussy."

## Commanding her Orgasm

When she is already very excited, move on to give her an orgasm. Remember that she won't be so exuberant as when she is awakened. She will only move and moan very lightly. When you feel that you have given her enough fantasy-telling and that she must be really excited, tell her to have an orgasm. This orgasm will only happen when you order it to happen, using a clear order, such as, "Come, sweetie!" To be on the safe side, tell her during the fantasy that she is only allowed to come when you order her to come.

## Setting a Trigger

After her orgasm and a little rest, inform her that she will not remember anything when you bring her out of hypnosis—until she hears you repeat the exact order that made her come. When she hears it, everything will come back to her mind, and she will come in the same way.

## Getting Her Out of Hypnosis

The last step is to bring her out of hypnosis, which is extremely simple. Just slowly do a simple counting (for instance, up to 5), informing her that at the end of it, she will be totally awaken.

## Pulling the Trigger

Over the next approximately thirteen days, you can pull the trigger you left in her unconscious mind, in any situation, by giving her the order to come. Be careful and use this power with responsibility.

## Using Triggers for Directing the Sexual Practice

There are lots of fantasies and triggers that can be used for different effects. Besides sentences, you can use nonverbal triggers that are mutually beneficial. For instance, you can order her to come when she feels your penis in her mouth (not unlike the "Deep Throat" movie). Surely you will have two weeks of intense oral sex!

Please note that this is not hypnotizing her to have the urge to give you oral sex, which would be tampering with her free will. What I am proposing is just to make it more pleasurable for her, if she, without any interference whatsoever from hypnosis, decides to do it.

Of course, hypnosis can also be used to trigger the urge or desire to have sex, or specific kinds of sex—thus tampering with her free will. You do that by stopping the session before she has an orgasm and then triggering that feeling on her later on. She will, of course, become extremely horny and willing to have sex. However, that is changing her free will and is not done with the aim of being pleasurable for her, so I don't recommend doing it at all. Don't do it unless she explicitly wishes that you hypnotize her with that intention.

**Precautions**

While hypnosis is huge fun, it brings you a lot of power that should be used with responsibility and foresight. Always think about what can go wrong, then think again and only then proceed with your action. For instance, you can hypnotize her to come when she reads a particular sentence in an e-mail or in a text message. That sounds really cool and she will think it is a great idea. However, look at the huge potential for disaster that comes with it: She can read your text message while driving and crash her car. She can read her e-mail while talking to her boss and harm her career. If you are not in control about everything in her surroundings, don't trigger an orgasm—even if she thinks it's a great idea.

Being dominant is to take the responsibility. So while she has to agree with everything you do, her agreement is not enough for you to do it. You have to be the one ensuring it will be safe. She may not if she assumes you have done that already.

Be careful also not to do anything illegal. Check about the laws regarding hypnosis in the country and state where you live (if there are any). While it might be a good idea for you to tape every session of hypnosis you do, if you decide to give her those tapes, consider how she might use them against you in case of a problematic split-up. So be extremely careful and think ahead.

Be also careful of triggering orgasms on top of orgasms. You can do that just by repeating your trigger. However, that is uncomfortable for her. Triggering orgasms in succession is not the same experience as multiple orgasms, where the excitement that was left from (or created by) a previous orgasm gives rise to the new one at the right time. The best thing to do is to explore with her the best way to use the trigger (and yes, here you can ask questions!).

In fact, try giving her the power to pull the trigger. You can do that by setting the sound of an object as the trigger for her orgasm, and then hand in the object to her. Use a charming object that is not widely available, as you don't want her to go around orgasming at the wrong moments.

Unless you have learned it from other sources than this book, don't try to use hypnosis for anything else than previously agreed-upon sexual play.

## How to Progress As a Hypnotist

### Self-hypnosis

Chances are that you will feel extremely insecure the first time you hypnotize someone. If you fail, you might look dorky. If you succeed, you will be doing something intrusive in the mind of someone you like, without any previous experience. Besides, you are not even sure that hypnosis really works, which will increase your insecurity. Therefore, I recommend that you start by hypnotizing someone very special and forgiving: yourself. (If the idea of hypnotizing yourself sounds silly, laugh for a while before you proceed reading. Once you are done, let's move on.)

Hypnotizing oneself has a name: self-hypnosis. Self-hypnosis is truly fascinating because it is so counterintuitive—and it works. Self-hypnosis is done by reading out loud a hypnotic script, similar to one you would say to your subject (after switching "you" for "I"). As a way to improve in hypnosis, there are three advantages in hypnotizing yourself compared to hypnotizing your partner:

1. The subject truly and deeply trusts the hypnotist and wishes to be hypnotized;
2. The hypnotist is not afraid or insecure; and
3. You can understand both sides of hypnosis and get better feedback.

Despite all these advantages, you will not be able to go beyond the lighter stages of hypnosis using self-hypnosis, because you would be unable to keep on reading. However, these lighter stages of hypnosis will be enough to show you the power of hypnosis.

Using self-hypnosis, you will be able to train your voice and your abilities to send yourself to a state of hypnotic trance. You will be able to induce yourself to feel or experience whatever you wish and see how that feels in reality. That will be the best training you can have.

As a guide to self-hypnosis, I suggest the book, *"Instant Self-Hypnosis"*, detailed in the "Sources" section.

**Important Details on How to Hypnotize**

*Logical Mistakes*

While you are sending her under, you need to be careful not to make any logical mistakes. Don't contradict yourself, don't say anything that is impossible, and don't leave loose ends. This is especially important while you are sending her under: the conscious mind can progressively "let go" as long as it trusts what it is hearing. If it detects an error, it immediately gets back in control.

When you describe a setting, her mind visualizes it. If you later commit a logical mistake, such as describing something during the day that you had previously described it as being during the night, it will "break the spell." This can also happen if you leave too many loose ends. She might fill the gaps of what you say with her imagination. If you later describe details that go against what she imagined, her conscious mind might take over again. So, describe using all the detail you will need from the start. This can be done either when describing beautiful relaxation settings or by simply stating which arm she is unable to move when you tell her so.

*Hypnosis is Dominance to the Extreme*

In hypnosis, the subject decides to be controlled by someone whom he or she trusts and feels to be superior in some field. He or she does so to gain something—either to get attention (in a hypnotist's show), to improve (using hypnotic therapy), or to experience pleasure (the kind of hypnosis I talk about here)—and always to satisfy his or her curiosity. It is a clear dominance–submission relationship. Therefore, the hypnotist needs to look and act extremely dominantly.

I advise you to watch several hypnotic shows, either on TV or live. You will see that the hypnotist usually has charisma and sends extremely strong dominance signs. He not only touches his subjects, he touches them in a very intrusive manner, gets very close and looks them deeply in the eyes without blinking. In the entire life of the subjects, probably only their parents were this deep inside their personal boundaries. However, given the setting, the subjects accept that intrusion and, in doing so, feel like a submissive child. So the subject automatically obeys, as a submissive child does.

Don't worry; you don't have to do anything like that to hypnotize your partner. You can be a thousand times worse than a hypnotic performer and still easily hypnotize her. His task, hypnotizing people he never met in a few minutes, is incomparably harder than using an entire half hour to hypnotize your loved one.

However, while you don't have to act as dominantly as a performer, it is still extremely important that you demonstrate total confidence when you hypnotize your partner. Don't doubt, don't babble, and don't ask anything (have I ever told you not to ask questions?). *Be totally sure that it will work fine, and it will.* Not because of some cosmic forces or positive energy, but *because her perception of your confidence is what allows hypnosis to work.* To illustrate this, nothing better than the following quote:

*"Try not. Do or not do. There is no try"*—Master Yoda

## Variations

After your first hypnotic session with your partner, you will be very inspired to start making variations and build your own new ways of giving her pleasure. Here are a few suggestions. When hearing the trigger, you can make her do any of the following:

- Come;
- Play an entire exciting situation in her mind and then come; or
- Come imagining that her strap-on is her real penis and that she is penetrating another woman.

You can also set some fun triggers instead. You can make her come when:

- Your dick is totally inside her;
- You slap her ass;
- You come; or
- Your dick begins to enter her.

I am sure you will have lots of other interesting and sexy ideas. Is a never-ending source of fun.

## Example Hypnotic Script

I am providing an entire hypnotic script for you to use. However, it is a bit succinct. That is, I describe the entire process but I avoid repeating myself. When doing hypnosis, however, repeat yourself. Repeat, repeat. When using the script, then, cycle through some parts. Repeat the sentences.

### Stage 1: Describing the Relaxation

*Relax as you are comfortably sitting down listening to my voice. Listening to my voice will make your mind become clearer and calmer. My words will bring clarity to your mind. Each word making you feel more and more relaxed. Breathe in... and out. In... and out. In... and out. At each breath, you become more and more relaxed. Breathe in... and out. In... and out. In... and out. Let the tension and stress leave your body. Become more and more relaxed, only listening to my soothing voice. Listening to my voice and feeling my presence makes you feel more and more relaxed.*

*Let us now go on a small journey. You are now sitting on a beautiful and comfortable chair full of pillows. It lies on a wooden deck. In the middle of it is a beautiful swimming pool, full of cyan water. This deck is on the top of a beautiful and large house, with a beautiful view: green fields, trees, and mountains in the distance. You enjoy this amazing view. It is a beautiful view. There are no clouds in the sky, and the sun is shining in its afternoon colors.*

*You feel very relaxed. The sun warms your skin just right. Not too warm, not too cold. There is no wind. It is so relaxing and so perfect here. You can feel your skin being warmed by the sun, all your skin enjoying the perfect temperature and the heat of the sun. The pillows you are lying on are so soft. You feel so relaxed...*

## Stage 2: Ordering the Relaxation

*You enjoy the feeling of the sun heating your face. It is so pleasurable. You feel like smiling with all the relaxation you now feel. You feel like just enjoying the relaxation the sun gives you while letting go of any thoughts... and tension. You feel the relaxation of the sun entering you, through your face. The sun is telling you to relax. Let go of any tension in your face. All the muscles in your face relax to enjoy the sun. Feel the sun on your face and relax your face, relax your jaw, relax your mouth.*

*Your face is now relaxed and you enjoy the sun smoothly warming it. Your neck starts to relax as well. Let it relax even more. Let it relax more and more. Your neck is totally relaxed without any tension. This relaxation feeling now moves down your chest. You feel an inner peace blossoming in your chest. No tension. No tension. That feeling now moves down from your shoulders, elbows, arms, hands to the tips of your fingers. Feel how your upper body is now basking in the*

*sun in total relaxation and comfort. Your hips now feel this relaxation feeling. They become totally relaxed and without tension. The feeling continues moving down your thighs. Your thighs now feel extremely relaxed. So relaxed...*
*Those long muscles in your thighs are now deeply relaxed. Feel your hips and your knees and feel how there is no tension between them. No tension at all. Your thighs are so relaxed, enjoying being under the warm sun. The relaxation feeling starts traveling down from your knees, along your lower legs. Your calves and other muscles just feel so relaxed. So relaxed...*

*Finally, total relaxation reaches your feet. Like a wave, it passes along your feet. Keeping your body totally relaxed and in joy, the wave of relaxation from the sun slowly leaves your body through your toes. The sunlight smoothly enters through your head and slowly leaves through your toes. You are part of a circle of relaxation. The light enters you and leaves you more and more relaxed as you feel it traveling down your spine. You are one with the sun. The light enters through your head and travels down your spine. Feel it traveling down your spine. It travels down your spine and through your legs until it leaves you, through your feet, leaving you more and more relaxed. You feel more and more relaxed. Your entire body feels totally relaxed. Deeply relaxed...*

(Repeat this last part a few times and then move to Stage 4.)

### Stage 4: Putting Her into a Deep Hypnotic Trance

*You will now start moving towards the inner parts of your mind. There are ten levels of consciousness. We live our regular lives at level ten. But you are now at level eight and you can feel how much calmer, deeper, still, and powerful your mind is now. Feel how much calmer, deeper, still, and powerful your mind is now. Your mind has now superior control over your body, but you don't want to use that yet. You want to go into more deeper, calmer, still and powerful levels of consciousness. You will now move into the deeper levels of consciousness. When you reach the lower levels, you will be totally hypnotized.*

*Feel the cycle of sun energy though your body. I will now direct your energy to take you down. Breathe in and feel the energy take you to level seven. Breathe out. See the numeral "7" in front of you and keep it there in front of you. Breathe in, breathe out. Breathe in, breathe out. Keep "7" in front of you. Breathe in, breathe out.*

*If you have seen "7" in front of you, you are now on level seven. Feel how more relaxed you feel. Feel how in level seven you feel twice more relaxed. Twice more relaxed, twice more quiet. Feel how more quiet your mind is. At level seven you are more deep into hypnosis and closer to your inner self. Your inner mind. Your real wonderful self.*

*Now breathe in... and breathe out. Prepare to use the sun energy to take you down. Prepare to go down to level six, where you will feel twice as relaxed. Now, breathe in and go down to level six! See the numeral "6" in front of you and keep it there in front of you...*

(Repeat this part to levels five and four until you reach level three.)

*You are now in a supreme relaxation state. If feels so good. Your mind is now really calm. Really deep. Really calm. Really deep. You are now totally hypnotized. Your mind is now very powerful. It will do exactly what my voice tells it to do.*

(If this is the first time you hypnotize her, read the following paragraph. If not, jump to "Stage 5")

*Feel how good it is to be here at level three. Some other day, in the future, I will ask you if you want me to hypnotize you. If you say yes, and I answer, "Go now to level three," you will immediately return to where you are now. Your mind will become as calm and deep as it is now. You will immediately arrive at level three.*

### Stage 5: Putting Her into a Deeper Hypnotic Trance

*I will now direct your energy to take you down, to the deepest levels of consciousness. Breathe in and feel as you go down to level two. Breathe out. See the numeral "2" in front of you and keep it there in front of you. Breathe in, breathe out. Breathe in, breathe out. Keep "2" in front of you. Breathe in, breathe out.*

*If you have seen "2" in front of you, you are now on level two. Feel how more relaxed you feel. Feel how in level two you feel twice more relaxed. Twice more relaxed, twice more quiet. Feel how more quiet your mind is. At level two you are even deeper into hypnosis and closer to your inner self. At level two your mind is already in control of your body. Your mind is in total control of your body; In total control of your body.*

(Repeat for levels 1 and 0)

### Stage 6: Erotic Induction

*You are now at level zero and your mind is in total control of your body. Your mind is now extremely powerful.*

*Feel your right nipple. Feel a bit of pleasure on your right nipple. Feel a bit of pleasure on your right nipple and feel how it gets hard. Yes, feel your right nipple getting hard. Feel pleasure on that right nipple. Enjoy the pleasure on that right nipple.*

(Repeat.)

*Now... feel pleasure on both your nipples. Feel the pleasure on both your nipples. Keep feeling the pleasure on both your nipples. They feel like they are clamped. Clamped giving you pleasure.*

*Now, you are starting to feel something at the entrance of your pussy. Something very light. Something nice. Something pushing slowly into your pussy. Feel how good that feels. Feel how good that feels slowly pushing into your pussy. Feel how good it feels at the entrance of your pussy.*

*Feel your nipples getting clamped tighter. More pleasure on your nipples, more pleasure on your nipples as something good pushes a bit more into your pussy. Pushes against the inside of your pussy. Feel the walls of your pussy being pushed. Feel how good it feels. Feel how good that thing pushing into your pussy feels. It is something nice, soft and large... and it pushes so good into your pussy. If feels so good on the walls of your pussy. Feel how wet your pussy is. Feel how wet your pussy is. Feel how you are getting that soft large and nice thing in your really wet pussy. Feel how it starts moving back and forth slowly. It is now wet inside you, and your pussy is being slowly fucked so well. Your nipples are being clamped so good. You feel so much pleasure from your nipples. So much pleasure from your pussy. Your pussy feels so full and so well fucked. You feel so much pleasure from your pussy and from your nipples. So much pleasure from your pussy and your nipples.*

*But you can't come yet. You can't come because you want to come much harder later. You want to come harder than you ever did. So you don't come now.*

*You keep feeling your pussy being so well fucked and your nipples being so well clamped. Feel that pleasure on your nipples and pussy.*

*Feel your clitoris now. Nothing is touching your clitoris... yet. It wants to be touched, but nothing is touching it. Feel it. Feel it not being touched.*

*Oh, something is touching it now. Is so good. Feel how good it is. Now it started vibrating. Feel that vibrating feeling in your clitoris. Feel that. Feel how it wants to make you come but you won't come yet. Feel how good it feels in your clito-*

ris, your pussy, and your nipples.

Oh... Something is different now in your pussy! Yes, now it is fucking you really deep. Feel it hitting really deep in your pussy. Your pussy is totally full now and this just feels so good. This feels even better than everything before. Oh this is so much deeper and better than everything else, you would come really hard if you came. It feels so good in your pussy and your clitoris and your nipples. If feels so good. Feel how good it feels and how you are blocking your orgasm. Feel how much pleasure you are feeling without coming. Feel that pleasure, feel that pussy, feel that clitoris, and feel those nipples. It feels so good, it feels so strong, you have to come soon, but you will come only when I tell you to.

(Repeat.)

Come now, sweetie!

It feels so good in your filled pussy, amazing on your vibrating clitoris and so good on your clamped nipples. It feels so good coming like that. It feels so good coming all over and tightening that soft thing in your pussy. It feels so good to come so hard.

(She comes. Let her rest for a while.)

Relax now. Relax deeply.

Soon I will wake you up. I will take you back to level ten. You will not remember anything of what happened. You will just feel extremely happy and relaxed.

However, in the future, whenever you hear me saying, "Come now, sweetie!" you will feel exactly the same as you did just before you started coming, and you will come exactly in the same way.

I will now count to ten. At each number, you will move up to its consciousness level. When I reach ten you will be fully awakened.

*Let's move up...*

(Slowly count...)

*...four, five, six, seven, eight... You are now almost waking up... nine... wake up, ten."*

(Talk to her in your normal voice from then on, but give her some time to get herself together and don't be scared if it takes a while.)

Chapter 16:

# Toys, Beatings, Bondage, and Imagination

*Arriving home with her, you lead her into the bedroom. She is surprised by all that lies on your bed: handcuffs, extensors, ropes, dildos, vibrators, and a computer. You tie her up, play her favorite porn on the computer and start talking to her in a very dominant manner. Soon after, you are whipping her butt. She is so happy to be in pain. You then start teasing her with the dildos and the vibrators. She is so excited she almost starts coming, so you stop... and then beat her some more. Then you go back to tease her with dildos and vibrators. After some tease-stop-beat-tease-stop-beat repetitions, you decide to be nice to her. You put it all together to give her an extremely violent orgasm that almost breaks her handcuffs apart.*

\*

*"If you start soon enough, you won't have to run to catch up."*
—Unknown author

## TOYS

Despite the hard work Evolution put into each man a fine lover, we have to admit that twenty-first century technology can sometimes give a helping hand. In terms of purely physical stimulation, the effect of one vibrating dildo in her pussy, another in her butt, and one vibrator against her clitoris are hard to compete against. Of course, the psychological side of sex is so strong that we should not fear being replaced by our cybernetic friends, in the same way that no perfectly designed doll will ever replace a real, hot woman. The best thing to do then is to get some help from these friends, combining their abilities for physical stimulation with our own abilities for psychological stimulation.

MATERIAL

There are some materials you can consider buying if you want to start playing with restriction and sex toys.

### Restriction Materials

- Handcuffs (play handcuffs, that she can open by herself)
- Ropes
- Leg extensor
- Blindfold

### Beating Materials

- Flogger
- Paddle

### Sexual Stimulation Materials

- Dildos (preferably vibrating ones)
- Anal butt plug
- Vibrator
- Powerful vibrator (to plug into the wall, such as the Magic Wand or other kind of massager)
- Cucumber

HOW TO LEARN MORE

More important than buying materials is to gain knowledge. I advise you not to use any restriction or beating materials before you have gained sufficient knowledge. Some things in life you can learn by trial and error, but beating your sexual partner for her pleasure is probably not one of them. I advise that you buy one good book on SM (I mention one in the "Sources" section).

When you buy a dildo, be aware that its flexibility is very important. If it is too rigid—and many are—it can harm your partner during her orgasm or with more harsh or tight applications (like double penetration). I advise having dildos of different dimensions. You can apply the shorter, thinner ones more harshly without the risk of hurting her (as long as they are soft). The larger ones need to be handled with care. Despite having the potential for being erotic and pleasurable, they can hurt her if they are too big or destroy your manly self-confidence if they are very pleasurable—so use them with care.

If you are concerned about the ecological footprint of your sexual activities (which I am not), you can use an alternative to dildos: cucumbers. Cucumbers are cheap, come in an array of sizes, and are disposable, nutritious, biodegradable and discrete to have around your place. They can also be very exciting as they are such an everyday item. On the other hand, they are not very romantic. But hey, you never know what tragedy can happen if a dolphin accidentally swims against your disposed dildo one hundred years from now, specially if swimming backwards. Always use a condom over your cucumber, especially if you plan to reuse it for a salad (but let me warn you, a vagina-crushed cucumber does not keep its freshness).

Now for the vibrators. They come in all kinds of sizes, shapes, colors, and textures. Some are sweet, for they look like a cute pet, others have a sleek design; and still others are instead small and practical. Most of them, however, work on batteries, which is not the best solution if you want powerful vibrations. And most women will prefer powerful vibrations. So, I definitely recommend getting a wall-pluggable, powerful vibrator. They are usually sold as massagers, not deliberately as sex toys. They are quite big and not sexy at all, but your partner will forget all about that as soon as you touch her clitoris with one of them. Besides this one, keep a normal small one, handy to use on her clitoris during intercourse.

## Small Intro to Beatings

Sometimes, to beat your partner can be an exciting sexual play. If a slap in the ass during sex can be very exciting, a flogging in the ass without sex can be equally exciting. If you do so, you will be entering the realm of sadomasochism that, contrary to what many people think, is not about the perversion of some crazy, cruel, and sadistic people. Well, at least is not only about the perversion of some crazy, cruel, and sadistic people. It is also about erotic play around the themes of power, dominance, and submission. As we have seen, the majority of women find it extremely attractive to add to her sex life a component of submission to her King, and domination of her underlings. The SM play allows for a much more extreme, exaggerated, and explicit way of doing this.

While serious SM is definitely not for most couples, a little slap here and there feels great to most women. So, the first rule as you enter SM is to move in small steps. Not only because you are playing with fire and you don't want to get burned, but also because you want to slowly find what is the appropriate level of SM for you and your partner, and you really don't want to overshoot.

The second rule is to always use your empathy and common sense.

The third rule is to ask your partner to give a safety word. Whenever she mentions that word during your play, you should stop what you are doing and give her full control of the situation. Use a word that she won't forget.

The fourth rule is to play as if on stage in a theater. Be dramatic in your voice, your acting, your beating, your fucking—everything should be part of a coherent fantasy that you play out for your partner. Build this fantasy from what you know about your partner. If you don't know anything that makes you think of a specific fantasy, try a general one.

A very general and popular thing to do is just to beat her as a punishment for being so naughty. You can start your acting from a normal bed conversation, pretending to be offended with her naughtiness (do this very theatrically, so that she immediately understands that you are playing, and plays along with you; you don't want her to think that you suddenly developed schizophrenia). Because she is so naughty, you decide to punish her, so you order her to lower her pants or raise her skirt. Place your partner in a submissive position, such as on her knees or lying over your legs as you sit. She will probably play along. If she doesn't obey, be smart and understand whether she is acting or for real. Not every woman likes to be slapped. So don't push!

If she complies, punish her in a symbolic manner. Just slapping is very boring. Using her belt to hit her buttocks is much more exciting. Of course, as a gentleman, you will test the belt first, and harder, on your own hand, so that you get a grip on how hard you should hit her buttocks not to overdo it. Every time you flog her, tell her how naughty or slutty she is for enjoying those things she enjoys. Mentioning these things will make her horny. The punishment will make her horny, too. Let's look at an example:

*"You are so naughty, aren't you?"*

*"No!"* or, *"I am..."*

*"You love to make man crazy for you, don't you? You love feeling how horny men get from looking at your cleavage as you talk to them, don't you?"*

*"Yes..."*

ZAP! Flogging! (No would also deserve a flogging. You would just call her liar! as well)

*"And you just love to know that many of them think of you at night wishing they could grab your boobies with their hands and suck on your nipples, isn't that right?"*

*"Yes..."*

ZAP! Flogging!

*"You are so naughty! Besides that, you love coming when a cock fucks your really hard, don't you?"*

*"Yes..."*

*"And you love coming with a cock fucking your ass as well, don't you?"*

*"Yes..."*

*"Didn't anyone ever told you how wrong that is? Something only a naughty little slut would do?"*

*"Yes..."*

ZAP! Flogging!

*"Ouch!"*

*"You know you have been a bad bad bad girl, don't you?"*

*"Yes..."*

*"So you understand that you deserve a beating, don't you?"*
*"Yes..."*
*"So, clench your teeth, I am going to flog your cute little ass because you are such a naughty little slut..."*

You can then flog her until you feel she has reached a plateau of excitement from beating alone and then bring the conversation to her passion for being penetrated—and start penetrating her. Or you can start placing some "medical devices" in her pussy that will cure her naughtiness (dildos and vibrators), with the explicit order that she is not allowed to come. If she starts disobeying you—ZAP! Flogging!—and stop stimulating her. After you flogged her, go back to use the dildos and vibrators. If she gets close to come, stop and flog her some more. Play like this until you finally make her come really hard. In this play you are being theatrically dominant, so there is no problem in exerting your dominance to the extreme and make her wait ages before letting her come.

After you have finished playing, be your old self again and kiss her plenty! Show how it was just acting and how you love her naughty personality.

Real SM is a world in itself and not for the majority of us. If you and your partner enjoyed the initial steps, you might want to go deeper. But again, be sure to learn more before you do.

BONDAGE

Tie her up so that she can be free. Free from the need to perform, free from thinking what to do next, free from evaluating if you are liking it, free to experience pleasure.

Lying in bed with her legs and arms spread apart, well tied, unable to move, and with a blindfold that prevents her from seeing, she can't do anything at all—she will just enjoy.

A submissive woman will feel very excited if you tell her you will tie her because you want to do whatever you feel like with her, including fucking her as much as you want to, because now she won't be able to escape you! (At least that's what you'll tell her, using a playful tone.) A dominant woman will not find that exciting at all.

However, more so than the other types, the altruistic domi-nant will love being tied if she overcomes her initial discomfort. She will love being tied to be worshiped and to finally disconnect from her need to perform, and be really able to feel pleasure. She will, of course, hate being tied to be dominated.

So, if she is an altruistic dominant, ask her sweetly and kindly if you can tie her up. Tell her how you will not be annoying and that she can stop it at any time by saying the safe word. You can even use gentle, well-meaning emotional blackmail here, such as, "Do you trust me?" Basically, tell her how she is so amazingly good to you that you would love if she would let you pay back a little bit of your debt.

When she is tied (and by the way, I recommend the following for altruistic dominants, but it is equally good for other personality types), worship her. Kiss her entire body for head to toe, toe to head, head to toe. Rub your body over hers. Take ages just kissing, rubbing over her and feeling her body, as if you were a blind man admiring Michelangelo's David. Give her as much good feeling as you can. Tease her by being very slow in your progress, but don't tease her in a way that shows that you are abusing the power you have acquired by restraining her. Don't tease her with your words. Don't act domi-nant. You should be dominant when she is free to resist you. When she voluntarily allows you to restrain her, forget about dominance. Doing demonstrations of dominance on a restrained person (unless in a clear SM setting) is a sign of weakness, not of strength.

As she lies in bed with spread arms and legs, without being able to see, make her feel loved, admired, and excited.

Slowly progress, build her excitement, and give her pleasure and tenderness until you start putting in the orgasms. Use your mouth, your hands, your toys, your penis, whatever feels more ap-propriate. In the end, use your penis, as she will enjoy knowing that even though you just wanted to give, you ended up not resisting her body...

IMAGINATION

The focus of this book has been on the instinctive side of sex, to understand and release all the power in that instinct. However, the non-instinctive, elaborate side of sex also has its charms and huge potential.

There are no limits to the human imagination and therefore there are no limits to what you can do in your sex life. You can apply your creative mind to imagine different settings, role-playing scenarios, objects to play with, fantasies, games, or whatever—or you can put other people's imaginations to work for you and buy one of the many books on the topic. Your creativity (or someone else's— you don't have to show her the book) will be deeply appreciated.

After you have a special evening set up, you can either surprise her or send her several SMSs during the day, teasing her for what's to come later...

Chapter 17:

# Being Sensual

*"Logic is a systematic method of coming to the wrong conclusion with confidence." —Unknown author*

*"He who lives without folly isn't so wise as he thinks." —Francois de La Rochefoucauld*

*"My life has been filled with terrible misfortune; most of which never happened." —Montaigne*

*"At the touch of love everyone becomes a poet." —Plato*

## WHAT IS SENSUALITY?

To be sensual is to exude pleasure and fun.[1] To be sensual is to exude to a woman that if she becomes your partner, she will have a great time and feel wonderful. The sensual is the opposite of the dull, the boring, the rational, and the brutish. The sensual is fun with a sexual undertone. To be sensual is not to be attractive—many men are initially attractive. When the woman feels a lack of sensuality, attraction fades.

Sensuality is about enjoying life, having fun, and exploring the pleasures of the senses. A woman wants her man to take her into a life of fun and pleasure, not to drag her down to a life of worries and obligations. Because of this, the professional/corporation man is not very sensual. Nor the stingy guy, the planner, the organizer, the se-

---

1 This is my own distorted definition. The official one in English dictionaries is slightly different.

rious guy, the nerd, the couch potato, the practical guy, the "very healthy" guy, etc...—all of them, not very sensual.

The artist and the playboy are much more sensual, and therefore enticing. Next to them, a woman will live a relaxed and fun life.

Fortunately, as everything in life, sensuality can be learned, so you don't need to be an artist or a playboy to be sensual.

DEVELOPING A SENSUAL MIND

### Don't Be Sexual Only During Sex

Don't keep your sexual verve only to your bedroom. Keep it alive during your daily interactions with your partner. Any moment is a good moment to show her how attractive she is. Actually, the more surprising that moment is, the better—as long as no one else hears or sees anything that could harm her image. So, when you are together with her in a public place but where no one can see what is happening, try telling how much you love having sex with her, compliment her, grab her ass slowly, etc. Start gradually with this kind of play, as not every partner is receptive to this. If she is—and most women are—keep on going. Make her come in elevators, buses, taxis, planes, public toilets, swimming pools, on the beach, etc. It is fun and exciting.

At home, start having sex impulsively wherever you are. Many women prefer having sex on a hard and cold living room table than on their sweet and soft bed. If you live in a flat, your building stairways are very appropriate: On the way home, play the part of being so hot to fuck her that you don't know whether you can wait until you get home. On the stairways show her that you couldn't resist her that long. If it is illegal to do so in the country or region where you live, fuck her against your apartment door as soon as you enter your flat.

Obviously, use your empathy when you play these kind of games. Be sure she is enjoying herself. A man who only talks and thinks about sex is extremely annoying. That is definitely not what I am talking about here. Do it very seldom, but don't do it only in the bedroom. Not only will this be very exciting, as it will build a stronger and more honest relationship between the two of you. She knows that you are the same wherever you are and wherever you are doing. She knows that you aren't shy, repressed, or playing roles. You are not Mr. Serious when going out and Mr. Crazy when closing the bedroom door. You are Mr. Serious when that is appropriate for her, and you are Mr. Crazy when that is appropriate for her.

### Enjoy the Pleasures of the Senses

The man who appreciates food, music, massage, etc., exudes the idea of pleasure, making every activity much more pleasant. The tough man who doesn't appreciate these earthly pleasures and lives life far from physical sensations makes everything unpleasant for his partner. Learn to appreciate the pleasures you don't yet care so much about, and to communicate to your partner how much you enjoy them.

### Touch

Touching communicates tenderness. Touch your partner often, both in private and in public (unless that is inappropriate or illegal where you live). Non-sensual people use touch with one of three purposes: to initiate sex, to call the other's attention, or to demonstrate possession in public environments. If you avoid touching your partner with any of these intentions, but instead touch her to show that you care and simply enjoy the feeling of your skin against hers, you will be extremely sensual.

### Be Fun

If you are a really funny guy, that is great for you! Women love it. If you are not a really funny guy, be very careful. Everything can be learned, but to be a really funny guy takes many years of practice: Each bad joke destroys the effect of many good jokes. Not surprisingly, most funny guys were terrible dorks saying plenty of bad jokes during their teenage years—they were learning back then. You probably don't want to go through the sacrifice of being a dork today to be really funny ten years from now. So give it up. And by the way, even if you are as funny as Seinfeld, never crack jokes during sex.

Sex is the time for emotions and urges—it doesn't go well with jokes.

Being fun, though, is not only about being funny. It is about having fun, being happy, not taking things too seriously, and creating situations/dates that are fun to do. How many men take dancing lessons with their partner and transform what should be hours of sensual fun together in a boring practice in search for perfection? When you are with her, focus on having a good time and not in being the best you can be in whatever activity you are doing.

## Be Irreverent and Don't Always Follow the Rules

Few things are a bigger turn off to women than being with a man who obeys all rules. That is a clearly submissive, over-rational, and cowardly trait. Sure, if everyone thought like this, the world would be a terrible place to live—but this book isn't the Bible. We are focusing on getting your partner hot, not on improving our society. You might be a fanatic garbage segregator, a speed-conscious driver, and very proud of having all your bills since 1990 very well archived. Just avoid showing this side of you to your partner[2], and definitely avoid giving the impression that you consider yourself to be a better person because you obey rules. When a woman sees an adult man happily showing her what a nice boy he is, her ovaries freeze in her belly and her sexual hormone production drops to zero.

Also, break some "common-sense" rules with her. For instance, just because you invited your partner for dinner at your place, you don't have to follow the "dine, drink wine, have sex, sleep" rule. How about "have sex, drink wine, have sex, dine, sleep?" Granted, the food might be a bit cold, but dinner will be more fun, and sex more surprising!

## Transmit Irrationality

Most women are quite irrational as they don't construct their opinions based on logical deductions. This is actually a good thing,

---

2 The only exception to this is if where you live, breaking rules gives an impression of being low-class. In general, the lowest strata in a society breaks some rules, the middle strata is very proud of obeying the rules (showing how they are not low strata) and the top strata is again very good at breaking rules.

as most logical deductions are wrong anyway, as they are based on wrong premises, but they give a false sense of certainty. However, in many environments, pure rationality is seen as a sign of intelligence (which is actually not true), and women often get treated as less intelligent, which is extremely annoying. So, be a bit less rational when you are with her. Having the most evidence-based opinion is not always so important. What do you have to lose by talking a bit less rationally, anyway? Sure, even if she is saying something that has no support from evidence and might be incorrect, you must remember that not all female conversation aims to transmit factual info—its goal is to have fun interacting with another person and analyzing his emotions and personality. Join in!

If you are interested, go for the next level. Pursue irrational interests: art, spirituality, astrology, etc. Many women find these topics more engaging during their "off-hours" than history, politics, technology, science, etc.

One final tip: you will be amazed how her opinion of you grows if you avoid questioning her mystical beliefs.

## Use Your Imagination

Imagination is one of those important words women use to describe men. Of course, when they say they want a man with imagination, they don't mean one that reads all of Tolkien's books, but one that surprises them in romance and in bed. They mean a man that never has the exact same sex twice, that sends her SMSs to meet at hotel rooms out of the blue, who hands her handcuffs when she gets home, or dresses in special clothes for the evening. One that buys surprise gifts, prepares special evenings, and role-plays. One that writes her long erotic e-mails for her to masturbate to while reading them. If she never knows what will happen next, she will be always thrilled to meet you.

Most women have erotic fantasies about their own man. Capitalize on that. Apply your imagination to please her.

## Don't Worry, Be Happy

Most of us were not born playboys with a large inheritance to spend. Quite the contrary, we do have plenty to worry about. But is not by worrying that things get better. Think and plan, but don't worry. Women are chronically anxious and worried. They need a dominant man who doesn't worry himself to calm them down. Adding your anxiety to hers is a no-go. If you can't stop worrying... keep it to yourself.

## Spend Money with Her

An outcome of not worrying, being irrational, fun and enjoying life's pleasures is that a sensual man spends quite a lot of money with his partners. On top of this, spending money makes his partner feel more like a Queen, which she enjoys.

While I say that you should spend money with her to increase her perception of your sensuality, I am not advising you do to that. For some people (like myself), personal finances are more important than the sensuality that spending brings. Nevertheless, I am aware that saving that money does have a cost in sensuality.

If you want to spend some and keep some, I advise you to spend in a controlled manner and focus on the symbolism and fun of each present—and its cost! Buying her presents suited for a woman and for a Queen have more sensual impact than paying bills. Taking her on a surprise trip during the weekend is more attractive than buying a really nice and expensive practical gift.

Also, be careful not to fall prey to all those social rules made to rip men off their money and subtly pay women for their affection. Yes, you want to make her feel like a Queen. Yes, you want to show your value. Yes, you want to make her friends feel jealous of her. However, you don't want to do that by showing how dorky you are and how much hard-earned money you can throw out the window—that is definitely something a real King won't do.

## Sensual Looks

If a woman quickly detects a non-sensual mind by its words and deeds, she is equally quick in detecting it by the way its owner looks like. It is therefore a very bad strategy to focus only on your mind and neglect your looks, especially because her friends will mostly evaluate you by your outside, and she is acutely aware of that. She wants a King—a man whom other women also perceive as a King. And other women will evaluate you by your taste. So it is extremely important that, in her eyes, you are a man with good taste.

Good taste is terribly relative, of course, but I want to avoid getting into aesthetic arguments. Good taste, for the purpose at hand, is what women consider good and feel attracted to. If that is real good taste or not, it is totally irrelevant. The important thing is for you to look like what the women in your environment consider to be tasteful, preventing their attraction to you from being hampered by a bad choice of clothes. Don't forget: they have to look at you as a King, and a King should not have obvious flaws. You have to allow her imagination to believe you are fantastic—don't give her obvious evidence that you are not.

# Conclusion

*"Reasoning draws a conclusion, but does not make the conclusion certain,
unless the mind discovers it by the path of experience."*—Roger Bacon

As we finish our journey together, I hope to have contributed a few new techniques with which you can give even more pleasure to your woman. Besides these techniques, I also gave you my views on how to behave sexually to match the powerful female unconscious desires.

Still, I suspect you might have a few questions for me: How ethical is all this? And how easy—isn't this a full time job? Even if it is totally ethical and easy, how and where should you start?

## Ethical Considerations

As you know by now, I firmly believe that to fully please the ones we love, we have to look at their unconscious mind as a wonderful part of the whole and communicate with it directly, without being tied by the ropes of proper behavior, morality, and religion. This is, of course, a questionable view. Am I being coherent? After all, while I talk so much about the unconscious mind, I don't profess a "let go" attitude; instead, I recommend a manipulative approach, that is, I advise saying the "right words" to cause a specific, desired effect on your partner. So, is this coherent and, more importantly, is this an ethical approach?

I take a manipulative approach for two reasons: first, because the goal of this book is to please our female partners, specifically, their unconscious. Not ours. Saying whatever crossed our manly minds would perhaps not be as effective as being manipulative. Second, because I don't think that there is anything wrong with being manipulative, when the goal is the good of others. After all, we are all manipulative to some extent, usually focusing on creating a particular image of ourselves in the people we interact with. Here, I recommend using manipulation to generate sexual pleasure instead of a good image. Is that wrong?

I think that the real moral test to this approach is the following:

Would you enjoy having a lover who would manipulate you to fulfill your conscious and unconscious sexual desires?

My own answer is a big and loud yes!

## Practical Considerations

I know that some of what I write sounds like hard work. First, it raises the bar; then it puts all the pressure on your shoulders; finally, it provides no silver bullet. Cherry on top, it tells you that you might have to change your way of interacting with your partners.

Wow.

But wait. That is the negative way of looking at it.

The positive way is that there are amazing rewards if you excel at sex. When you successfully apply even a part of what is inside this book, you will be able to please your partners effortlessly. And they will do their best to please you. Sex will mean only pleasure and success, never stress.

Rejection? Only having the kind of sex your partner deems proper? When she is in the mood for it? No, forget about all that. As you will have the ability to make her really hot, you will have sex whenever you feel like it and how you feel like it—and she will love it. Plus, your relationship will improve dramatically, as few things make a woman as happy as having great sex.

How about her being unfaithful? Many men are afraid of that. Not you. First, she won't have a reason to be. Second, you will know that even if she is, she will come running back, disappointed with her adventure.

If you are not in a monogamous relationship, your sex life will improve as well. Your eventual one-night stands will turn into "call me whenever you want" affairs. They might try to push you into a commitment, but if you reject, they will still be very happy to stay around.

## So, Where to Start?

If you are eager to try out everything in this book, you still might have a problem... where to start? For the sake of the argument, and while this is probably not the case, let's say that all of the material is new to you and that you want to try it all. Where is the best place to begin? How to progress?

I recommend that you start by applying the soft physical techniques: the touch, oral sex, doing foreplay during the entire sexual interaction... Then make your partner feel more like a Queen, complimenting her during sex. Progressively turn your compliments into more sexual comments. After a quick practice session in front of the mirror, you can start applying the powerful penetration movement. Try the turbo missionary position. After that, go for the fingering techniques, adapting them as described in the respective chapter.

As you practice all these and get increasingly better at it, you will feel much more confident. You will be ready to try everything else in this book. As you feel your partner appreciating your more dominant attitudes, you will feel more comfortable taking them, in a virtuous cycle. Soon after, you will have successfully applied everything in the book.

With nothing else to say, I wish you the best of luck and that you use your abilities and talent to develop much beyond this book.

Your own findings and views are very welcome. E-mail me at rg@rodgovea.com.

# Sources

In this first section, I mention the books that have influenced my views the most or that I consider a good-follow up to this book. In the second section I mention other interesting books.

BOOKS:

## Concepts in sexuality:

*David Shade Products at Davidshade.com*

In the online seduction community, David Shade is considered the master of sex. In his first e-book, "The David Shade's Manual," David collected information from many different sources and added a lot of his own very interesting ideas and experiences. While that book has been discontinued, David nowadays has an array of more detailed products on different topics: how to talk in bed, phone sex, erotic hypnosis, the A-spot and a lot about dominance and understanding women.

*"Screw the roses, send me the thorns—the romance and sexual sorcery of sadomasochism," 2009, Philip Miller and Molly Devon, Mystic Rose Books, US$24.95*

A very good introduction and explanation of SM from two very smart authors. It is fun to read and brings plenty of interesting insights.

**Hypnosis:**

*"Comprehensive stage hypnosis guide to mastering hypnosis," 2003,*

*Trickshop.com Inc., US$12.95*

This book is a manual on how to perform stage hypnosis and it brings detailed and exhaustive information on hypnosis. It can be bought at www.trickshop.com in PDF format. Well worth the money.

*"Instant Self-Hypnosis," 2004, Forbes Robbins Blair—Sourcebooks, Inc., US$14.95*

This book gives a good—albeit short—explanation on self-hypnosis and brings 35 hypnotic scripts for you to try on yourself. Very handy for your self-hypnosis sessions.

**Sexual techniques:**

*"Red hot touch," 2008, Jayna and Jon Hanauer, Broadway books, US$10.95*

This book explains in detail an enormous amount of techniques to stimulate your partner (mostly using the hands, but not only). You will never run out of techniques to try if you have this book.

*"ESO—How you and your lover can give each other hours of Extended Sexual Orgasm," 1983, Alan P. Brauer, Donna J. Brauer, Warner Wellness, US$14.95*

28 years after its publication, this is probably still one of the key books regarding orgasms. Very interesting and detailed, with plenty of information on techniques and the physiology of orgasm, its key message is the extended sexual orgasm.

*"Nina Hartley's guide to total sex," 2006, Nina Hartley, I. S. Levine, Avery, US$25.95*

This book is written by a proven expert. Nina writes in a very charming tone, covers many topics and is quite insightful. Definitely worth reading.

## Seduction:

*"The Art of Seduction," Robert Greene, Joost Elffers, 2001, US$18.00*

This book is an art piece. It describes seduction and how to seduce in an extremely seductive manner. A must have. The book is so big and beautiful that it is actually cheap for US $18.

*"The Mystery Method—How to get beautiful women into bed," Mystery and Chris Odom, St. Martin's Press, 2007, US$19,99*

This book is a revolutionary manual on how to pickup women. It is very original, rational, deep into female psychology and it works wonders. If you walk into a bar some night and see a guy wearing some funny clothes, looking social and relaxed and getting loads of female attention– he is probably one of the many men who has read the book.

*"The Game—penetrating the secret society of pickup artists," Neil Strauss, ReganBooks, 2005, US$29.95*

Neil Strauss describes his journey from average frustrated man to a renowned pickup artist through the Mystery Method. Neil is a very good writer and the topic is very interesting to most men, so this book deservedly became a best-seller.

*"Double your dating," www.doubleyourdatingebook.org, David DeAngelo, US$19.97*

David deAngelo is a pickup guru from the online seduction community. This book is a "classic" introductory book on seduction. Yet, it has some very fundamental concepts in place, especially David's views on dominance during the seduction/attraction stages.

## Scientific books:

*"The Mating mind," 2000, Geoffrey Miller, Anchor Books, US$16.95*

A brilliant book that puts forward the thesis that, in the same way that bulls compete for mates by fighting and birds by singing, humans compete by being charming, fun, talented in the arts, etc. The author proposes that both men and women have evolved to be seductive—in a single sweep explaining why we are so irrational, creative and why love and romance are so important to us.

*"Primate Sexuality,"* 1998, Alan F. Dixson, Oxford University Press

A 500-page long authoritative book on the sexuality of primates from a scientific point of view. While it is well written and unbiased, it will probably only cater the very scientific and biologically minded readers, as it does not give any special relevance to *Homo sapiens.*

*"The Blank Slate—the modern denial of human nature,"* Steven Pinker, Penguin Books 2002, US$17.00

This book makes the case against the blank slate hypothesis—that humans have neither instincts nor innate differences between each other—and explains why this scientifically unsound hypothesis became so popular and politically correct.

*"Our Inner Ape—a leading primatologist explains why we are who we are,"* Frans De Waal, Riverhead Books 2006, US$24.95

The title says it all. In this great book, Frans De Waal, based on his lifelong experience studying Bonobos and Chimpanzees, tells us how these animals see the world and what makes them tick.

SCIENTIFIC ARTICLES:

*Buss, D. M., Larsen, R. J., Westen, D., & Semmelroth, J. (1992)." Sex differences in jealousy: Evolution, physiology, and psychology." Psychological Science, 3, 251–255.*

The authors show that men feel more jealous if their partners have sex with another man than if they fall in love with another man, while the opposite is true for women.

*Meredith L. Chivers, Gerulf Rieger, Elizabeth Latty, J. Michael Bailey (2004). "A sex difference in the specificity of sexual arousal" Psy-*

*chological science 16(8): 579-84*

The authors show that sexual arousal in women follows a bisexual pattern (women enjoy watching both genders, together or separately), while it clearly divides men in two exclusive groups: homosexual or heterosexual.

*Patricia H. Hawley and William A. Hensley IV (2009). "Social Dominance and Forceful Submission Fantasies: Feminine Pathology or Power?" Journal of Sex Research 46(6): 568-85*

The authors review the state of the art on dominance and submission and show that most people (from both genders) prefer a fantasy of submission to one of dominance.

*M.G. Alexander and T.D. Fisher (2003). "Truth and consequences: using the bogus pipeline to examine sex differences in self-reported sexuality." Journal of Sex Research 40(1): 27-35*

By asking sexual questions to their subjects with the threat of using a lie-detector, the authors showed that it is women that hide their sexual experience, not men that exaggerate theirs.

OTHER INTERESTING BOOKS

*"Inside her mind," Rod Govea, pum! Press, 2012?*

*"Secrets of being a gigolo" Gary Brodsky, 2009*

*"The happy hooker's guide to sex—69 orgasmic ways to pleasure a woman," Xaviera Hollander, Skyhorse Publishing, 2008*

*"Getting the sex you want—shed your inhibitions and reach new heights of passion together," Tammy Nelson, Quiver, 2008*

*"Oral sex she'll never forget—50 positions & techniques that will make her orgasm like she never has before," Sonia Borg, Quiver, 2010*

*"Sex talk: how to tell your lover exactly what you want, exactly when*

*you want it,"* Carole Altman, Sourcebooks Casablanca, 2004

*"Don't have sex again until you read this book,"* Carole Altman, Caster Pub., 2007

*"How to make love all night (and drive a woman wild)—male multiple orgasms and other secrets for prolonged lovemaking,"* Barbara Keesling, Harper Paperbacks, 1995

*"A little bit kinky—a couples guide to rediscovering the thrill of sex,"* Natasha Valdez, Three Rivers Press, 2010

*"Crazy hot sex secrets,"* Adrianna Savine, 2010

*"Just fuck me!—what women want men to know about taking control in the bedroom,"* Eve Kingsley, KRE, LLC, 2008

*"She comes first—the thinking man's guide to pleasuring a woman,"* Ian Kerner, Collins Living, 2004

*"The sex bible—the complete guide to sexual love,"* Susan Crain Bakos, Quiver, 2006

*"How to tell a naked man what to do—sexual advice from a woman who knows,"* Candida Royalle, Fireside, 2006

*"Secrets from the sex lab—from first kiss to last gasp...how you can be better in bed,"* Judy Dutton, Broadway, 2010

*"The sex god method,"* Daniel Rose, 2008

*"How to dominate women,"* Gary Brodsky, 2002

*"How to give her absolute pleasure— totally explicit techniques ev-*

ery woman wants her man to know," Lou Paget, 2000

"Rock her world—the sex guide for the modern man," Adam Glasser, aka Seymore Butts, Gotham books, 2009

"Male sexuality: Why women don't understand it—and men don't either", Michael Bader, Rowman & Littlefield, 2010

"The seven principles for making marriage work—a practical guide from the country's foremost relationship expert", John M. Gottman and Nan Silver, Three Rivers Press, 1999

"I love female orgasm—an extraordinary orgasm guide," Dorian Solot, Marshall Miller, Da Capo Press 2007

"Sex, time and power—how women's sexuality shaped human evolution," Leonard Shlain, Penguin Books, 2003

"Warrior Lovers—erotic fiction, evolution and female sexuality," Catherine Salmon and Donald Symons, Yale University Press, 2003

# Your annotations: